ESSAYS ON PAUL

BOOKS BY C. K. BARRETT
Published by The Westminster Press

Essays on Paul
Essays on John
The Gospel According to St. John, Second Edition

ESSAYS ON PAUL

C. K. Barrett

THE WESTMINSTER PRESS
PHILADELPHIA

Published by The Westminster Press®
Philadelphia, Pennsylvania

PRINTED IN THE UNITED STATES OF AMERICA
9 8 7 6 5 4 3 2 1

Library of Congress Cataloging in Publication Data

Barrett, C. K. (Charles Kingsley), 1917–
Essays on Paul.

Includes index.
1. Bible. N.T. Epistles of Paul—Criticism, inter-
pretation, etc.—Addresses, essays, lectures.
I. Title.
BS2650.2.B37   227'.06   82-2764
ISBN 0-664-21390-1   AACR2

CONTENTS

ACKNOWLEDGEMENTS

The publishers acknowledge the following sources for the essays in this volume:

'Christianity at Corinth' was a T. W. Manson Memorial Lecture given at Manchester on 26 November 1963, and was first published in the *Bulletin of the John Rylands Library* (March 1964).

'Cephas and Corinth' first appeared in *Abraham unser Vater, Festschrift für Otto Michel*, published by E. J. Brill (1963).

'Things Sacrificed to Idols' was first published in *New Testament Studies* (January 1965), and 'Paul's Opponents in 2 Corinthians' in the same publication (April 1971).

ΨΕΥΔΑΠΟΣΤΟΛΟΙ first appeared in *Mélanges Bibliques en Hommage au R. P. Béda Rigaux*, published by Editions J. Duculot (1970).

Ο ΑΔΙΚΗΣΑΣ was first published in *Verborum Veritas, Festschrift für Gustav Stählin* by Theologischer Verlag Rolf Brockhaus (1970).

'Titus' first appeared in *Neotestamentica et Semitica, Studies in Honour of Matthew Black*, published by T. & T. Clark (1969).

'Romans 9.30—10.21: Fall and Responsibility of Israel' was first published in *Die Israelfrage nach Röm. 9–11*; Monographische Reihe von *Benedictina*, Biblisch-ökumenische Abteilung 3, Abtei von St Paul vor den Mauern (1977).

'The Allegory of Abraham, Sarah, and Hagar in the Argument of Galatians' first appeared in *Rechtfertigung, Festschrift für Ernst Käsemann*, published by Mohr and Vandenhoeck & Ruprecht (1976).

PREFACE

I have often been asked to republish, in collected form, some of the essays and lectures I have written on Paul and John. A few have already appeared in *New Testament Essays* (1972). I have been hesitant to act on this suggestion because the essence of what I have to say about the two great New Testament theologians is contained in the second edition of my Commentary on St John (1978), in the Commentaries on Romans (1957), on 1 Corinthians (1968), and on 2 Corinthians (1973), and in *From First Adam to Last* (1962). Those, however, whom I have consulted have made the point that some of the matters considered are dealt with more fully than in the Commentaries, and sometimes from different points of view; and, looking back, I myself find it interesting to trace how my views on the historical setting and theological content of the Pauline and Johannine writings have developed, interacted and gradually built up into what I hope is a reasonably coherent structure. Full coherency is, in my opinion, an end-product, which I know that I have not yet attained; this means that no one need be surprised if he finds minor, and indeed a few major, contradictions between the essays, and between the essays and the Commentaries. If I have a few more years of writing I may succeed in producing a truly consistent account of Christian origins; I suspect however that if it is truly consistent with itself it will not be wholly right.

It has been decided to publish the Essays on Paul and the Essays on John separately. The present volume contains the former; the latter, it is hoped, will follow next year. Most of the Essays on Paul are connected with people or places, and it gives me pleasure to recall their original contexts. 'Christianity at Corinth', one of my first attempts to deal with the problems, and the rich contents, of the Corinthian letters, was a T. W. Manson Memorial Lecture. Other papers are drawn from volumes honouring Matthew Black, Ernst Käsemann, Otto Michel, Béda Rigaux and Gustav Stählin. To all these friends I am glad to renew my salutations. 'Things sacrificed to Idols' and 'Paul's Opponents in 2 Corinthians' were given at meetings of Studiorum Novi Testamenti Societas, to whose members I owe much. In some ways I owe perhaps even more to the small group that has met from time to time at S. Paolo fuori le Mura in Rome to conduct a Colloquium Paulinum. My paper on Romans 9.30—10.21 is sadly lost without the contributions and criticisms of my colleagues, but it gives me an opportunity of greeting them.

With the correction of a small number of misprints, the bringing up to date of three footnotes, and accommodation to a uniform house style, the papers are reprinted exactly as they first appeared, with no attempt to multiply bibliographical references.

Durham, April 1981   C. K. BARRETT

ABBREVIATIONS

AGSU	*Arbeiten zur Geschichte des Spätjudentums und Urchristentums*, Leiden/Köln.
Bauer, *Wörterbuch*	W. Bauer, *Griechisch-Deutsches Wörterbuch zu den Schriften des Neuen Testaments und der übrigen urchristlichen Literatur.* Berlin ⁴1952.
BC = Beginnings of Christianity	F. J. Foakes Jackson and K. Lake (eds.), *The Beginnings of Christianity*, Part I: *The Acts of the Apostles.* Five volumes. London 1920–33.
Bibl	*Biblica*, Rome.
Bill	*see* S.-B.
BJRL	*Bulletin of the John Rylands Library*, Manchester.
Blass-Debrunner	F. Blass, *Grammatik des Neutestamentlichen Griechisch*, rev. A. Debrunner. Göttingen ⁸1949.
ET	English Translation.
ExpB	*Expositor's Bible*, London.
ExpT	*Expository Times*, Edinburgh.
FRLANT	*Forschungen zur Religion und Literatur des Alten und Neuen Testaments*, Göttingen.
HNT	*Handbuch zum Neuen Testament*, Tübingen.
ICC	*International Critical Commentary*, Edinburgh.
JBL	*Journal of Biblical Literature*, Missoula.
JTS	*Journal of Theological Studies*, Oxford.
Liddell-Scott	H. G. Liddell and R. Scott, *A Greek-English Lexicon*, a new edition rev. H. S. Jones and R. McKenzie. Oxford 1940.
MeyerK	*Kritisch-Exegetischer Kommentar über das Neue Testament*, begründet von H. A. W. Meyer, Göttingen.
NEB	*New English Bible*

NF	Neue Folge.
NTD	*Das Neue Testament Deutsch,* Göttingen.
NTS	*New Testament Studies,* Cambridge.
Pauly-Wissowa	A. Pauly and G. Wissowa, *Real-Encyclopädie der klassischen Altertumswissenschaft.* Stuttgart 1894ff.
S.-B. = Bill = Strack-Billerbeck	H. L. Strack and P. Billerbeck, *Kommentar zum Neuen Testament aus Talmud und Midrasch.* Munich 1922–55.
SBU	*Symbolae Biblicae Upsalienses,* Uppsala.
SHAW	*Sitzungsberichte der Heidelberger Akademie der Wissenschaften,* Heidelberg.
THK	*Theologischer Handkommentar zum Neuen Testament,* Berlin.
TR	*Theologische Rundschau,* Tübingen.
TWNT = ThW	G. Kittel and G. Friedrich, *Theologisches Wörterbuch zum Neuen Testament.* Stuttgart 1933–79.
WMANT	*Wissenschaftliche Monographien zum Alten und Neuen Testament,* Neukirchen/Vluyn.
WUNT	*Wissenschaftliche Untersuchungen zum Neuen Testament,* Tübingen.
ZNTW = ZNW	*Zeitschrift für die neutestamentliche Wissenschaft und die Kunde der älteren Kirche,* Berlin.

1
CHRISTIANITY AT CORINTH

Not the least of the merits of this subject is that it enables me to build on the work of T. W. Manson himself.[1] I shall do my best to observe the warning of 1 Cor. 3.10, and take heed how I build. But the subject has other merits. If Romans gives us the most systematic presentation of Paul's theology, it is nevertheless from the Corinthian epistles that we gain the most complete and many-sided picture of how Paul believed that his theological convictions should be expressed in the life of a church. To say this is not to claim that the Corinthian church was a paragon of all churches; there was often a wide divergence between what happened in Corinth and what Paul thought ought to happen. But both pictures—the actual and the ideal—contribute to our understanding of Pauline Christianity in its practical expression, and we learn much of what Paul thought right from what the Corinthians got wrong. In the Corinthian epistles Paul deals with an exceptionally large number of practical problems, always on the basis of a theological grasp of the situation, so that there is in fact no more important source for Paul's conception of the Christian way of life.

It is also true that 1 and 2 Corinthians provide the most valuable information we have about early non-Pauline Christianity. There is no epistle (apart from Philemon) in which Paul does not deal with some deviation from or perversion of the Christian faith, but nowhere else is so great a variety of deviations and perversions so fully displayed; and their advocates were able to develop their views and consolidate their adherents to such an extent as almost to disintegrate the originally Pauline church.

Full as the Corinthian letters are of valuable raw material, it is no easy task to win from them a clear account of what was going on in the Corinthian church of the 50s of the first century. The difficulties that stand in the way of historical reconstruction are well known. First stands the fact, which we shall encounter from time to time, that among the verses of crucial importance there is scarcely one of which the interpretation is not disputed. This difficulty is one that often presents itself in the form of a vicious circle: a certain and unambiguous interpretation of a particular verse would give one a clear insight into part at least of the Corinthian history; yet only if one has a clear picture of the history is it possible to interpret the verse with confidence. There is a trap here, evident enough, yet one that has snared a number of students. How easy to make a hurried inference from a text of one of the epistles to historical circumstances, and then to use the supposedly known historical circumstances to confirm the interpretation of the text!

The outstanding literary problem involved in the Corinthian letters is that of their integrity, and this, as can easily be seen, has important consequences for precisely the kind of historical question that is to be dealt with in this lecture. The view of the matter perhaps most commonly held in this country may be briefly set out as follows:[2]

Paul wrote four letters to Corinth.

The *first* has been lost, unless a part of it is preserved in 2 Cor. 6.14—7.1.

The *second* consists of what we call 1 Corinthians.

The *third* has been partially preserved in 2 Cor. 10—13.

The *fourth* is contained in 2 Cor. 1—9 (omitting perhaps 6.14—7.1).

This hypothetical reconstruction has the effect of knitting the two epistles (as contained in our Bibles) very closely together; in particular, 2 Cor. 10—13 stands next in time to 1 Corinthians. The more elaborate reconstructions,[3] in which 1 Corinthians also is partitioned, 2 Cor. 2.14—7.5 attached to 2 Cor. 10—13 and 2 Cor. 8 and 9 separated from each other, have the effect of dovetailing the two epistles even more completely. If however the unity of 2 Corinthians is maintained, or if, as is perhaps more probable, 2 Cor. 10—13 is detached from the rest of the epistle but regarded as subsequent to it,[4] the two documents preserved to us stand further apart; in particular, it becomes less likely that the disturbances of 2 Cor. 10—13 should be regarded as a simple continuation of the divisions of 1 Cor. 1.12, and more likely that the Corinthian troubles had by this time taken a new turn.

Corinth was a place in which a rich development of Christian forms of thought, worship and life was to be expected. Not that it was a centre of intellectual activity; it had no such reputation. But it was a commercial centre in which men of many races, and of many faiths, met, and were in constant contact. New Corinth was not a Greek city. The old πόλις had lain in desolation for a hundred years when the new foundation of Laus Julia Corinthus was made by the Romans in 44 BC.⁵ The town that commanded the Isthmus was bound to become a busy entrepôt; and so it was. Roman colonists, more or less local Greeks, and levantine traders, among them a community of Jews large and wealthy enough to have their own synagogue building,⁶ probably made up the greater part of the population. It is probable that, before the Christian gospel reached Corinth, Isis from Egypt, the Great Mother from Phrygia, Dionysus from Thrace and elsewhere, and the strange nameless deity from Judaea, had already met there, and added the spice of speculation and of ecstasy to the more formal, and politically inspired, worship that came from the west.

Moreover, we have in the epistles themselves the plainest evidence that Christian propagandists, other than, and some of them very different from, Paul had been at work in the city; Apollos certainly; Peter, with very great probability; and if not Peter himself disciples of his who made free with his name.⁷ These may have been embarrassing but comparatively harmless; there were others, and a different gospel, another Jesus and another Spirit were preached. Alexandrian Judaism, Jewish Christianity, Hellenism, all seem to have played upon the already inflammatory material assembled at Corinth. It is no wonder there was a blaze; no wonder the city could add to its trade fairs as fine an exhibition of Christian deviations as was to be seen anywhere in the world. There will be all too little time in this lecture to discuss them.

At this point we cannot do otherwise than turn to 1 Cor. 1.12. Surely it is only by a *tour de force* that Johannes Munck can, in the heading of a chapter in his *Paulus und die Heilsgeschichte*,⁸ describe Corinth as '*Die Gemeinde ohne Parteien*'. True, he has done well to remind us that, when 1 Corinthians was written, the church remained united: Paul could address all its members with a comprehensive 'you', and expect that all would read or hear what he had to say. The ἔριδες of 1.11 do not refer to separate, schismatic bodies, and the αἱρέσεις of 11.19 become manifest συνερχομένων ὑμῶν ἐν ἐκκλησίᾳ (11.18); they are not such as to prevent all from meeting in one place. Dr Munck has also very properly reminded us how little we know about these groups.⁹ Yet divided loyalties, and ecclesiastical preferences were certainly visible, and caused Paul deep anxiety; and the unity of the church, so far as it continued to exist, must have been an uneasy unity.

'I am of Paul', said some, doubtless a reactionary group.[10] As long as no influence but Paul's was felt in Corinth such a slogan would have been meaningless. Other influences were now at work, into which we must shortly look, and in opposition some fell back on the old and familiar. How far the Paulinists understood Paul, and how far he approved of their tenets, are questions to which we may be able to give brief attention.

'I am of Apollos': here there is a familiar and almost certainly correct explanation.[11] According to Acts 18.27 f Apollos formed and carried out the intention of visiting Achaea; the probability that such a journey would include Corinth is immediately confirmed by 19.1. That Apollos was a Jew (18.24) need not be disputed; that he was Ἀλεξανδρεὺς τῷ γένει is probably insignificant, for there is no ground for supposing that every Alexandrian Jew was a potential Philo (though some writers seem to think so); that he was ἀνὴρ λόγιος[12] would account for his acquiring a following of his own. Many no doubt found him a refreshing change after an apostle who could be dismissed as ἰδιώτης τῷ λόγῳ (2 Cor. 11.6). Paul had no quarrel with him;[13] they may well be right who see in Apollos's disinclination to visit Corinth again (1 Cor. 16.12) a delicacy of sentiment that made him unwilling to appear even unintentionally in the character of a rival. It is nevertheless probable that Apollos contributed to the Corinthian development of thought about γνῶσις, λόγος, and σοφία.

'I am of Cephas' probably implies the presence of Peter himself in Corinth.[14] T. W. Manson's argument[15] that the group that made use of his name is to be detected (for example) in the way in which Paul handles such questions as litigation, the eating of sacrificial foods, and the Lord's Supper, is convincing. It adopted a Jewish Christian 'nomistic' attitude, not extreme enough actually to divide the church (as a demand for circumcision would have done), or to disfranchise Paul from the apostolic body, but awkward enough to raise difficulties, and to cast a certain amount of doubt on Paul's status.[16]

'I am of Christ': here's the rub. Who said these words? According to some,[17] a copyist, who inserted in the margin of his New Testament the pious comment: These Corinthians had their various party leaders—ἐγὼ δὲ Χριστοῦ. It is sometimes replied that there is no textual evidence in support of this view, but this is not strictly true. There is no MS evidence; but it could be urged that the earliest textual authority for I Cor. 1.12 is I Clem. 47.3, where Clement says of Paul that ἐπ' ἀληθείας πνευματικῶς ἐπέστειλεν ὑμῖν περὶ αὐτοῦ τε καὶ Κηφᾶ τε καὶ Ἀπολλῶ, διὰ τὸ καὶ τότε προσκλίσεις ὑμᾶς πεποιῆσθαι. In this context there is no reference to Christ, or to οἱ Χριστοῦ. It is at least possible to maintain that Clement did not read ἐγὼ δὲ Χριστοῦ in I Cor. 1.12. There are however other possible explanations of Clement's silence. Lightfoot[18] thinks that Clement made no reference to the Christ-group because to refer to it would have 'complicated his argument', and adds that the exact theological position of this group was probably not known to him.[19] A further possibility is that Clement, who did not always verify his references, was thinking of, or was confused by, I Cor. 3.22, where only Paul, Apollos and Cephas are mentioned. It would be rash to conclude that ἐγὼ δὲ Χριστοῦ did not stand in Paul's own copy of I Corinthians.

We must still ask, however, Who said these words? Are they another party cry, parallel with and analogous to the other three? Or are they Paul's own comment? The latter is an attractive view,[20] for there is at least a superficial difficulty in supposing that the name Christ could be taken as in any sense on the same level as those of Paul, Apollos, and Cephas, and it could be argued that Clement, if the words ἐγὼ δὲ Χριστοῦ did stand in his text, understood them as a comment and not as referring to a fourth party. More-over, the words seem—superficially again—to be an apt rejoinder to a church making too much of its human leaders. Against this is the strict parallelism of the four clauses, and the complete lack of indication that in the fourth Paul has ceased to quote. The awkwardness, often remarked on, of the following words is perhaps to be explained by the fact that it was an embarrassment to Paul that one group had adopted as a party cry what should have been the watchword of all.

Perhaps the strongest argument for regarding the words ἐγὼ δὲ Χριστοῦ as indicating the existence of a fourth group is that when we have eliminated from I Corinthians everything that can reasonably be ascribed to a Paul-group, an Apollos-group and a Cephas-group, there remains a well-defined body of opinion, distinct from the views of the first three groups, consistent with itself and explicable in the context of events in Corinth. The mere existence of such a body of opinion does not prove the existence of a fourth distinct section of the church, still less that ἐγὼ δὲ Χριστοῦ was the slogan of this group, but it seems to weight the balance of probability in this direction.

If then we ask what Corinthian Christianity was like, we shall not be surprised if the answer is complicated rather than simple, and that even if we confine our attention to doctrinal matters and exclude almost completely literary and historical problems. The complexity of the situation does not diminish, and, at first at least, the student's own perplexity may increase, when he makes some attempt to master the range of modern literature that Corinthian problems have evoked.[21] It will, I think, be clear that if (as I hope) I am to give some account of the data, refer to suggestions made by others, and try to offer a few new suggestions, I shall have to be selective, and omit a good deal that could profitably have been included in this lecture if its compass had permitted.

Σοφία and Γνῶσις at Corinth

No problem arising out of Christianity at Corinth has been more discussed during recent years than that which is suggested by these words.[22] In what sense or senses were they used at Corinth? What theological presuppositions and theological systems lie behind them? How far was Paul himself prepared to use this terminology and adopt the systems and presuppositions involved?

The distribution of the words suggests that we are dealing with a problem belonging mainly to the period of 1 Corinthians.[23] Σοφία occurs sixteen times in 1 Cor. 1—3, once in 1 Cor. 12.8 and once in 2 Cor. 1.12. The occurrence of the adjective σοφός follows precisely the same pattern: ten times in 1 Cor. 1—3, once in 1 Cor. 6.5 (but this is not a technical use) and nowhere else in the two letters. That the theme of wisdom is connected with the divisions in the Corinthian church, which are in mind throughout 1 Cor. 1—3, is hardly to be questioned. The distribution of γνῶσις is less significant. The word occurs once in 1 Cor. 1, five times in 1 Cor. 8, once in 1 Cor. 12, twice in 1 Cor. 13, once in 1 Cor. 14, four times in 2 Cor. 1—9, twice in 2 Cor. 10—13. The cognate verbs (γινώσκειν, ἀναγινώσκειν, ἐπιγινώσκειν) have even less to tell us. It seems that γνῶσις was connected less with speculation than with the practical question whether a Christian might or might not eat sacrificial food.

I shall deal mainly with σοφία in relation to speculative Christianity at Corinth, and I propose to take as a starting-point the recently stated and undoubtedly important views of Ulrich Wilckens.[24]

Dr Wilckens asserts, and lays great emphasis upon, the unity of 1 Cor. 1.18—2.16, and refuses to accept the notion that there is any disharmony between 1.18–25 and 2.6–16. The latter section is determinative of the meaning of the whole, and shows against what adversaries Paul is arguing throughout. 'The adversaries are thus gnostics, not Greek philosophers'[25] using the rhetorical methods of the Greek philosophical schools. It is true (Dr Wilckens allows) that Paul speaks of these adversaries as Greeks,[26] but in fact 'the Corinthian gnosis was nourished ultimately upon hellenized Jewish apocalyptic speculation'.[27] When Paul speaks of λόγος he is thinking 'not of traditional Greek rhetoric . . . but of gnostic charismatic speech, as is shown not only by a comparison of 2.1 with 12.8, but also especially by Paul's argument in 2 Corinthians: cf. especially 11.6 and 10.10'.[28] When Paul attacks the Corinthians' σοφία λόγου (1.17) it is not as a rhetorical method, but as a gnostic pneuma-Christology. Only this view makes sense of Paul's argument that the cross of Christ was being made of no effect. 'That a Christian preaching in the style of Greek philosophy was fundamentally impossible, and a distortion of the Christian kerygma, this Paul did not say in 1 Corinthians—and, considering the range of his experience, probably could not have said.'[29] For Paul had not been educated in Greek philosophy.[30]

So far Dr Wilckens. There is some truth in his view, but taken as a whole it seems to me an unconvincing over-simplification of the facts. He denies the existence of disharmony in the various uses of σοφία in 1 Cor. 1—3, but if there is no disharmony there is at least a good deal of polyphony. His argument that Paul could not have been opposing a rhetorical expression of Christianity because he knew nothing of the rhetorical styles of the formal philosophies ignores the fact that in Paul's day there were plenty of journalistic market-place arguers who themselves had not been trained in and were not exponents of a particular kind of philosophical oratory, but knew all there was to know about the tricks of windy rhetoric.

It is scarcely an exaggeration to say that there is a different shade of meaning in the word σοφία (and σοφός) every time it occurs; analysis of the material, however, suggests that the occurrences of the word may be grouped into two categories, good and bad, each with two sub-divisions. Any attempt to draw the lines too sharply would lead to error; there are close relations between all four groups.

First (*pace* Wilckens) there is a considerable group of passages where σοφία denotes a kind of eloquence, a technique for persuading the hearer.[31] In itself this is harmless; it becomes vicious only when the user of it comes to rely on human device and artifice, and not on the divine power resident in Christ crucified and transferred by the Spirit to the preaching which has Christ crucified as its theme. It was this sort of wisdom Paul refused to adopt when he first preached at Corinth.[32] So 1.17; 2.1. It is instructive to note how in both these verses λόγος and σοφία are combined. 2.4 is equally clear:[33] here λόγος is used twice, once for preaching and once for mere words. Preaching is not a matter of verbal arguments, however clever (σοφίας λόγοι); it is accompanied by the manifestation of the Spirit and of power. Similarly, wise men (σοφοί) are those who try to win over their fellows by the exercise of clever talk. This appears in the quotation of 1.19, and even more clearly in 1.20, where the σοφός stands in parallel with the γραμματεύς and the συζητητὴς τοῦ αἰῶνος τούτου. Cf. 1.26 f.

We must however pause for a moment over 1.20, for here we may see one meaning of σοφία moving over into another. After scornfully apostrophizing the wise man, the scribe, the debater, Paul asks, οὐχὶ ἐμώρανεν ὁ θεὸς τὴν σοφίαν τοῦ κόσμου; This question includes the meaning, Has not God, by giving up his Son to the cross, made human arguments look silly? But the human arguments are not merely rhetorical or logical; they rest upon presuppositions, such as the undesirability of suffering, and the necessity of imposing one's will on others. That is, σοφία is more than technique; it has come to be a way of estimating and assessing life. A similar shift of meaning can be seen in 2.5 (cf. 2.13), and in 3.18, 19, 20.

There is thus a σοφία of speech, no bad thing (cf. 12.8), but dangerous; dangerous when preachers think they can use it as a substitute for Christ crucified, and most dangerous of all when it ceases to be a human technique and becomes a humanistic philosophy.[34]

Second, there is the σοφία that wisdom of speech develops into when it ceases to be controlled by Christ crucified. We have already noted passages (1.20; 2.5, 13; 3.19) where this development takes place. 2.6 is particularly important in its implication that there is (though Paul rejects it) a wisdom of this age, of the rulers of this age.

What is this? The expression οἱ ἄρχοντες τοῦ αἰῶνος τούτου occurs only in 2.6, 8 in the Pauline letters; cf. however 2 Cor. 4.4, where the meaning will not be widely different.[35] Paul is referring to the heavenly angelic powers, whom he elsewhere describes in other terms. It is easier to understand their lack of true wisdom than the wisdom they may themselves be said to possess. They showed their failure to grasp God's wisdom by crucifying his Son, and thus unwittingly compassing their own ruin. This is sometimes[36] taken to mean that they simply failed to recognize in the man Jesus the (personal) wisdom of God, and thus thought that they might safely put him out of the way. But this interpretation fails to take into account (a) the recognition of Jesus by supernatural powers,[37] and (b) the fact that if the ἄρχοντες had thought Jesus to be merely a man they would have had no ground for crucifying him—what harm could a man do them? It is more probable that the wisdom the rulers failed to understand was God's purpose of redemption[38] not simply through Christ but through Christ crucified; this indeed is God's wisdom ἐν μυστηρίῳ.[39]

Now it may be that in 2.6f Paul is merely denying that the divine wisdom belongs to this age, or to its rulers, without asserting that they have a wisdom of their own.[40] This might cover 1.22—the wisdom sought by the Greeks is a mirage having no real existence. But it would not do justice to 1.21, which implies that the world has a wisdom—that is, a wisdom which it regards as wisdom, though it is totally inadequate for acquiring knowledge of God. There is in fact a close substantial parallel—perhaps in the end substantial identity—between the human wisdom that is confident of its own powers and resources both to attain to the truth and also to commend that truth to others, and the supernatural, demonic wisdom that is incapable of recognizing the wisdom of God in Christ crucified; and though Paul himself no doubt believed in the personal existence of the ἄρχοντες τοῦ αἰῶνος τούτου, it may not be improper for us to demythologize them as a sublimation of anthropocentricity—the spirit of the age, if you will.[41] Their wisdom is one that arises within this αἰών, or (and Paul uses both terms) within the κόσμος. Like other gnostic systems it is a way of escape from this world[42] to the upper world of divine existence, based upon the authority of the ἄρχοντες. More than this we can hardly say, since Paul is writing allusively, and tells us no more.

We turn next to the good uses of σοφία; of these the first arises

directly out of the last observations, and can be stated quickly. The
σοφία of the rulers is a self-regarding, self-preserving σοφία; over
against it stands God's wisdom, that is, his mysterious—and by
human standards foolish—plan for destroying the rulers and thereby
delivering men who were living in subjection to their authority. In
this sense, σοφία is essentially a *Heilsplan*. It has a negative aspect,
which is expressed in two ways, mythological and anthropological.
(a) It was a means of overthrowing the rulers of this age, who, since
their foolish act in crucifying the Lord of glory, are καταργούμενοι,
in process of destruction (2.6 f). The destruction of these rulers is a
necessary condition of the bringing in of the age to come.[43] Paul
stands at the point where the two conceptions, of two ages, and of
two worlds, meet. Because the new age is at hand the angelic powers
no longer decide who shall have access to the heavenly world;
through Christ crucified the way is open. (b) It was part of God's
wise plan (1.21) that men should not know him by the exercise of
their own wisdom, since this, being a self-seeking wisdom, was
orientated in a direction opposite to his own. Like the angelic
rulers, man must himself be καταργούμενος if he is to receive the gift
of salvation. Elsewhere[44] Paul expresses this truth in terms of death
and resurrection with Christ; in 1 Corinthians he has a significantly
different way of putting it:

3.18: If anyone among you thinks he is wise in this age, let him
become a fool, in order that he may become wise (cf. 1.25).

8.2 f: If anyone thinks he has come to know something, he has
not yet come to knowledge as he ought: if anyone loves
God, he has been known by him.

Already in speaking of the negative aspect of God's *Heilsplan* we
have reached the positive. By destroying the rulers of this age God
brings near the age to come. By demonstrating the falsehood of
human wisdom and gnosis he opens the door to the truth. It will
suffice here to draw attention to the implications of 2.13. With
'words taught by human wisdom' Paul contrasts words that come
from the instruction of the Spirit. It is the Spirit who supplies the
knowledge of things which eye has not seen or ear heard (2.9), of
the things that God has given (2.12), and indeed of God himself
(2.11).

From this point, the transition to the second 'good' use of σοφία
is easy. It is sometimes disputed whether, in these chapters of 1

Corinthians, σοφία is better understood as *Heilsplan* or as *Heilsgut*.[45] The answer is that it is both. We have seen passages where it means *Heilsplan*; there are (in addition to the hints we have already noted) at least two where it means *Heilsgut*. In 1.24, 30 Christ himself is σοφία,[46] and, in both, other terms used in parallel with σοφία make the meaning clear. Christ is also δύναμις, δικαιοσύνη, ἁγιασμός, and ἀπολύτρωσις. The overlap between *Heilsplan* and *Heilsgut* is a function of the absolute centrality of Christ crucified in Paul's conception of God and of salvation. The placarding of a crucified Christ before men's eyes (Gal. 3.1) is the means by which God destroys all human wisdom, overthrows the cosmic powers and establishes his kingdom; but during the establishing the kingdom is Christ's and he himself is the substance of it, as he is also the ground and basis of reigning humanity, the heavenly Man in whose image man will be created anew.

We can tidy up the evidence by noting that we now have the explanation of the fact that, notwithstanding 1.17, Paul can declare in 2.6 that he does, in the right circumstances,[47] speak wisdom.[48] His wisdom is identical with the λόγος τοῦ σταυροῦ (1.18).

Among Paul's many virtues is not to be counted a strict consistency in the use of terminology. This observation is not least true of his use of σοφία; but as far as this word is concerned Paul is hardly to be blamed. He was dealing with a complicated situation, and the complicated situation and inconsistent terminology are to some extent mutually explanatory.

It is, to say the least, a not unreasonable guess that it was Apollos who popularized in Corinth what we may call the wisdom method of preaching—a method which Paul acknowledged was not his own, a method of which he was clearly (perhaps more clearly than Apollos) aware of the dangers, but one which he could not and did not reject out of hand; if he had done so he could not have written 1 Cor. 2.6; 12.8. It is true that Dr Wilckens warns us[49] not to build on the ἀνὴρ λόγιος of Acts 18.24, but it is not improper to ask where, if not at this point, Apollos differed from Paul. The two were in substantial agreement, and 3.6–9 suggests that the contribution of Apollos may have been a version of Christianity more advanced in its presentation even if no more fundamental in its content. Apollos's use of the wisdom method would have been harmless enough if others—and is there any good reason why we should not think of the Christ-group?—had not developed form into substance,

and produced out of a technique of preaching and teaching a radically changed gospel, accommodated to Greek tastes—a wisdom of
this age. It is worth noting that we have in Corinth precisely the
accumulation of factors out of which gnosticism (in its mature form)
may be supposed to have emerged.[50] It seems to me that we lack
clear exegetical evidence that any adversaries of Paul's in Corinth
taught a σοφία-myth, in the sense of a story about a figure called
σοφία who descended through the powers for the redemption of
mankind: this sort of myth arose rather in Paul's response to a
σοφία which was that of the powers themselves. It was the necessity
of combating this σοφία, which may well have laid more stress on
charismata than on myth, together with the apocalyptic-eschato-
logical consideration that the powers were now in process of being
overthrown, that led Paul himself to the development of a myth,
which spoke of the descent of Christ, his crucifixion by and victory
over the powers, and the consequent redemption of mankind.

The development of the Christ-group, with its σοφία and γνῶσις
(8.1), may have been due to reaction to the Peter-group.[51] Paul in
turn reacted creatively as well as negatively to both groups. The
adherents of Peter had to be vigorously resisted so far as they
represented a legalistic perversion of the gospel, even though in
practice Paul might agree with some of their conclusions, on the
different ground of Christian love and consideration for weaker
brothers. The Christ-group too had to be resisted if it taught or
implied that human wisdom offered a way of placating the rulers
and thus of ascending independently into heaven; yet (as Apollos's
colleague could not deny) there was a Christian σοφία whose theme,
whose very substance, was Christ crucified.[52]

It was characteristic of Paul that he should see, in the new situation, precisely in the dangerous errors that were being propagated
in Corinth, the possibility of advance in the understanding and
statement of the Gospel. Few men in his own, or in any other, age
have had minds big enough to do this. In Corinth there were some
who adhered to the old Pauline gospel, as they had first received it.
Their watchword was, 'Εγώ εἰμι Παύλου. There is little clear indication of their presence in the epistles (one could not expect Paul to
blame them severely, though they may well have embarrassed him),
but we may, I think, point to one place where their views are
expressed.

There can be little doubt that at several points in 1 Corinthians

Paul quotes opinions that were current in Corinth. One example[53] is to be found at 6.13. It seems probable that some at Corinth were arguing from analogy: τὰ βρώματα τῇ κοιλίᾳ, καὶ ἡ κοιλία τοῖς βρώμασιν. This is incontestable truth, and it is consistent with it that neither food nor belly has permanent existence. From this some would conclude: τὸ σῶμα τῇ πορνείᾳ—other physical organs may be used as freely as those of digestion. Paul firmly denies this conclusion, but it is evident that some at Corinth accepted it.

Dr J. Jeremias[54] has shown that 1 Cor. 7.1 also contains a quotation: καλὸν ἀνθρώπῳ γυναικὸς μὴ ἅπτεσθαι, a judgement accepted by Paul only with severe qualifications. Dr Jeremias's analysis of the opening verses of this chapter seems to me convincing, but it presents us with the difficulty, which he does not discuss, of attributing to the Corinthians two diametrically opposed views: on the one hand, fornication is a natural function of the body and is therefore not merely pardonable but inevitable; on the other, it is a good thing for a man to avoid any sexual contact with a woman. Is it reasonable to suppose that both views were maintained in the one community?

Schlatter[55] thought so, and that both views could be ascribed to the Christ-group. It is wrong, he says, to explain the two attitudes as Jewish and Hellenistic. 'The desire for celibacy breaks off every connection with Judaism, but it is not for that reason Greek. It is thinkable only under the protection of the slogan "All things are lawful for me", and this has nothing to do with the traditions of Greece, but was the Christian answer to Jewish subservience to the law'.[56] Schlatter continues,[57] 'They evaluated celibacy just as much as access to a harlot as the putting into effect of Christian strength, as the fulfilment of the liberty grounded in Christ. The continent man is strong; he proves his strength by dispensing with a wife. This does not take us beyond the profession, "We are of Christ".'

Thus the watchword of the Christ-group is Christian freedom; and this may be expressed both in sexual licence, and by dispensing with the opportunities of sexual expression that most men need, or desire. We are reminded of the varying moral practices of various second-century gnostic groups.[58] It is doubtful however whether Schlatter's explanation is the best available. It seems more probable that those who proclaimed καλὸν ἀνθρώπῳ γυναικὸς μὴ ἅπτεσθαι were the Pauline group. Certainly Paul comes much closer to their opinion than to approving Christian freedom in fornication.[59] He was himself unmarried (1 Cor. 7.7), and gives limited agreement to the Corinthian view: abstinence has a good deal to be said for it, but it cannot be required of Christians because it fails to take account of all the facts of the human situation.

Paul was a great enough Christian thinker to learn from the changing facts of his environment, as well as from his friends and from his adversaries. We can scarcely say so much of all Paulinists—whether of the first century or of later ages.

2 Corinthians 10—13

It has too often been assumed that the troubles with which Paul deals in these chapters were a simple continuation of those that appear in the first epistle;[60] in particular that the trouble-makers of the second epistle are the same persons as those described in 1 Cor. 1.12 as the Christ-group. There is some superficial justification for this belief, especially in the fact that in 2 Cor. 10.7 Paul deals with an unnamed person who πέποιθεν ἑαυτῷ Χριστοῦ εἶναι and makes a reply not widely different from that of 1 Cor. 1.13: it is not wrong to claim to belong to Christ; indeed any Christian may and must make such a profession (1 Cor. 3.23). But to make it exclusively, so as to deny that others belong to Christ, is to divide Christ. So in 2 Cor. 10.7 Paul rejoins, καθὼς αὐτὸς Χριστοῦ (this is not denied), οὕτως καὶ ἡμεῖς. Moreover, there is common material. There is at least some reason to think that the Christ-group in 1 Corinthians were Christians of a gnostic type, who laid stress on charismatic and spiritual phenomena, against whom Paul found himself obliged to defend his apostleship. It seems that his opponents in 2 Cor. 10—13 also laid some stress on charismatic speech and visions, and despised Paul for his deficiencies in these respects; in reply, Paul vehemently defends his apostleship.

This assimilation of 2 Cor. 10—13, and the anti-Pauline movement to which these chapters bear witness, to the evidence of the earlier letter, is nevertheless to be rejected.[61] It is bound to appear in a new light if we cease to think of the four chapters as constituting the intermediate 'severe' letter (or a part of it),[62] but take them to be not earlier, and perhaps later, than 2 Cor. 1—9. More important still, however, is the simple but too often neglected observation that whereas 1 Cor. 1.12 deals with native inhabitants of the Corinthian church,[63] 2 Cor. 10—13 is directed against strangers who intrude themselves into the church from without.[64] It is true that from time to time Paul speaks of the Corinthians themselves with some bitterness, because they have allowed themselves to be deceived and corrupted by those who have visited their church: Paul needs to commend himself to those who should spontaneously have taken his part. But the source of the trouble is outside the church not within it; and it follows that the problems of 2 Cor. 10—13 must be treated separately from those of 1 Corinthians—though naturally this is not to say that there was no resemblance, or connection, between them.

Who then were these latest opponents of Paul's, and what, in addition to personal animosity, which does not seem to have been absent, were the grounds of their opposition to him?

The old view, which goes back to F. C. Baur,[65] was that the trouble-makers, ironically described as ὑπερλίαν ἀπόστολοι, were the Jerusalem apostles, who were now beginning, in person or through deputies, to carry on in Corinth the same kind of Judaizing propaganda that they had earlier conducted in the churches of Galatia. This view found support in the fact that the opponents claimed that they were the seed of Abraham, servants of Christ (that is, perhaps, disciples during his earthly ministry), and servants of righteousness (that is, perhaps, upholders of righteousness according to the law).[66] It was however vigorously assailed by Lütgert,[67] who at least succeeded in making it very difficult to hold the old view in the old form. That the adversaries were Jews is incontrovertible; but it does not follow from this, said Lütgert, that they were Judaizers. The unmistakable badge of the Judaizers was an insistence on circumcision, as we see in Acts and Galatians; of this insistence there is no trace in 2 Corinthians. Lütgert proceeded to make merry over his predecessors, who, aware of this difficulty, tried to devise means of getting round it—suggesting, for example, that the supposed Judaizers were keeping circumcision up their sleeve as a card they would play at a later date when first they had won the confidence of their victims. It need not be said that there is no evidence of such plans; if they had existed it is more than likely that Paul would have seen through them, and that we should have heard a good deal of the duplicity of these crypto-circumcisionists.[68] According to Lütgert, the intruders in Corinth were *Schwarmgeister*, gnostics and charismatics of Jewish origin,[69] libertine in their interpretation and practice of Christian freedom.[70] The greater part of Lütgert's thesis was difficult to refute, though some, for example E. B. Allo,[71] questioned the assertion that the opponents were in any proper sense gnostics. They were (according to Allo) hellenized Jews of the dispersion, who did not preach circumcision, suspecting that this would not go down well at Corinth, but exalted Moses at the expense of Christ.[72]

Lütgert's work remains of great importance, but it cannot be said that he answered satisfactorily all the questions raised by 2 Cor. 10—13. Another very important contribution is that made by E. Käsemann.[73]

According to Dr Käsemann, Paul was accused by his adversaries of deficiency in spiritual gifts; because of this deficiency he could be no independent apostle, but must be subordinate to the original group. Since he claimed to be an independent apostle when he was not, he must be acting for unworthy ends; hence his whole Christian existence, his Χριστοῦ εἶναι, was called in question.[74] The adversaries themselves were Jews but not Judaizers,[75] spiritual men (*Pneumatiker*) but not gnostics, since no specifically mythological gnosis is attributed to them. In fact, it is necessary to ask why, in so fierce a battle, Paul said so little about his opponents' beliefs. The answer is that the ὑπερλίαν ἀπόστολοι of 2 Cor. 11.5; 12.11 (to be distinguished —according to Käsemann—from the false apostles of 11.13) were the Jerusalem apostles; the opponents in Corinth were 'a delegation sent out from the primitive community'.[76] This is why the central theme of 2 Cor. 10—13 is not myth, not charismata (as in 1 Corinthians), but spiritual freedom, the authority of the apostle. The fact that his immediate adversaries could invoke the Jerusalem apostles was an embarrassment to Paul. 'He intends to reckon relentlessly with the intruders in Corinth, yet he is neither able nor willing to come into conflict with Jerusalem and the primitive apostles ... Perhaps we may formulate the matter thus: He defends himself against the primitive apostles, and smites the intruders in Corinth.'[77]

In this disputing of his apostleship Paul saw at the same time a falsifying of the gospel—hence he traces it back to satanic deception (11.3 f). In this respect at least Baur was right.[78] The adversaries' position led to an insistence on tradition (*Traditionsprinzip*), according to which every new-founded Christian community must recognize the authority of Jerusalem. Only so could the work of the Spirit be guaranteed. Paul was accordingly accused of walking after the flesh (10.3).[79]

The issue at Corinth was not merely personal; it touched the 'constitution of the early Christian church'.[80] Gospel, Christ, and Spirit (11.4) were all viewed in a way different from Paul's. 'In his own person he is merely the example in which, for the first time in church history, the question of the Christian ministry (*Amt*) appears with a radical demonstration of the problems involved (*mit radikaler Problematik*)'.[81]

The most searching criticism of Dr Käsemann's essay is that of Dr Bultmann.[82] Dr Bultmann does not find convincing the argument that Paul's adversaries were *Pneumatiker*, but not gnostics. Why should Paul say explicitly that his adversaries had a mythological, speculative, saving gnosis? He had one himself. The fact that material from 1 Corinthians is not repeated in 2 Cor. 10—13 is no proof that it was not applicable to the adversaries there; in 2 Cor. 10—13 Paul had more important matters to discuss. It is true that the opponents were Jews; but they need not have come from Jerusalem, still less need they have been an official delegation. 'Since there is no indication that leads us to think of Judaizers we may have to do throughout with a hellenistic gnostic Jewish Christianity ... the spirituality against which Paul contends can only be the hellenistic spirituality which we know as characteristic of the gnostic movement'.[83]

Dr Käsemann's distinction between the adversaries in Corinth and the ὑπερλίαν ἀπόστολοι will not stand. According to him, Paul would not have said (11.5) of those whom he describes as the servants of Satan (11.14 f), 'I am no less than they'. But why not (says Dr Bultmann), if this were necessary in order to open the Corinthians' eyes? In 11.3 f Paul accuses his adversaries of satanic deception. But, the Corinthians could reply, these men have proved themselves in λόγος and γνῶσις. Paul answers—I no less! Moreover, 12.11 refers to activity in Corinth itself;[84] thus the ὑπερλίαν ἀπόστολοι had been in Corinth. And the reserve which, according to Dr Käsemann, Paul shows in attacking his adversaries is due not to respect for the Jerusalem apostles, whose backing the adversaries are supposed to have, but to the situation itself.

Our discussion of divergent views of 2 Cor. 10—13 leaves us with a number of outstanding questions, of which three may now be briefly considered. If in these we can reach firm ground we shall have made considerable progress towards the solution of a very difficult problem.

(1) The interpretation of 2 Cor. 10.12–18.[85] Paul writes ironic-

ally. He[86] will not count himself among, or compare himself with, those who commend themselves.[87] His language is thus consistent with his ironical description of certain men as ὑπερλίαν ἀπόστολοι— naturally, no one would think of comparing himself with super-apostles! This creates at least a presumption that, in this paragraph, Paul is thinking of the same persons as in 11.5; 12.11. Paul does not dare to make such comparisons; they however measure themselves by themselves and compare themselves with themselves, because they recognize no authority or standards external to themselves. Doing so they fail to understand[88] what apostleship, and even Christian existence, are. They glory εἰς τὰ ἄμετρα (cf. 11.22 f), as Paul will not do. εἰς τὰ ἄμετρα, used by Paul only in this paragraph, was no doubt suggested by the foolish self-measurement (μετροῦντες) of v. 12; to measure oneself by oneself is inevitably to fall into unmeasured excesses of boasting, which there is no objective, external standard to check. This, 'we' will not do. What 'we' will do would have been easier to understand if Paul had seen fit to use a verb to express it; the reader must repeat καυχησόμεθα, or, perhaps better, understand (ἑαυτοὺς) μετροῦμεν. The latter alternative is suggested by κατὰ τὸ μέτρον τοῦ κανόνος.[89]

According to Dr Käsemann, Dr Kümmel, and others, κανών means a 'standard of judgement',[90] relating to the mandate for evangelism which the success of the mission demonstrated (cf. 1 Cor. 9.2). This interpretation is not satisfactory. (a) It involves redundancy, for μέτρον also means a measure or rule,[91] and μέτρον τοῦ κανόνος, if κανών means 'measuring-rod', is absurd. (b) The words ἐφικέσθαι ἄχρι καὶ ὑμῶν[92] point clearly to the extension of Paul's mission in space, rather than its success in any particular place. In view of these facts it is better to take κανών in the sense of limit or boundary, and thus of measured space. Not that Paul's thought is exclusively geographical:[93] the geographical bounds of his apostleship are such as to include Corinth, and his apostleship includes not merely a visit to Corinth but the foundation of a church there.

Verse 14 brings this point home yet more clearly. If Paul had not legitimately and effectively reached the Corinthians as an apostle he would in dealing with them be stretching himself out (ὑπερεκτείνομεν) beyond his appointed limit; but this is not so. He did get so far (ἐφθάσαμεν), and that not merely as a sight-seer; he came ἐν τῷ εὐαγγελίῳ.

In verse 15 Paul's rivals appear once more by implication. They do what Paul does not. The participial clause οὐκ . . . καυχώμενοι is parallel to and takes up the clause οὐ . . . ὑπερεκτείνομεν, re-introducing the theme of glorying, as in verse 13 with the adverbial phrase εἰς τὰ ἄμετρα. In his relations with the church at Corinth Paul is neither extending himself beyond limit nor glorying beyond measure, for the church is (under God) his own work, and he is adhering strictly to his rule (cf. Rom. 15.20) of not interfering with other men's work. This, it is implied, is exactly what his opponents in Corinth are doing; they are illegitimately extending the scope of their apostolic activity, and that with a view to glorying in the work of others.

With the next participial clause (ἐλπίδα δὲ ἔχοντες) the grammar becomes yet more confused, and we might excuse ourselves from continuing to the end of the chapter were it not that there are two further uses of the word κανών that must be noted in confirmation of what was said above. The hope Paul cherishes is that, as the faith of the Corinthian church grows, he may be magnified among them[94] according to his κανών (κατὰ τὸν κανόνα ἡμῶν), that is, in terms of the field of apostolic work assigned to him (which includes Corinth). He adds, εἰς περισσείαν. The grammatical construction is not clear, but the sense, added as an afterthought, is that Paul hopes to be magnified yet further, and this will be by preaching the gospel in parts beyond Corinth. The fundamentally spatial use of κανών is emphasized here, and again in the epexegetical clause οὐκ . . . καυχήσασθαι, which refers by implication to Paul's adversaries, who, instead of seeking out new mission-fields, invade the fields of others (ἐν ἀλλοτρίῳ κανόνι), and for their boasting make use of what they find ready to hand (εἰς τὰ ἕτοιμα).

The point of this exegetical sketch is as simple as the details of the passage are obscure. Two or three questions are superimposed one upon another. Within whose area of apostolic activity does Corinth fall? Whose work has justified itself (in Corinth, for example) in the creation of new churches, and not in a mere facade of boasting about the achievements of others? Whose ministry shows the true marks of apostleship?[95] It is impossible to state these questions without calling to mind Gal. 2.1–10, where there is not only a mutual recognition of apostolic ministries but also an agreed division of apostolic labour. Paul is to go to the Gentiles, Cephas to the Jews. This was an agreement the practice of which was bound to cause difficulty because there were few places that were purely Jewish or purely Gentile in population, and there is no reason to be surprised that trouble of precisely this kind arose in Corinth. We have here an important pointer to a solution of the problems of 2 Cor. 10—13, and are directed to a new question.

(2) Should we distinguish between the ὑπερλίαν ἀπόστολοι and the ψευδαπόστολοι? Our examination of 2 Cor. 10.12–18 has led to a clear suggestion that Paul had in mind those with whom the agreement of Gal. 2.9 was made—in the first instance Cephas, next the so-called 'pillars', and perhaps the Jerusalem apostles as a whole. It is reasonable to suppose that these are the persons whom he describes as ὑπερλίαν ἀπόστολοι (2 Cor. 11.5; 12.11). Dr Kümmel[96] says that even so indirect a polemic against the original apostles is nowhere to be found in Paul, but in fact the irony of οἱ ὑπερλίαν ἀπόστολοι is precisely parallel to that of οἱ δοκοῦντες (Gal. 2.6).[97] In both 2 Cor. 11.5 and 12.11 Paul claims that he does not fall behind (ὑστερεῖν) these exalted persons. This is exactly what he does elsewhere (Gal. 1.1, 18f; 2.6; 1 Cor. 9.4 ff) with reference to the same apostles.

That οἱ ὑπερλίαν ἀπόστολοι are the Jerusalem apostles is confirmed by study of the contexts in which the expression occurs. It has been argued[98] that in 2 Cor. 11.5 the Twelve cannot be intended because in 11.2f Paul has spoken of the seduction of the Corinthian church by satanic agencies, and in 11.4 of one who comes and preaches another Jesus, a different Spirit, a different gospel. The conclusion is valid only if it is known that Paul was unable to conceive radical divergence between himself and the Jerusalem authorities. That Paul was quite able to do this is proved by Gal. 1.8 f; 2.5 f, 11,14. Further, the difficulty is severe only if we try to establish a direct connection between 2 Cor. 11.5[99] and 11.4. But 11.5 looks back to 11.1, and the run of thought (which is no more irregular than many a passage in Paul) goes as follows: Please put up with a little folly from me (11.1). I must speak, for I have reason to be extremely anxious about you (11.2f). You are willing even to put up with one who preaches a false gospel to you (11.4). You should put up with me, for I do not come behind (those whom you consider) the highest apostles of all (11.5). It is true that some despise my power of speech, but I do not lack knowledge (11.6). Or perhaps I injured you by preaching the gospel for nothing (11.7). This last point had already been noted in 1 Cor. 9 as a point of difference between Paul and the Jerusalem apostles.

In 12.11 similar points arise. Paul has uttered his folly; he has become a fool. He affirms once more that he does not fall behind the ὑπερλίαν ἀπόστολοι—εἰ καὶ οὐδέν εἰμι. This recalls the unfavourable comparison of Paul with the earlier witnesses to the resurrection in I Cor. 15.8; and almost immediately (2 Cor. 12.13) we return to the theme of the payment of apostles.[100]

It is unlikely that Paul felt any inhibition in speaking ironically of the Jerusalem apostles, but unlikely also that he would call them false apostles, evil workers masquerading as servants of Christ, servants of Satan masquerading as servants of righteousness (11.13 ff). We may be confident that those whom he so bitterly attacked formed a different group. If we look for an analogy we may turn again to Galatians: to the envoys of James who, in 2.12, succeeded in turning Peter from the 'right road toward the truth of the gospel';[101] and disrupting the alliance between him, Paul and Barnabas. To say this is not to give a complete answer to the question: Who were the evil intruders in Corinth? We know little about the process by which the Jewish Christianity of the first generation became the hellenized, gnostic, Jewish Christianity of a later time; we may for the present be content to locate the Jewish Christianity of Corinth somewhere between the two extremes.

This observation suggests the last question that calls for brief discussion.

(3) Were there Judaizers who did not circumcise? Lütgert, it will be remembered,[102] argued that Paul's opponents in Corinth could not have been Judaizers because there is no indication that they required that Gentile Christians in Corinth should be circumcised. The argument has often been repeated, but it is not conclusive. There were Judaizers who did not call for circumcision, and one of them had most probably been in Corinth already before I Corinthians was written—Cephas. Without demanding circumcision he had attempted to impose a Judaic pattern of thought and religious life upon a Gentile community; for the evidence I may refer once more to T. W. Manson's convincing paper.[103] The verb 'to Judaize' can be used of Peter and of his influence on the authority of Paul himself: πῶς τὰ ἔθνη ἀναγκάζεις ἰουδαΐζειν; (Gal. 2.14). With Peter we may class the group (which can hardly have included Paul) that promulgated the Apostolic Decrees[104] of Acts 15.20, 29.

Thus, if there is a connection between the troubles of 2 Cor.

10—13 and those of 1 Corinthians, it is to be found, not, as is often supposed, in the Christ-group, but in the group of Cephas; though indeed there has been much development between the two epistles.

When the curtain falls on the last scene of the first act of the story of Christianity at Corinth the stage is in confusion. It has cleared but little when, forty years on, Clement of Rome raises the curtain for us once more. The Corinthians are still divided,[105] and in themselves they have perhaps little to teach us except the important truth that the apostolic age was not one of primitive perfection and unbroken unity. But Paul, who learnt at Corinth what it is to be weak in Christ, shows there perhaps more clearly than elsewhere his full stature of Christian intelligence, firmness and magnanimity.

NOTES

1   T. W. Manson, *Studies in the Gospels and Epistles* (Manchester 1962), 'The Corinthian Correspondence', pp. 190–224.

2   See e.g. T. W. Manson, op. cit., pp. 190f.

3   See e.g. J. Weiss, *The History of Primitive Christianity* (London, ET, 1937), pp. 356f; G. Bornkamm, 'Die Vorgeschichte des sogenannten Zweiten Korintherbriefes', in *Sitzungsberichte der Heidelberger Akademie der Wissenschaften*, Philosophisch-historische Klasse, Jahrgang 1961: 2 (Heidelberg 1961), pp. 16–23.

4   See e.g. J. Munck, *Paulus und die Heilsgeschichte*, Aarsskrift for Aarhus Universitet XXVI, 1, Teologisk Serie 6 (Aarhus-Copenhagen 1954), pp. 162–6.

5   See Pauly-Wissowa, *Suppl.* IV, pp. 991–1036; VI, pp. 182–99, 1350 f. There is slight uncertainty about the date, and a few other forms of the name appear to have been in use.

6   A. Deissmann, *Light from the Ancient East* (London 1927), p. 16.

7   T. W. Manson, op. cit., pp. 194–207; also see below, pp. 28–39.

8   See note 4.

9   Op. cit., pp. 134, 141.

10   See below, pp. 12 ff.

11   See below, pp. 11 f.

12   Eloquent, probably, rather than learned, though it is a fault of the ancient world that it often confused the two. For Wilckens's view see below, p. 11.

13   See below, p. 11.

14   See note 7.

15   Op. cit., pp. 197–206.

16   And perhaps to provide a foundation for more severe trouble at a later time; see below, pp. 21 f.

17   Notably J. Weiss, ad loc.; also Einleitung, pp. xxxvi ff.

18 *The Apostolic Fathers: Part I, Clement of Rome* ii (London 1890), p. 143.

19 R. Knopf, in *Handbuch zum Neuen Testament* Ergänzungsband (Tübingen 1920), p. 123, mentioning this view, adds that the Christ-group may have been enigmatic to Clement 'wie sie es der neueren Auslegung ist'.

20 It finds some support in 3.22. See J. Héring ad loc., with a reference to H. von Dobschütz, *Die urchristlichen Gemeinden* (Leipzig 1902), p. 58.

21 In addition to Commentaries, and to works mentioned in other notes, I name here by way of example some of the contributions of which I have made most use in preparing this lecture:

R. Bultmann, *Exegetische Probleme des zweiten Korintherbriefes* (Uppsala 1947).

G. Friedrich, 'Die Gegner des Paulus im 2. Korintherbrief', in *Abraham unser Vater, Juden und Christen im Gespräch über die Bibel*, Festschrift für Otto Michel, ed. O. Betz, M. Hengel, P. Schmidt (Leiden-Cologne 1963), pp. 1–12.

E. Käsemann, 'Die Legitimität des Apostels', in *ZNTW* xli (1942), pp. 33–71 (reprinted Darmstadt 1956).

W. Lütgert, *Freiheitspredigt und Schwarmgeister in Korinth* (Gütersloh 1908).

A. Schlatter, *Die korinthische Theologie* (Gütersloh 1914).

W. Schmithals, *Die Gnosis in Korinth* (Göttingen 1956).

U. Wilckens, *Weisheit und Torheit* (Tübingen 1959).

22 See especially the works by Schmithals and Wilckens (note 21), and reviews and articles prompted by them.

23 From the time of Lütgert (see p. 15, and notes 21, 75) it has been customary to apply material drawn from 1 Corinthians to the elucidation of 2 Cor. 10—13; but the change in vocabulary suggests that 2 Cor. 10—13 deals with a new situation.

24 See note 21; also the article σοφία, κτλ. in Kittel/Friedrich, *Theologisches Wörterbuch zum Neuen Testament* vii, 465–529. The latter is more convenient for quotation in a brief summary, and will be cited below by page and line.

25 523.25.

26 But are the Greeks of 1 Cor. 1. 22, 24 in any sense adversaries (*Gegner*)? or even a 'Christ-party'? Are they not non-Christians?

27 523.26 f.

28 523.33 8.

29 523.45–8.

30 That Paul had not had a formal Greek education is doubtless true, but it is also true that his writing shows marks of Greek rhetorical style, especially of the diatribe.

31 Wilckens gives too much attention to the philosophical uses of σοφία. Essentially the word means '*cleverness* or *skill* in handicraft and art' (Liddell-Scott); see the discussion in Aristotle, *Eth. Nic.*, 1141a. It can refer to skill in speech, though, it seems, more often of poets than of orators; cf. e.g. the ἀγὼν σοφίας between Aeschylus and Euripides in

Aristophanes *Frogs*, 882. The most important evidence of all, however, for our purpose is simply the figure of the Sophist, who for
centuries dominated Greek education. The Sophist offers σοφία for
money (e.g. Xenophon, *Mem.* 1.6.13: καὶ τὴν σοφίαν ὡσαύτως τοὺς μὲν
ἀργυρίου τῷ βουλομένῳ πωλοῦντας σοφιστὰς ὥσπερ πόρνους ἀποκαλοῦσιν), and
what he teaches is the art of disputation (e.g. Plato, *Sophist*, 232b
ἀντιλογικὸν αὐτὸν ἔφαμεν εἶναί που . . . οὐ καὶ τῶν ἄλλων αὐτοῦ τούτου διδάσκαλον
γίγνεσθαι; and much more).

32 He determined not to use this σοφία before he reached Corinth, and
thus before any Corinthian Christian gnosis existed—a clear indication of the meaning of σοφία here, though one that is often overlooked.

33 Apart from the linguistic problems of the word πειθοῖς which need
not be discussed here.

34 Cf. 2 Cor. 1.12 οὐκ ἐν σοφίᾳ σαρκικῇ, with which is contrasted ἐν χάριτι
θεοῦ. Wisdom, though regarded by those who cherish it as supremely
spiritual, is, if man-centred, fleshly, and ultimately forms a contrasting
counterpart to grace, since by means of it man seeks his own glory
and satisfaction. The real trouble with σοφία is that it is very difficult
to dissociate it from upward aspirations of the human mind.

35 See also John 12.31; 14.30; 16.11; also Eph. 2.2. Cf. Ignatius, Eph.
19. 1. Earthly rulers (such as Pilate) are not intended by Paul's words.

36 E.g. Lietzmann, ad loc.

37 Especially in the synoptic gospels, e.g. Mark 1.24.

38 See R. Liechtenhan, *Die urchristliche Mission* (Zürich 1946), p. 71,
n. 12.

39 See below, pp. 10 f.

40 As e.g. at Rom. 8.15 he contrasts a πνεῦμα δουλείας with the πνεῦμα
υἱοθεσίας, without meaning to imply that the former has as real and
distinct an existence as the latter.

41 See *From First Adam to Last* (London 1962), p. 90 (and elsewhere).

42 The notion of escape, of disentanglement from the evil (material)
world, seems to be primary. Whether the redeemer-figure of gnosticism existed independently of Christian influence is at present a
notoriously controversial question.

43 Cf. especially 1 Cor. 10.11.

44 E.g. Rom. 6.3 ff, 11; Col. 2.12; 3.1–4.

45 See Wilckens in *TWNT* vii, 520, n. 382.

46 Other passages, notably 1 Cor. 8.6, are often taken to imply the same
identification without use of the word.

47 ἐν τοῖς τελείοις. The sense of the word is disputed. Cf. 3.1, where the
τελεῖοι are πνευματικοί, contrasted with σάρκινοι, νήπιοι. The meaning is
certainly 'mature Christians', but it seems to have been borrowed
from the gnostic background.

48 Cf. 1 Cor. 12.8, where a λόγος σοφίας is a gift of the Spirit.

49 *TWNT* vii, 523, 35 f.

50 There seems to be a connection between gnosticism and Jewish
apocalyptic. See R. M. Grant, *A Historical Introduction to the New
Testament* (London 1963), pp. 204 ff.

51 See T. W. Manson, op. cit., especially p. 207: 'It [the Christ party] seems to stand at the opposite extreme to the Cephas party.'

52 This is confirmed by 1 Cor. 1.25: true wisdom, the wisdom that is the gospel, is described by a striking oxymoron as God's folly (τὸ μωρὸν τοῦ θεοῦ). This is more than a rhetorical device; by human standards the cross was folly.

53 See e.g. Allo, ad loc., 'Si Paul n'avait pas supposé qu'un tel sophisme avait cours à Corinthe . . ., alors sa comparaison serait un hors-d'oeuvre assez inutile, pour ne pas dire un peu trop brutal.'

54 In *Studia Paulina in honorem J. de Zwaan*, ed. J. N. Sevenster and W. C. van Unnik (Haarlem 1953), pp. 151 f.

55 *Paulus der Bote Jesu* (Stuttgart 1962).

56 Op. cit., p. 212.

57 Op. cit., p. 213.

58 See e.g. H. M. Gwatkin, *Early Church History* (Cambridge 1927), ii pp. 26 f.

59 It is possible that in the 'previous letter' Paul may have said, or have appeared to say, more than he intended (cf. 1 Cor. 5.9).

60 Cf. Käsemann's note on Lütgert quoted in note 75 below; also note 70.

61 See Kümmel's additional note in H. Lietzmann—W. G. Kümmel, *An die Korinther I, II* (Tübingen 1949), p. 208, on the view that 2 Cor. 10.7 refers to the Christ-group; also note 75.

62 See note 4.

63 Paul, Apollos and Cephas [and Christ], are certainly not Corinthian figures; but at least as far as the first two are concerned we can be confident that they did not desire the formation of groups in their names; the fault lay with the Corinthians, not with their missionaries and ministers.

64 See especially 10.12–18 (discussed below); 11.4 f., 12–15, 22 f.; 12.11 ff.

65 See *Paulus, der Apostel Jesu Christi* (Stuttgart 1845), pp. 259–332 (this theme is the main subject of the chapter); also 'Die Christuspartei in der korinthischen Gemeinde', reprinted in *Ausgewählte Werke* i, herausgegeben von K. Scholder (Stuttgart—Bad Cannstatt 1963), pp. 1–76.

66 This is not a necessary interpretation of διάκονοι δικαιοσύνης (2 Cor. 11.15), in which the genitive may well be adjectival—not satanic but righteous ministers.

67 See note 21.

68 For Paul's ability to see through such tricks cf. e.g. Gal. 4.17; ζηλοῦσιν ὑμᾶς οὐ καλῶς.

69 'Sie bekämpfen ihn [Paulus] nicht wie die Judaisten in Galatien als einen Irrlehrer, der die Gemeinde verführt, nicht als Sündendiener, der sie vom göttlichen Gesetz weglockt, nicht als Antinomisten, nicht als gefährlichen Gegner der alten Frömmigkeit, als Neuerer und Revolutionär, der zu weit geht,—sondern umgekehrt: als Schwächling, sie hassen und fürchten ihn nicht, sie verachten ihn' (op. cit., p. 68).

70   'Sie [die Gegner] entstammen einer Richtung, die aus der urchrist-
      lichen Freiheitspredigt erstanden ist . . . Sie sind libertinistiche Pneu-
      matiker" (op. cit., p. 86). It is unfortunate that both Lütgert and
      Schlatter (see note 21), who followed him closely, took 2 Cor. 10—13
      closely with data deduced from 1 Corinthians about the Christ-group.
71   *Première Epître aux Corinthiens* (Paris 1956). See also below, p. 16.
72   'Ainsi nous n'allons pas, comme *Lütgert*, jusqu'à prendre ces opposants
      déclarés pour des libertins "gnostiques" proprement dits, mais pour
      des faiseurs de spéculations où, sur la base prétendue des enseigne-
      ments évangélique et mosaïque combinés, se dressait quelque
      mystique d'allure gnosticisante. On comprendrait fort bien alors
      comment ils pouvaient grouper autour d'eux les mécontents des
      partis les plus divers' (op. cit., p. 272).
73   See note 21. Käsemann treats the problem with special reference to
      the conceptions of apostleship involved. It is very important that he
      does not make the mistake of confusing the situation of 2 Cor. 10—13
      with that of 1 Corinthians.
74   Thus, 2 Cor. 10.7 does not mean that 2 Cor. 10—13 is to be closely
      connected with the Christ-group (1 Cor. 1.12).
75   'Kennzeichnend ist jedoch, dass Lütgerts These—in der Negation
      durchschlagend—in ihrer positiven Beweisführung solange farblos
      bleibt, wie sie ihre Argumente nicht aus 1 Cor. entleiht' (op. cit.,
      p. 40 (18 of the reprint)).
76   Op. cit., p. 46 (27 of the reprint).
77   Op. cit., pp. 48 f. (30 of the reprint).
78   Op. cit., p. 50 (33 of the reprint).
79   At this point (op. cit., p. 51 (36 of the reprint)) Käsemann makes the
      interesting suggestion: 'Hier ist vor allem das שליח—Institut zu
      erwähnen, das zwar kaum die Entstehung des christlichen Apostolates
      ausreichend erklärt, wohl aber die Entsendung urgemeindlicher
      Emissäre in das Missionsgebiet.'
80   Op. cit., p. 51 (35 of the reprint).
81   Ibid.
82   See note 21.
83   Op. cit., p. 25.
84   'Denn 12.11 heisst es im Aor. οὐδὲν γὰρ ὑστέρησα τ. ὑπερλ. ἀπ., und das
      κατειργάσθη ἐν ὑμῖν (v. 12) bestätigt es. Dann müssen aber doch die ὑπερλίαν
      ἀπόστολοι eben in Korinth den Paulus durch ihr Wirken . . . in den
      Schatten gestellt haben' (op. cit., p. 28).
85   I have no space to show in detail how my interpretation of this
      passage is indebted—both positively and negatively—to Käsemann
      and Bultmann, as well as to the commentators. I am however unable
      to follow Käsemann and Bultmann in accepting the reading of the
      Western text, which omits the last words (οὐ συνιᾶσιν) of verse 12 and
      the first words (ἡμεῖς δέ) of verse 13, thus running the two verses to-
      gether. The Western reading is smoother than that of the other MSS
      (with its abrupt change of person and absolute use of συνιᾶσιν), and
      not to be preferred.

86 Paul uses the first person plural. He may be associating colleagues with himself; this makes no difference to the argument.

87 Cf. 3.1; 5.12.

88 N. Turner, in J. H. Moulton, *A Grammar of New Testament Greek*, iii *Syntax* (Edinburgh 1963), p. 160, translates, 'they do not realize that they are measuring themselves by their own standards'. But cf. the other uses of συνίημι in Paul (Rom. 3.11; 15.21).

89 For the construction of οὗ ἐμέρισεν see Blass-Debrunner, 294.5 (Anhang).

90 'Beurteilungsmassstab' (Kümmel, p. 209).

91 μέτρον has other meanings also, but none that is applicable here.

92 Cf. ἐφικνούμενοι εἰς ὑμᾶς, ὑπερεκτείνομεν, ἄχρι καὶ ὑμῶν ἐφθάσαμεν (v. 14), ὑπερέκεινα (v. 16).

93 For this use of κανών cf. 1 Clem. 41.1: ... μὴ παρεκβαίνων τὸν ὡρισμένον τῆς λειτουργίας αὐτοῦ κανόνα.

94 ἐν ὑμῖν: perhaps 'on account of them'.

95 See 12.12; and Käsemann, op. cit., pp. 61–71 (51–66 of the reprint).

96 Op. cit., p. 210.

97 See *Studia Paulina* (note 54), pp. 1–4.

98 See Kümmel, p. 210; Bultmann, op. cit., pp. 27 f.

99 The γάρ (B: δέ) seems to demand such a connection, but it is by no means every γάρ in Paul that links directly with the immediately preceding sentence.

100 All the signs of an apostle (verse 12) were present—except the demand for payment.

101 See G. D. Kilpatrick, 'Gal. 2.14 ὀρθοποδοῦσιν', in *Neutestamentliche Studien für Rudolf Bultmann* (Berlin 1954), pp. 269–74.

102 See above, p. 15.

103 Op. cit., especially p. 205: 'I suggest that the demand [for glossolalia] came from the leaders of the Cephas party, and was part of the concerted move to instil Palestinian piety and Palestinian orthodoxy into the Corinthian Church.'

104 See *From First Adam to Last*, pp. 25 f.

105 See especially 1 Clement 47, with specific reference to 1 Cor. 1.10 ff.

2
CEPHAS AND CORINTH

The enigmatic position of Peter in the development of the primitive church has not yet been fully resolved—by the traditions of the patristic age, the controversies of the Reformation period, the critical reconstruction made by F. C. Baur and his followers, or the more recent works of Dr Cullmann[1] and the late Dean Lowe[2] (to name no others). The question as a whole cannot be handled in a short essay; all that will be attempted here is a re-examination of the references, and possible allusions, to Peter (Cephas) in the Corinthian letters, and a tentative assessment of their bearing on the wider issues. These letters, written during the 'Ephesian period' of Paul's activity, are of central importance as historical sources, and it may well be hoped that they will provide useful pointers which it will be worth while to collect.[3]

Cephas is not mentioned by name in 2 Corinthians. In 1 Corinthians he is mentioned at 1.12; 3.22; 9.5; 15.5, and a brief exegetical account of these passages must be given first.

1.12. The opening words, λέγω δὲ τοῦτο, introduce an expansion and explanation of what has been said in the preceding verse,[4] in which Paul repeats the information given him by members of the household of Chloe: there are ἔριδες among you. It would be wrong to take this statement in itself to mean that the Corinthian church was split into factions, for ἔρις means not 'party' but 'strife'; here, perhaps, 'wrangling'. But verse 11 has in turn grown out of verse 10 (γάρ), which refers to σχίσματα.[5] Paul does not say in this verse that σχίσματα already exist, but warns his readers of the danger that they may come into being, if all do not endeavour to 'say the same thing', and to be framed together in one mind and one opinion. It is however probable that for reasons of tact Paul is here saying less than the truth. According to 11.18 he has already heard that σχίσματα exist, and, in the circumstances, considers it inevitable that there should be αἱρέσεις (11.19). Further, if each one has his slogan,[6] those who adopt the same rallying-cry will inevitably fall into the same group.

Thus we must think of a church still outwardly united,[7] but, when it meets, divided into parties, one saying Ἐγὼ Παύλου, another Ἐγὼ Ἀπολλῶ, and another Ἐγὼ Κηφᾶ.[8] A pointer to the meaning of the genitives is given in the context by the reference to οἱ Χλόης (1.11), who are probably slaves, or freed household dependants, of Chloe. This supports Bachmann's view that 'die Genitive nicht ein Verhalten *subjektiver* Anhänglichkeit, sondern ein Verhältnis wirklicher, *objektiver* Zugehörigkeit bezeichnen',[9] though it is evident that in such a context subjective assent to the views of the leader in question must be included. The fact that Paul immediately (in verse 13) goes on to speak of baptism suggests that converts tended to align themselves with the evangelist under whom they had been won to the faith.

3.22. Here the name Cephas appears in a list which expands the word πάντα, which occurs in the preceding verse, and is taken up again at the end of verse 22. All things are yours; and this 'all' includes persons (Paul, Apollos, Cephas), and things (the world, life, death, things present and things to come). This is a strange list, and its constituents cannot all be said to be 'yours' in the same way. The general sense is given by the fact that the list as a whole forms a concessive clause. No one should glory in men, for though all things are yours you are yourselves Christ's.[10] The application of the personal names in verse 22 is thus determined by μηδεὶς καυχάσθω ἐν ἀνθρώποις. Some would (if unchecked) glory in Paul, in Apollos, in Cephas. Paul not infrequently uses καυχᾶσθαι with ἐν,[11] and in these epistles twice quotes Jer. 9.22 to the effect that men ought to glory only in the Lord. To glory in men, in the flesh, in the law, is wrong because to do so is to rob God of his due. Men have been placing boastful confidence in Paul, Apollos and Cephas; the next verse emphasizes the wrongfulness of this, by underlining the fact that they are men—not κύριοι in whom one might boast, but ὑπηρέται and οἰκονόμοι.

9.5. In this verse (as in verse 4) μή is the interrogative particle, and οὐκ negatives the verb:[12] You don't suppose, do you, that we do not have the right to take about with us a Christian wife? It is almost certain that the ἤ that introduces verse 6 leads to a new kind of question, in which the stress lies upon the subject (not the verb). If this is so, μὴ ἐργάζεσθαι corresponds to eating and drinking, and to taking about a wife, 'at the expense of the community' being understood in each case, and Paul implies that he (and Barnabas) had the right to be supported, and to claim support for their wives (if they had wives).

The list of persons in verse 5 b is ambiguous, and its sense depends on the way in which λοιποί is taken. οἱ λοιποὶ ἀπόστολοι could mean (a) the apostles other than the brothers of the Lord and Cephas (about to be mentioned). In this case, it is implied that the brothers and Cephas are apostles. This raises no difficulty with regard to Cephas, but (notwithstanding Gal. 1.19) there is no good ground for supposing that the brothers as a body were counted apostles; and the position of λοιποί (preceding the exceptions) would be at least surprising. It is better to suppose (b) that λοιποί makes a contrast with Paul (and Barnabas). In this case we should have a reference to the two great groups of leading Jewish Christians—the (twelve) apostles, and the brothers of the Lord. If we take λοιποί in this way, the question is raised the more sharply why Cephas should be mentioned by name, since he has already been included as one of οἱ λοιποὶ ἀπόστολοι.

15.5.   In the passage of which this verse forms part Paul is undoubtedly recalling to his readers traditional material which he had himself received, and had previously handed on to them (verse 3). The question has been raised,[13] where the traditional material ends—certainly before verse 8, which at least is Paul's own addition: probably earlier. Whatever be the answer to this question it is scarcely open to doubt that the appearance to Peter, the first to be mentioned, was part of the tradition. It is the more surprising that it is not narrated in any of the Gospels.

Only one question need be taken up here. At the end of the paragraph (15.11) Paul sums up in the words εἴτε οὖν ἐγὼ εἴτε ἐκεῖνοι, οὕτως κηρύσσομεν—the resurrection of Christ is common apostolic proclamation. But who are ἐκεῖνοι? There is no clear antecedent to this pronoun, but we are bound to look back to the αὐτῶν πάντων of verse 10. But who are these? Presumably the apostles of verse 9, apart from their 'least' (ἐλάχιστος) member, Paul himself; that is, substantially the same group as those described in 9.5 as οἱ λοιποὶ ἀπόστολοι. As in that passage, so here, Peter is singled out as an outstanding representative of the apostolic group; as there 'the brothers of the Lord' stand with the apostles, so here James (the Lord's brother is surely intended) is mentioned as having seen the risen Jesus. The point of the paragraph appears to be that though the Corinthians might be familiar with an apostolic preaching other than Paul's, and have been informed that, in comparison with such figures as Peter and James, Paul was a mere ἔκτρωμα,[14] yet on this point at least (not necessarily on others) complete unity prevailed: Christ was raised from the dead according to the Scriptures. From this the rest of the chapter follows.

These few references are sufficient to raise a number of questions of great difficulty and equally great importance. They may be divided into two groups: (a) Local questions, such as, Had Cephas visited Corinth? Who were οἱ Κηφᾶ? and (b) general questions, such as, How were the mission of Peter and the mission of Paul related to each other theologically, and in scope, method and success? The local questions have been answered so variously that it is not surprising that the more general problems remain unsolved. When scholars such as J. Weiss and E. Meyer, H. Lietzmann and M. Goguel, can be ranged on opposite sides it is temerarious to suppose that a convincing case for one alternative can be made; yet the evidence seems to point in one direction. Let us collect our inferences so far.

(1) The Cephas adherents were objectively related to their leader. It is surprising that Bachmann, who stresses the objectivity of the relationship, should refuse to draw the conclusion that Cephas had been in Corinth, though his suggestion that οἱ Κηφᾶ were eastern Christians who owed their conversion and baptism to Peter but had subsequently migrated to Corinth must be allowed to be possible. It is however much less likely that such chance visitors should form a coherent group, parallel to those attaching themselves to Paul and Apollos, than that the group should have been constituted in Corinth itself, the objective relationship coming into being there, probably in the context of instruction and baptism.

(2) Again, in 3.22 the three missionaries are placed side by side on equal terms. This is striking in view of the fact that, throughout the passage as a whole (3.1—4.13), only Paul and Apollos are mentioned. That this restriction was deliberate is a probable inference from 4.6, where the sense appears to be: I have made these things (ταῦτα) look as if they applied to Apollos and me (only), in order that you may learn with reference to us (ἐν ἡμῖν, us and not anyone else) not to go beyond what is written (in the Old Testament about ministers)—though in fact the lesson really applies to a third party.[15] The name of this third party slips in at

3.22, because here Paul is writing somewhat rhetorically and is off his guard. Peter was in fact a more dangerous potential cause of schism in Corinth than either Paul or Apollos.

(3) We have seen reason to think that, at 9.5, the name Cephas is logically pleonastic; he has already been included in οἱ λοιποὶ ἀπόστολοι. Why then is he named? Conceivably because he was an outstanding person and his circumstances were the talk of Christendom; much more probably (since we are dealing not with his public teaching but with his domestic affairs) because he had been in Corinth with his wife.

(4) It seems clear from 15.11 that the Corinthians were aware of more than one kind of apostolic preaching. The Pauline and the other preaching were agreed on the fact of the resurrection; how far they otherwise differed remains so far unclear.

It is evident that these observations, even when combined with others made incidentally in the discussion of 1.12; 3.22; 9.5; 15.5, do not amount to proof that Cephas visited Corinth. The well-known statement of Dionysius,[16] that both Peter and Paul 'planted and taught' the Corinthian church, is a worthless deduction from 1 Corinthians; but when we recall that Cephas certainly visited Antioch (Gal. 2.11), that he probably travelled as far as Rome,[17] that it was thought reasonable to represent him as writing to Christians in Pontus, Galatia, Cappadocia, Asia and Bithynia (1 Pet. 1.1), and that the Clementine literature, though itself fictitious, freely and without fear of contradiction ascribes to him widespread missionary activity, it seems far more probable that he had himself been in Corinth than that members of the church there had simply heard of him as a notable Palestinian Christian.

If Cephas did in fact play a personal part in the development of the Corinthian church it will be not unreasonable to suppose that traces of his presence may be found in the Corinthian letters in addition to those passages in which his name is mentioned. We must next consider this possibility.

The most notable recent attempt to detect the figure of Peter behind 1 Corinthians has been made by the late T. W. Manson in his Rylands lecture.[18] A brief sketch of his suggestions, together with a few comments, follows.

(a) In 3.1–9 Paul deals with the relation between himself and Apollos. In 3.10–17 an unnamed person is represented as trying to build on Paul's foundations, and indeed to interfere with the foundation Paul has laid—which is Christ himself (3.11). The situation must be understood in terms of Matt. 16.18: either Peter himself, or someone acting in his name, is making the claim that Peter is the rock on which the Church must be built.

This observation seems to me to be just; and I believe it to be supported by what I have said in an earlier discussion[19] of the 'pillars' of Gal. 2.

(b) In 5.9–13 (and in the 'previous letter') there may be an echo of the controversy at Antioch (Gal. 2.11 ff). 'May it not be that Paul was giving in this letter *his* idea of what constituted a "kosher" table for Christians with all the emphasis on the company rather than the viands?' (p. 197).

(c) 6.1–8 gives a double treatment of the problem raised by Corinthian litigation. The first part (verses 1–6) contains a characteristically Jewish criticism, such as might have been made by the Cephas-party: as Jewish disputes should be taken not to pagan but to Jewish courts, so Christian disputes should be confined to Christian courts. Paul does not disagree, but in verses 7 f adds his own view: there should be no disputes. That they exist at all indicates a failure in Christian charity.

(d) Behind the discussion of sexual problems in 1 Cor. 7 may lie a controversy Paul had been asked to settle. The members of the Apollos-party (or of the Christ-party), and the Jewish–Christian followers of Cephas, would probably not see eye to eye over the question of virgins and spiritual marriages. This point is (rightly) advanced somewhat tentatively.

(e) 1 Cor. 8, 9 and 10 contain a discussion of the legitimacy of certain foods, punctuated by an impassioned defence of Paul's apostleship, and his apostolic rights. The problem had been raised at Antioch (Gal. 2.12), and dealt with[20] at the council of Acts 15. Why then does Paul not refer to the decision of the assembled apostles and elders? 'I cannot help thinking that the question was raised at Corinth by the Cephas-party, and that Paul's way of dealing with it is, and is meant to be, a snub' (p. 200). In the end, Paul accepts the Jewish–Christian conclusion (10.21), but he 'insists on supplying it with an entirely Christian basis' (p. 202). 'Jewish–Christian visitors cannot presume to legislate in these matters for Gentile–Christian churches' (p. 200). It is no accident, or digression, that the discussion of apostleship intervenes; on this issue Paul's authority was directly challenged.

This is a convincing point, easily capable of restatement if a somewhat different view of Acts 15 is taken.

(f) Behind 1 ·Cor. 11.17–34 may be seen Gentile–Christian abuse of the Lord's Table, and criticism uttered by Jewish Christians, to whom 'the glaring scandal was that it was not a *kosher* table' (p. 202). Paul does not justify Gentile abuses, but argues that the real scandal lies in the lack of a true spirit of Christian brotherhood.

Here we may add that the σχίσματα and αἱρέσεις of 1 Cor. 11.18 f plainly recall the fact that at Antioch Peter ὑπέστελλεν καὶ ἀφώριζεν ἑαυτόν, carrying others with him (Gal. 2.12 f). It is at least possible that he had done the same thing at Corinth.

(g) Finally there is the question of *glossolalia* in 1 Cor. 12 and 14. Here Manson sees a demand that was being made by the leaders of the Cephas party that the Corinthian church should produce this particular fruit of the Spirit, as 'part of the concerted move to instil Palestinian piety and Palestinian orthodoxy into the Corinthian Church' (p. 205). Paul's own assessment of the importance of *glossolalia* is too familiar to need repetition here.

Manson's suggestion is attractive, but open to question, for it is not certain that *glossolalia* was practised in the Palestinian church[21]).

Before we leave Manson's suggestions it may be noted that if he is right in speaking of an organized attempt to 'instil Palestinian piety and Palestinian orthodoxy' into Gentile churches there is a heightened probability that the great Palestinian apostle himself will have been involved (though in what sense remains to be seen) in the movement, especially since questions of apostolic authority, apostolic privileges, and apostolic practices were explicitly raised. We cannot attempt even a brief summing up of these issues until we have looked for evidence in 2 Corinthians.

A full examination of the opposition to Paul implied by 2 Corinthians would require a literary analysis that would be out of place in this short note. There are other problems, too, of great importance for the interpretation of the epistle as a whole that must for the present be set aside. What can be affirmed, and will be supported by examination of the evidence, is that there was a Jewish Christian opposition to Paul which was concentrated in a single figure, never named but occasionally visible. No one can, or ought to approach, 2 Corinthians with a completely blank mind. 1 Corinthians teaches us in the plainest possible terms that there was in Corinth a party, or group, which did not consider Paul as its head, adopted a Jewish–

Christian standpoint and venerated one who could undoubtedly describe himself as an apostle, a Hebrew, an Israelite, of the seed of Abraham and a servant of Christ, and boast, if he wished, of his sufferings—stripes and imprisonments—and of his visions. It is with these facts in mind that we turn to 2 Corinthians.

We note first a number of passages where persons, or a person, are spoken of who behave in a way reprehended by Paul.

2.17. There are some[22] who traffic in the word of God. This appears to mean not that they falsify the word of God, but that they make profit from it;[23] it is however natural to compare 4.2 (δολοῦντες τὸν λόγον τοῦ θεοῦ), which may well refer to the same persons.

3.1. There are some (τινες—Paul presumably has definite persons in mind) who make use of commendatory letters, as Paul does not. Cf. also 10.12.

5.12. τοὺς ἐν προσώπῳ καυχωμένους is not an abstract statement but a description of particular persons. The use of the verb in 1 Cor. 3.21 (and cf. 2 Cor. 10.16 f) will be recalled. Glorying ἐν προσώπῳ is the same as glorying ἐν ἀνθρώποις, which could (in one case) mean glorying in Peter.

10.7. εἴ τις πέποιθεν could be a general statement, but more probably refers to a particular person who claims to be in a special way Χριστοῦ. Paul does not deny the claim, but urges that it could be made equally of himself. We may note here the use of the singular φησίν[24] in 10.10. This is usually taken to be the equivalent of Man sagt, and this is a possible translation; but the proximity of verse 7 suggests that the words quoted might be those of the man who is confident that he is 'Christ's'. This is confirmed by ὁ τοιοῦτος[25] in verse 11.

10.12–18. The remainder of the chapter is notoriously obscure, and cannot be discussed in detail here. It refers however to a specific group of persons (τῶν ἑαυτοὺς συνιστανόντων, verse 12; cf. 3.1) whose practices arouse Paul's vigorous, and at times sarcastic, condemnation. It will suffice to note that once more wrongful boasting (καυχᾶσθαι) is in mind, and especially that the question is raised whether the range of activity of the persons concerned may be rightly said to extend as far as Corinth. Paul claims that his evangelistic work legitimately extends as far as Corinth (ἄχρι ὑμῶν ἐφθάσαμεν ἐν τῷ εὐαγγελίῳ τοῦ Χριστοῦ) and indeed beyond (εἰς τὰ ὑπερέκεινα ὑμῶν); not so with his adversaries.[26] The reader cannot fail to recall the agreement reached in Gal. 2.9: Peter was to go to

the Circumcision, Paul to the Gentiles.[27] The Jewish–Christian
mission was within its rights at Antioch; it might claim to be equally
justified in evangelizing Corinth, where there was a συναγωγὴ
'Εβραίων,[28] but it had no right to invade an existing Gentile church
(10.15, ἐν ἀλλοτρίοις κόποις). Whether the mission had been headed
by Peter himself cannot be settled on the basis of 2 Corinthians
alone; but note (a) the evidence of 1 Corinthians; (b) the passages
in 2 Corinthians (see above and below) where the singular is used;
(c) the fact that the arrangement of Gal. 2 was made in the first
instance with Peter; and (d) the fact that in 2 Corinthians Paul
refrains from mentioning names—a reticence more easily com-
prehensible if the name that might have been mentioned was that
of the great apostle who was the primary witness of the resurrection.

11.4.   This verse seems at first to be perfectly clear. ὁ ἐρχόμενος
who preaches a 'different Jesus' may represent a group, but the
mode of expression suggests a representative person. The connection
with verse 5, however, is not clear, and the identification of οἱ
ὑπερλίαν ἀπόστολοι (cf. 12.11) is a notorious crux. The most natural
explanation will see in these words a reference to the original
Jerusalem apostles. Paul says: I do not consider that I come short
of what all will acknowledge as the standard of apostolic authority
and equipment. It is not entirely against this that one of those
concerned should be accused of proclaiming a 'different Jesus',
since in Gal. 2 Peter scarcely comes short of doing this.[29] It is more
serious that in 11.13 we read of ψευδαπόστολοι, who have been sent
not by Christ but by Satan. This can hardly have been said of the
original Jerusalem apostles. Nevertheless, in 11.19 f we again
encounter the verb ἀνέχεσθαι (cf. 11.4), and a 'τις' who καταδουλοῖ,
κατεσθίει, λαμβάνει, δέρει. The next verse moves into the plural,
and we meet with Hebrews, Israelites, the seed of Abraham, the
servants of Christ. The obscurity of the language, and its rapid
changes, reflect the confused and embarrassing situation Paul had
to deal with. In this section there is in fact a twofold oscillation
between singular and plural, and between envoys of Satan and
genuine if misguided apostles of Christ.

We have now reviewed passages where Paul plainly refers to
persons of whom he disapproves. There are a few other verses in
2 Corinthians that should be noted before we sum up.

1.24 might imply the existence of others who do lord it over the
Corinthians' faith.

2.9 might imply that the Corinthians in being disobedient to Paul had been not simply self-willed but obedient to others.

4.5. Perhaps there were others who did preach themselves, and not as δοῦλοι.

5.13. Some may actually have brought the charge that Paul was out of his mind.

11.7. For Paul's gratuitous preaching of the gospel, and the problems it caused for him, cf. 1 Cor. 9.4 ff, mentioned above.

12. 11: εἰ καὶ οὐδέν εἰμι (cf. 11.6). This may echo a slight— Paul is a mere nothing. Cf. ἔκτρωμα, in 1 Cor. 15.8.

We are now in a position to put the evidence together and sum up.

(1) The evidence of 1 Corinthians shows the certain influence, and probable presence, of Peter in Corinth. He was an embarrassment to Paul, and his characteristically Jewish–Christian opinions take some hard knocks; but Paul, who could not forget that Peter was the primary witness of the resurrection, and did preach Christ, crucified and risen according to the Scriptures, did not attack him. His name is mentioned with perfect propriety; of him and his colleagues it is said (15.11): εἴτε οὖν ἐγὼ εἴτε ἐκεῖνοι, οὕτως κηρύσσομεν.

(2) It was probably only in the general deterioration of the Corinthian situation, after the writing of 1 Corinthians (whether this letter be a unity or not), that Paul saw how serious the effects of the intervention of Jewish–Christian emissaries in Corinth were likely to prove, or were proving. It was no longer possible to use the words of 1 Cor. 15.11 (just quoted). A different Jesus (2 Cor. 11.4) was being preached, and the agreement of Gal. 2 flagrantly contravened; and the consequences were such as might have been expected.

(3) Yet in 2 Corinthians there is no specific reference to Peter, and Paul's most combative and indignant passages are couched in allusive terms, which show little respect for the original Jerusalem apostles, but reserve vigorous antipathy for other agents apparently at work in Corinth.

(4) The key to the situation may be found, by analogy, in Gal. 2.12. The New Testament evidence as a whole suggests that Peter's heart was in the right place, and that 'the root of the matter' was in him. But he was easily frightened, and therefore easily influenced and used. More subtle and less scrupulous ecclesiastical politicians found him useful as a figure-head. Hence Paul's embarrassment.

38 ESSAYS ON PAUL

He could not simply repudiate Peter; yet Peter, in the hands of those who made use of him, was on the way to ruining Paul's work at Corinth. Some such view as this may prove to be the clue that will lead to the solution of the very complex, and sometimes apparently contradictory, material in 2 Corinthians.

NOTES

1 O. Cullmann, *Petrus: Jünger—Apostel—Märtyrer* (Zürich/Stuttgart 1960²).

2 J. Lowe, *Saint Peter* (Oxford 1956).

3 The related material in Galatians is referred to in my essay: 'Paul and the "Pillar" Apostles', in *Studia Paulina in honorem J. de Zwaan*, ed. J. N. Sevenster and W. C. van Unnik (Haarlem 1953), pp. 1–19).

4 For this explanatory τοῦτο δὲ λέγω cf. Gal. 3. 17; also 4.1.

5 Unless with P⁴⁶ 33 sah we read the singular, σχίσμα. This reading is best explained as due to assimilation to 1 Cor. 11.18; 12.25.

6 On the inexact expression ἕκαστος ὑμῶν λέγει see e.g. J. Weiss ad loc.

7 Cf. J. Munck, *Paulus und die Heilsgeschichte* (Copenhagen 1954), pp. 127–61. I do not however find it possible to share all Munck's conclusions.

8 I do not discuss the words ἐγὼ δὲ Χριστοῦ, which raise problems too large to be included here with others.

9 *Der erste Brief des Paulus an die Korinther*, 4. Auflage, mit Nachträgen von E. Stauffer (Leipzig 1936), p. 64.

10 The sequence may contribute to the interpretation of ἐγὼ δὲ Χριστοῦ in 1.12.

11 The use of the nouns καύχημα (in 2 Cor. 1.14; 9.3; Phil. 1.26; 2.16) and καύχησις (in 2 Cor. 7.4, 14; 8.24; 1 Thess. 2.19) points to the relation between an evangelist and his converts.

12 See e.g. A. T. Robertson, *A Grammar of the Greek New Testament* (London 1919³), p. 1169.

13 See especially J. Jeremias, *Die Abendmahlsworte Jesu* (Göttingen 1949²), pp. 95 ff.

14 On this point see, however, J. Munck, 'Paulus tanquam abortivus' in *New Testament Essays: Studies in Memory of T. W. Manson*, ed. A. J. B. Higgins (Manchester 1959), pp. 180–93.

15 The use in this verse of μετασχηματίζειν with εἰς is difficult. In Paul cf. 2 Cor. 11.13–15; see also Philo, *Leg. Gai.* 80: ... ἑνὸς σώματος οὐσίαν μετασχηματίζων καὶ μεταχαράττων εἰς πολυτρόπους μορφάς. See M. D. Hooker in *NTS* 10 (1963–4), pp. 131 f.

16 In Eusebius, *Hist. Eccl.*, II, 25, 8.

17 See Cullmann, op. cit., pp. 78–178.

18 'The Corinthian Correspondence (1)', reprinted in *Studies in the Gospels and Epistles* (Manchester 1962), pp. 190–209.

19 See note 3.

20 So Manson. I should myself prefer a somewhat different account of the Council and of Paul's relations with it.

21 See M. Goguel, *La Naissance du Christianisme* (Paris 1946), pp. 112–115.
22 According to some texts (including ℵ A B C K), these are the majority (or at least numerous: οἱ πολλοί). Others (including P⁴⁶ D G Marcion) read οἱ λοιποί, which might recall 1 Cor. 9.5—the rest of the apostles, who, by accepting payment, do trade on the word of God.
23 So for example Lietzmann, ad loc.
24 This is undoubtedly the correct text, though B lat syr have the plural.
25 12.2 shows that ὁ τοιοῦτος may refer to a specific person.
26 See however E. Käsemann, 'Die Legitimität des Apostels', in *ZNW* xli, 1942, pp. 59 ff. (48–51 of the reprint, Darmstadt 1956). But ἐφθάσαμεν and ὑπερέκεινα seem to me decisively in favour of the view taken above.
27 Cf. T. W. Manson, as quoted and summarized on page 33 above.
28 See A. Deissmann, *Light from the Ancient East* (ET) (London 1927²) p. 16.
29 Cf. also Gal. 1.8 f.

3
THINGS SACRIFICED TO IDOLS

The problem raised by the use of food offered in sacrifice to idols, remote though it is from modern western Christianity, played a large part in Christian thought in and for some time after the New Testament period. The evidence for this statement, so far as the New Testament is concerned, is, briefly, as follows.

The subject evidently occupied part of a letter written to Paul by the church at Corinth,[1] and in turn makes up a substantial sub-division of the document we call 1 Corinthians.[2] In 1 Cor. 8 and 10, with allusions elsewhere, the question whether it is or is not proper for a Christian to eat food that has at some stage in its history passed through a pagan rite and been offered in sacrifice to an idol is explicitly discussed. The discussion raises a number of problems, some of which will be mentioned below: in addition to linguistic and exegetical cruces there are the questions, first, why Chapter 9 should intrude between the two treatments of the subject in Chapters 8 and 10, and, secondly, whether Paul is consistent in what he says in the various places where the eating of εἰδωλόθυτα is discussed. The subject is one that raises several of the most pressing problems in the literary study of 1 Corinthians and the historical study of the life of Paul, to say nothing of important theological issues.

Of importance equal to that of 1 Corinthians is the evidence of the so-called Apostolic Decree, of which the relevant words, in the form given by Nestle,[3] are as follows:

Acts 15.20: ... ἀπέχεσθαι τῶν ἀλισγημάτων τῶν εἰδώλων καὶ τῆς πορνείας καὶ πνικτοῦ καὶ τοῦ αἵματος.

15.29: ... ἀπέχεσθαι εἰδωλοθύτων καὶ αἵματος καὶ πνικτῶν καὶ πορνείας.

21.25: ... φυλάσσεσθαι αὐτοὺς τό τε εἰδωλόθυτον καὶ αἷμα καὶ πνικτὸν καὶ πορνείαν.

It will be noted that the expressions used in the three verses all differ. We may reasonably suppose that Luke took them all in the sense of 15.29, which he gives as the text of the Decree itself: Gentile

Christians must abstain from the use of articles of food (εἰδωλόθυτα, plural) which have been offered in sacrifice in idolatrous worship. That Luke simply invented this decree seems highly improbable; that he has placed it in the right historical context is perhaps equally improbable. Two further points may be noted at this stage, as we collect evidence. (1) With abstention from εἰδωλόθυτα goes abstention from blood and from strangled carcasses. It was natural for a Jew to put these together: for him, food was forbidden if it was idolatrous, even though (supposing it to be meat) it had been correctly slaughtered, and equally food was forbidden if, though untainted by idolatry, it had been improperly slaughtered. In 1 Corinthians the question of methods of slaughtering does not arise at all. (2) With abstention from idolatrous food goes abstention from fornication (πορνεία). This at first sight surprising combination recurs in 1 Corinthians and Revelation.

Next come the references to εἰδωλόθυτα in the letters to the Seven Churches, in Revelation. In the letter to Pergamum there is a reference to those who hold the teaching of Balaam, ὃς ἐδίδασκεν τῷ Βαλὰκ βαλεῖν σκάνδαλον ἐνώπιον τῶν υἱῶν Ἰσραήλ, φαγεῖν εἰδωλόθυτα καὶ πορνεῦσαι (Rev. 2.14). This 'teaching of Balaam' may possibly be related to the teaching of the Nicolaitans mentioned in the next verse; if so, we must look back to the letter to Ephesus, in which the works of the Nicolaitans are reprobated (Rev. 2.6). Here it is important to note the recurring connection with fornication, and the reference to Balaam; compare the reference to the incident of Baal Peor (in the context of the Balaam stories) in 1 Cor. 10.8.

In the next letter, to Thyatira, stands the condemnation of the woman Jezebel, who calls herself a prophetess, καὶ διδάσκει καὶ πλανᾷ τοὺς ἐμοὺς δούλους πορνεῦσαι καὶ φαγεῖν εἰδωλόθυτα (Rev. 2.20). Here too the eating of εἰδωλόθυτα is connected with fornication, and with Old Testament precedent, though here the figure of Jezebel is substituted for that of Balaam. Jezebel is described at 3 Reg. 16.31 as leading her husband into idolatry, and at 4 Reg. 9.22 as guilty of fornication; see also 3 Reg. 18.19 . . . τοὺς προφήτας τῆς αἰσχύνης . . . καὶ τοὺς προφήτας τῶν ἀλσῶν . . . ἐσθίοντας τράπεζαν Ἰεζάβελ.

To these passages which speak directly of the eating of sacrificial food we should perhaps add Rev. 2.24: οὐ βάλλω ἐφ' ὑμᾶς ἄλλο βάρος. Many commentators[4] have seen here an allusion to the Decree; cf. Acts 15.28, μηδὲν πλέον ἐπιτίθεσθαι ὑμῖν βάρος πλὴν τούτων τῶν ἐπάναγκες. There is at least no difficulty in supposing that the Decree was current in the circles from which Revelation arose. Compare also Rev. 9.20 f, which puts together the worship of demons and idols, and fornication (with other sins).

Rev. 2.14 sends us to the story of Balaam; Balaam sends us next to Jude and 2 Peter.

Jude 11: τῇ πλάνῃ τοῦ Βαλαὰμ μισθοῦ ἐξεχύθησαν.

2 Pet. 2.15: καταλείποντες εὐθεῖαν ὁδὸν ἐπλανήθησαν, ἐξακολουθήσαντες τῇ ὁδῷ τοῦ Βαλαὰμ τοῦ Βοσόρ, ὃς μισθὸν ἀδικίας ἠγάπησεν.

Here there is no clear reference to the eating of εἰδωλόθυτα, but there is some reason to think that this lurks in the background. In Revelation (cf. also 1 Cor. 10) the story of Balaam is linked (as it is also in the Old Testament)[5] with both sexual immorality and participation in idolatrous rites, and it would be natural to expect the same connection in Jude and 2 Peter also. Undoubtedly sexual vice is in mind (Jude 7; 2 Pet. 2.6 f, 14), and there are some indications of idolatry too. In Jude 10, where the theme of vice has given place to that of disrespect to angels, the point may be failure to recognize spiritual forces behind sacrificial foods, by which, in consequence, men are destroyed (φθείρονται); and in Jude 15 the ungodly works (ἔργα ἀσεβείας) of the sinners seem to be religious rather than moral offences, and thus in all probability to consist of some kind of compromise with idolatry. In 2 Pet. 2.10, 20 the use of the words μίασμα and μιασμός should be noted; these have a close connection in the Greek Old Testament with the defilements of idolatry.[6] In both epistles (Jude 12; 2 Pet. 2.13) it is possible that the more or less oblique references to the profaned or improper love-feasts[7] of the schismatics may imply that the food used on these occasions was objectionable to orthodox Christians.[8]

Finally, in our collection of evidence we return to Paul.

(1) We do not know why the weak Christian of Rom. 14.2 ate only vegetables. One possible interpretation of Paul's statement is that the man in question was a Jew, no longer able to obtain Jewish-killed meat because he had become a Christian and had therefore been cast out of the synagogue, and thus obliged to abstain from flesh altogether because only the heathen product, improperly killed and perhaps even offered in sacrifice, was available. There are parallels between Paul's treatment of the situation in Rom. 14; 15, and 1 Cor. 8; 10; there is, however, no definite indication in Rom. 14; 15 that either idolatry or Judaism is in mind.

(2) Together with the material in 1 Corinthians must be put the enigmatic paragraph 2 Cor. 6.14—7.1, on account of the words, quoted in 6.17 from Isa. 52.11, ... ἀκαθάρτου μὴ ἅπτεσθε. Taken in the light of 6.16 (τίς δὲ συγκατάθεσις ναῷ θεοῦ μετὰ εἰδώλων;) it seems that the ἀκάθαρτον envisaged here is (as in Deutero-Isaiah) connected with idolatry. It has become so usual to read this paragraph as part of the 'previous letter', the misunderstanding of which seems to have led to Paul's disclaimer in 1 Cor. 5.9–13, which in turn is read in the light of 1 Cor. 5.1 (the case of πορνεία), that it is often given an almost exclusively sexual interpretation. This, however, is mistaken. Fornicators are given prominence in 1 Cor. 5.9 f, but they are followed by others, including idolaters (5.10 f). Idolatry is at least one of the themes of 2 Cor. 6.14—7.1, and if it is accompanied by a reference to sexual sin (perhaps in 7.1) this is in line with almost all the other material we have considered. But it must not be assumed that 2 Cor. 6.14—7.1 is anything other than part of a letter to Corinth subsequent to 1 Corinthians.

So much may serve as a sketch of the necessary evidence. If for the moment we set aside the Pauline material it appears that the eating of εἰδωλόθυτα was reprobated in the strongest possible terms, and that it was coupled with fornication. There is no doubt that this attitude persisted in the primitive Church for centuries. Meat that had been offered to idols, and blood, had to be avoided by Christians at all costs. The evidence for this has recently been collected and set forth by Dr Ehrhardt.[9]

In the *Didache* food regulations are introduced as follows (6.3): περὶ δὲ τῆς βρώσεως, ὃ δύνασαι βάστασον.[10] As Knopf (ad loc.) says, this suggests 'eine recht entwickelte Speisen- und Fastenordnung in der Gemeinde'; but it also suggests that there were limits to Christian willingness to accept such a rule, and perhaps also limits to the availability of the foods prescribed. On εἰδωλόθυτα, however, no compromise was permissible: ἀπὸ δὲ τοῦ εἰδωλοθύτου λίαν πρόσεχε· λατρεία γάρ ἐστιν θεῶν νεκρῶν.[11] This falls, as we have seen, under the heading περὶ τῆς βρώσεως, and there can be no doubt that the author of the *Didache* believed that to eat food sacrificed to idols was to fall into the practically unforgivable sin of idolatry.

Justin treats the issue as a touchstone of orthodoxy. Thus in *Trypho* 34 he says that Gentile Christians (and this will apply *a fortiori* to Jewish Christians) πᾶσαν αἰκίαν καὶ τιμωρίαν μέχρις ἐσχάτου θανάτου ὑπομένουσι περὶ τοῦ μήτε εἰδωλολατρῆσαι μήτε εἰδωλόθυτα φαγεῖν.

Trypho replies (35) that he has found many who profess to be Christians ἐσθίειν τὰ εἰδωλόθυτα καὶ μηδὲν ἐκ τούτου βλάπτεσθαι λέγειν. Justin points out that these are those false Christians whose coming Jesus himself foretold. Irenaeus (*Haer.* 1, 6, 3) has a similar comment on the Valentinians.[12]

Western writers extend the prohibition beyond εἰδωλόθυτα in the strict sense to meat containing blood;[13] see, for example, Minucius Felix, *Octavius* 30; Tertullian, *Apology* 9; Eusebius, *Hist. Ecc.* v, 1, 26 (quoting the epistle of the Churches of Lugdunum and Vienna). In view of this confusion we need not hesitate to add a passage which bears witness to the impression made by Christians on the outside world. In *de Morte Peregrini* 16 Lucian says that Peregrinus offended the Christians who no longer ministered to him in prison, ὤφθη γάρ τι, ὡς οἶμαι, ἐσθίων τῶν ἀπορρήτων αὐτοῖς.

Another essay that should be mentioned along with Dr Ehrhardt's is that in which Einar Molland[14] argues for the continuing knowledge of and reverence for the Apostolic Decree among Jewish Christians who, because they abominated Paul, did not recognize the authority of Acts. Dr Molland shows, I think convincingly, that the Jewish Christians responsible for the *Preaching of Peter* (which appears to stand behind the Pseudo-Clementine literature) preserved and obeyed the Decree, respecting it both positively and negatively; that is, they not only observed its precepts but also refrained from insisting, as they would have liked to do, on circumcision, vegetarianism, and washings after the Jewish model, because these were not required by the Decree.

Not only did these Jewish Christians retain, though independently of Acts, the substance of the Apostolic Decree, they preserved (according to Dr Molland) the correct interpretation of the prohibition of εἰδωλόθυτα.

Les Pseudo-Clémentines nous donnent l'interprétation juste de cette prohibition. Ce qui est interdit, c'est [*participare daemonum mensae, hoc est*] *immolata degustare*, [*vel sanguinem, vel morticinum, quod est suffocatum,*] *et si quid aliud est quod daemonibus oblatum est* (*Rec.* IV, 36), toute forme de κοινωνεῖν τῆς τραπέζης τῶν δαιμόνων μιαρᾶς (*Hom.* VIII, 23; VII, 4; VII, 8; VIII, 19). La seule divergence à l'égard de la forme du décret dans les *Actes des Apôtres* est que les Pseudo-Clémentines ont une prédilection pour l'expression τράπεζα τῶν δαιμόνων, et que par la participation à la table des démons elles comprennent la manducation de tous les aliments interdits.[15]

It is possible that the expression τράπεζα τῶν δαιμόνων may owe something to Paul (cf. 1 Cor. 10.21), though the borrowing will scarcely be direct.

For the moment we may simply take this Clementine material as adding to the evidence for the widespread acceptance of the prohibition of the eating of εἰδωλόθυτα; it will be necessary to recall it later when we inquire into the fate of the Pauline attitude to this prohibition.

It is Paul's attitude we must now examine. Dr Ehrhardt believes that it changed. He contrasts Paul's attitude to the Jerusalem 'brasshats' in Gal. 2 with his discussion of sacrificial food in 1 Cor. 8. 'It is . . . remarkable that only a short time afterwards, namely after the visit of St Peter to Corinth, St Paul greatly changed his tune' (op. cit., p. 277). Peter, Dr Ehrhardt thinks, had insisted upon the general validity of the Decree, even at Corinth. He continues, 'The way in which St Paul now accepted the decree, and in particular the prohibition of the eating of sacrificial meat, is highly significant for the mutual relations between the two apostles. Not only did he not reject it any longer, but he even supported it strongly as a command of charity in favour of "the weak" ' (ibid.). Later he goes on,

Two conclusions may be drawn: the first, that St Paul apparently did eat sacrificial meat at his first stay at Corinth; the second, that without being conscious of any sin against the Holy Spirit, he abandoned this practice at St Peter's remonstrations 'for conscience sake', which means because of the testimony not only of any pagan scoffers, but even more so because of the 'weak' amongst the Christians, an expression which appears not to be entirely without a certain acerbity directed at the address of St Peter (p. 278).

With this we may compare the view of T. W. Manson,[16] who also thought that the question was raised at Corinth by Peter, or at least in his name.

Why does Paul now discuss the problem as if the Jerusalem Council had never met? I cannot help thinking that the question was raised at Corinth by the Cephas party, and that Paul's way of dealing with it is, and is meant to be, a snub. He takes it as a matter of purely domestic concern within the Gentile–Christian community, the implication being that the Jerusalem compromise is doubtless suitable for Churches like that of Antioch with a mixed membership, but that in predominantly Gentile–Christian communities Jewish taboos do not count and Jewish–Christian visitors cannot presume to legislate in these matters for Gentile–Christian churches (op. cit., p. 200).

Manson seems to imply, with Dr Ehrhardt, that Paul did accept the substance of the Jewish–Christian Decree. 'Here as elsewhere Paul, even when accepting the Jewish–Christian conclusion, insists on supplying it with an entirely Christian basis' (p. 202)—namely that the intimacy of Christian fellowship with Christ himself and with other Christians admits no rivalry: You cannot drink the cup of the Lord, and the cup of demons; you cannot partake of the table of the Lord, and the table of demons (1 Cor. 10.21).

Neither of these writers seems to me to do full justice to the facts in 1 Corinthians. That Paul found himself in some difficulty over the question of sacrificial food is certainly true. It is possible that he did in some respects change his opinion. But at no point in 1 Cor. 8; 9; 10 does he admit the view that a Christian must never eat what has been sacrificed to an idol, still less that he must never eat meat that has not been slaughtered in conformity with the Jewish regulations. On the contrary, he specifically states that sacrificial food may be eaten. The following verses are explicit:

10.25: πᾶν τὸ ἐν μακέλλῳ πωλούμενον ἐσθίετε μηδὲν ἀνακρίνοντες διὰ τὴν συνείδησιν.

10.27: εἴ τις καλεῖ ὑμᾶς τῶν ἀπίστων καὶ θέλετε πορεύεσθαι, πᾶν τὸ παρατιθέμενον ὑμῖν ἐσθίετε μηδὲν ἀνακρίνοντες διὰ τὴν συνείδησιν.

Certainly, Paul hedges these statements by reference to the conscience, not of the eater, or potential eater, but of his weak Christian brother. The Christian's ἐξουσία must not be allowed to become a πρόσκομμα (8.9). To eat publicly in an εἰδωλεῖον would be, he says, wantonly to bruise consciences (he does not say that it is in itself idolatry), and it would be better never to eat flesh at all than to drive a fellow-Christian to his doom (8.10, 11, 13). But this does not constitute acceptance of the Decree; at most it is a matter of tenderness towards those who did accept it. The Christian has ἐξουσία, though he must not abuse it.

There is evidence, though it is not conclusive, that if Paul did, between his first visit to Corinth and the writing of 1 Corinthians, execute a volte-face it was in a liberal rather than a conservative direction. He had written a letter[17] which the Corinthians (rightly or wrongly) had taken to mean that they must cut themselves off completely from the immoral and idolatrous life of Corinth—no easy task. In 1 Cor. 5.9–13 Paul corrects this impression. The Corinthians are not to break off relations with non-Corinthians who are πόρνοι, or (to pick out one significant word from Paul's list) idolaters. With such persons they may συναναμίγνυσθαι, and the context makes it clear that this includes συνεσθίειν (5.11).[18] The point is that Paul is concerned here with Christian discipline within the community; συνεσθίειν with those outside, which would almost certainly involve eating εἰδωλόθυτα, remains possible.

We now turn to more detailed study of 1 Cor. 10.25, 27. What was sold in the *macellum*? The answer is, food of almost every description.[19] Thus Cicero (*de Div.* II, 27 (59)), sarcastically, 'Si Epicuri de Voluptate liber rosus esset, putarem annonam in macello cariorem fore.' Compare Suetonius, *Tiberius* 34, 2. Here *annona* means the price of food in general; the 'cost of living', we might say. The *macellum*, however, was mainly concerned with the sale of meat and fish. When Plautus's Euclio (*Aulularia* 329 ff) visits the *macellum* his comment not only awakens the sympathy of the modern shopper but shows what he was looking for:

> Venio ad macellum, rogito pisces; indicant
> Caros, agninam caram, caram bubulam,
> Vitulinam, cetum, porcinam: cara omnia.

Plutarch does not even think of fish but only of meat when he raises the question (*Quaest. Rom.* 54), διὰ τί τὰ κρεοπώλια μάκελλα καὶ μακέλλας καλοῦσι; Plutarch's two suggested etymologies are distinguished rather by ingenuity than probability, but the question must reflect popular usage.[20]

Dr Ehrhardt[21] accepts Lietzmann's[22] argument that all, or very nearly all, of the meat sold in the *macellum* was εἰδωλόθυτον, sacrificed probably in nearby temples, but the argument is not wholly convincing; see Dr H. J. Cadbury's article on the *macellum* in Corinth in *JBL* liii (1934), pp. 134–41, with, not least important, the simple observation that *macella* and temples must often have been contiguous not on account of any religious connection but because public buildings are almost inevitably grouped together in the middle of a city. Dr Cadbury adds, 'The presence also in one shop [in Pompeii] of entire skeletons of sheep suggests that the meat may have been sold on the hoof or slaughtered in the *macellum* as well as sold already butchered or sacrificed in a temple' (op. cit., p. 141).

That meat was to be had that was not ἱερόθυτον is confirmed by Plutarch, *Sympos.* VIII, 8, 3, where it is said that the Pythagoreans ὡς μάλιστα μὲν ἐγεύοντο τῶν ἱεροθύτων ἀπαρχόμενοι τοῖς θεοῖς, which seems to mean that the Pythagoreans, who took flesh very sparingly, ate it only in the form of ἱερόθυτα. It is implied that others, who did not share the vegetarian principles of the Pythagoreans, would eat it when it had not been sacrificed—that is, that non-sacrificed meat was available.

The extent to which the Christian shopping in the Corinthian *macellum* would be forced to purchase goods with a religious history behind them must therefore not be exaggerated. According to Professor Kitto,[23] 'Barley-meal, olives, a little wine, fish as a relish, meat only on high holidays—such was the normal diet. As Zimmern has said, the usual Attic dinner consisted of two courses, the first a kind of porridge, and the second, a kind of porridge.'[24] This goes for the Mediterranean world in general; and there is even evidence to suggest that meat, though rarely eaten, was not the highly esteemed luxury that Professor Kitto suggests. F. R. Cowell writes,[25] 'On one of Caesar's campaigns it was apparently accounted a hardship when Roman soldiers were forced to eat meat because their corn supplies had been exhausted.' No reference is given, but I suppose Mr Cowell has in mind *Bell. Gal.* VII, 17: 'Summa difficultate rei frumentariae adfecto exercitu ... usque eo, ut complures dies frumento milites caruerint, et, pecore ex longinquioribus vicis adacto, extremam famem sustentarent; nulla tamen vox est ab eis audita populi Romani majestate et superioribus victoriis indigna.' Too much, however, should not be built upon this; compare on the other side *Bell. Civ.* III, 47: 'Non illis hordeum cum daretur non legumina recusabant: pecus vero, cujus rei summa erat ex Epiro copia, magno in honore habebant.' It may be that the latter statement is given as exceptional, and therefore confirms the point.

In addition to cereals and vegetables the most common food was fish. This was certainly true in Athens, and it would be surprising if, in *bimaris Corinthus*, nearer to Lechaeum and little further from Cenchreae than Athens from Peiraeus, the same conditions did not apply. Plutarch, in a passage quoted above (*Sympos.* VIII, 8, 3), adds ἰχθύων δὲ θύσιμος οὐδείς, οὐδὲ ἱερεύσιμός ἐστιν; and this statement appears to be correct.

It follows from this that a middle- to lower-class household in Corinth (1 Cor. 1.26), buying its supplies in the *macellum*, would very often make purchases that had no connection with idolatry. The problem of εἰδωλόθυτα would seldom arise, and possibly would never have arisen in a Gentile Church like that of Corinth if Jewish Christians (the Cephas group, perhaps) had not raised it. But this infrequency of occurrence is not the point. The point is that πᾶν τὸ ἐν μακέλλῳ πωλούμενον would include ἱερόθυτα, and that Paul says that these may be bought and eaten, and that the purchaser is not to ἀνακρίνειν. This, however, is exactly what a Jew would do.[26] The briefest way of illustrating this is to quote Billerbeck[27] on 1 Cor. 10.25:

> Dem Juden war es erlaubt, Fleisch aus einem heidnischen Fleischladen zu beziehen, wenn das Tier nicht von einem Nichtisraeliten geschlachtet war, wenn das Fleisch nicht mit dem heidnischen Kultus in Berührung gekommen war und wenn der Inhaber der Verkaufsstelle die Sicherheit gewährte, dass er minderwertiges, den Juden zum Genuss verbotenes Fleisch (טריפה) in seinem Geschäft nicht führte.

It is clear that only by careful inquiry (ἀνάκρισις) could a Jew satisfy himself on these points; and a quick reading of *Abodah Zarah* suffices to show the repeated investigations διὰ τὴν συνείδησιν that were incumbent upon the devout Jew.[28] Paul is nowhere more un-Jewish than in this μηδὲν ἀνακρίνοντες. His whole life as a Pharisee had been essentially one of ἀνάκρισις, not least into foods.

We turn to 1 Cor. 10.27. Some discussions of this point have been fogged by confusion with the situation implied by 8.10 (cf. 10.20 f), where the meal takes place in a religious establishment (εἰδωλεῖον), at the table (τράπεζα) of a god. It is this situation that is reflected by the well-known papyri quoted by Deissmann[29] and others. These should not be quoted with reference to 10.27, which deals with a meal given in a private house, where the religious character of the food is at least as uncertain as that of the goods displayed for sale in the *macellum*. The language of 10.27 is illustrated by Xenophon, *Mem.* 1, 3, 6, εἰ δέ ποτε κληθεὶς ἐθελήσειεν ἐπὶ δεῖπνον ἐλθεῖν; the use of (ἐ)θέλω is neutral, so that there is no ground for Calvin's note, 'he

[Paul] is tacitly hinting that he himself does not approve of this very much, and that it would be better if they declined'. Xenophon, however, in the same work (*Mem.* II, 9, 4) indicates the danger involved. Speaking of Crito's kindness to Archedemus he says ὁπότε θύοι, ἐκάλει. It is probable that private invitations were at least sometimes connected with sacrifices, though evidently this was not invariably so, or there would be no point in 10.28 f. If, however, a Christian had made up his mind in advance that he would eat nowhere where there was any possibility of encountering εἰδωλόθυτα he would have had to withdraw into a self-imposed ghetto; this, it appears, is what the Jewish Christians did,[30] and is pretty nearly what all Christians eventually did.[31] The question of the place of the Christian in ordinary life was raised, and Paul decisively took the view that the Christian (though his relation to the world is governed by the ὡς μή of 1 Cor. 7.29 ff) must not separate himself from it. There is to be no Christian ghetto. This was an attitude of extraordinary liberalism,[32] the more striking in that it led Paul into almost verbal contradiction of Exod. 34.15 (μήποτε . . . καλέσωσίν σε καὶ φάγῃς τῶν θυμάτων αὐτῶν).

It would be wrong to underestimate the importance of what Paul says about the claim other men's consciences make upon ours, but equally wrong not to grasp the fact that Paul's own view was that, provided no other Christian was hurt thereby, a Christian might freely buy sacrificial food in the open market, might sit at table with non-Christians (who were also non-Jews), and might eat food of any kind whatsoever. That these are all acts that we ourselves perform frequently should not blind us either to the Pauline revolution, or to the counter-revolution that followed it.

It is evident that on this question Paul took a line of his own; it is natural therefore to continue our discussion by considering the light thrown by his attitude on a number of important subjects.

(1) The affair of the εἰδωλόθυτα casts light upon the relation between Paul and Judaism. The essential Jewishness of Paul has been strongly emphasized of late. 'Throughout his life Paul was a practising Jew ... any deviation from orthopraxy would irretrievably close the doors of Judaism against him.'[33] It seems that the first part of this statement must be abandoned—in the matter of εἰδωλόθυτα (to mention no others) Paul was not a practising Jew; and the second part must be reworded—his deviations from orthopraxy did in the end close the doors of Judaism against him. To say

this is not to deny the important truth in Dr Davies's contention that Paul's thought continued to work within a rabbinic framework, but rather to underline Dr Chadwick's emphasis[34] on the flexibility of Paul's attitude.

We cannot think that Paul changed lightly the habits of a lifetime, nor is there reason to suppose that, as a Christian, he thought in a completely new way about idolatry, and the rites and objects connected with it. That he no longer lived in accordance with the 'most straitest sect of our religion' as a Pharisee does not mean that he gave up all his Jewish beliefs. It is important to see precisely where he differed from Judaism.

It will serve the interests of clarity and brevity if I quote Billerbeck's careful summary[35] of the attitude of the ancient synagogue to heathen gods.

> A. Die Götter der Heiden sind Engel, denen Gott die 70 Völker der Welt unterstellt hat. . . . B. Die Götter der Heiden sind Dämonen; ihre Anbetung ist Teufelswerk. . . . C. Die Götter der Heiden sind verstorbene Menschen, die sich während ihres Lebens als Herrscher von Völkern oder als Wohltäter ihrer Generation verdient gemacht hatten, und denen deshalb die dankbare Nachwelt göttliche Verehrung zollte. Diese euhemeristische Erklärung des Götzendienstes scheint sich nur in der hellenistisch-jüdischen Literatur zu finden. . . . D. Die Götter der Heiden sind 'Nichtse' אלילים, 'Nichtigkeiten' הבלים, 'Tote' מתים, an denen nichts Wesenhaftes oder Wirkliches ist שאין בהן ממש, die zu Herren erst dadurch geworden sind, dass die Menschen sie zu Herren gemacht haben. . . . E. Speziell die Teraphim sind Hausgötter, die dem Eigentümer als Orakel dienten.[36]

The reader of 1 Corinthians will immediately recognize B and D, in 10.20 f and 8.4; 10.19 respectively. How did Paul combine these distinct views?[37] and how, so far as he held to the belief that food sacrificed to idols was sacrificed to demons, could he permit the eating of εἰδωλόθυτα?

The basic answer is to be found in the new eschatological circumstances in which Paul believed himself to be living, circumstances which gave him a completely new outlook on the demon world. The position is stated epigrammatically in the context under discussion: . . . ἡμῶν, εἰς οὓς τὰ τέλη τῶν αἰώνων κατήντηκεν (1 Cor. 10.11). Since their defeat in the death and resurrection of Jesus the demons have come to occupy a changed position. They have not ceased to exist, nor have they ceased to be inimical to men, but they have lost their power to inflict radical injury upon the elect.[38] From this conviction, which is fundamental in Paul's thinking, follows his apparently confused and inconsistent[39] treatment of idolatry and idolatrous practices. With idolatry itself he will have no dealings: φεύγετε ἀπὸ τῆς εἰδωλολατρίας (1 Cor. 10.14). To worship a demon is to deny God his due; more, it is to throw in one's lot with the defeated, anti-God forces of the universe, to embrace the ultimately lost cause and to perish with it. But precisely because the cause of the demons is lost, they have no power to infest or infect a piece of meat. Hence (conscientious scruples permitting) the Christian may freely use εἰδωλόθυτα and eat with unbelieving friends. To take part in idolatrous ritual is another matter. To do this is to place oneself in the context of worship in which the demons still exercise power. This cannot be dismissed as a merely mythological statement. We may borrow the words of Billerbeck quoted above, and say that the demons are 'nothings' who become lords precisely in that men (in worship) treat them as lords; or, as Paul puts the matter elsewhere, οὐκ οἴδατε ὅτι ᾧ παριστάνετε ἑαυτοὺς δούλους εἰς ὑπακοήν, δοῦλοί ἐστε ᾧ ὑπακούετε; (Rom. 6.16).

This answer is crystallized in the quotation, in 1 Cor. 10.26, of Ps. 24.1. This verse was used not as itself a benediction but to justify the use of benedictions over food:... לא יטעם אדם כלם עד שיברך שנאמר (Tos. Ber. 4. 1). The psalm was also one of the seven appropriated weekly to worship in the Temple, and was used on the first day of the week.[40] R. Aqiba connected these seven psalms with the seven days of creation, the first perhaps more appropriately than most: בראשון מה היו אומרים? לה׳ הארץ ומלואה על שם שקנה והקנה ושליט בעולמו (Rosh Ha-Sh. 31 a). The psalm thus looked back to the beginning of creation. For the Jew, God's creation had been marred because it had come under the control of demons; one aspect of this was that food sacrificed to a demon became the demon's property. But for Paul, the new creation had begun, and the end was as the beginning. It was possible to believe in a new sense: The earth is the Lord's, and the fullness thereof; and to act upon the belief.

(2) In permitting the eating of εἰδωλόθυτα, Paul allows what elsewhere in the New Testament was strictly forbidden. In particular he contradicts the requirements of the Apostolic Decree.[41] The difficulty raised here is only partly mitigated by the suggestion that

the Decree was intended only for mixed Jewish and Gentile churches such as that at Antioch, and not for predominantly Gentile churches such as that at Corinth, for Paul thought it relevant to mention his dispute with Cephas (at Antioch) when writing to Galatia, and the Corinthian church itself was not without a Jewish element, to which incoming Jewish Christians would be able to attach themselves.

The problem of Paul and the Decree, which is raised by 1 Cor. 8—10, belongs to a context which is at least partially known to us. The relations between Paul, the 'pillar' Apostles at Jerusalem, and their envoys, were complicated and probably fluctuating, but Galatians and 2 Corinthians give us at least some insights into them.[42] We have already noted the views of T. W. Manson and Dr Ehrhardt, and though they cannot be accepted *in toto* these scholars are probably right in thinking of an attempt, made by or at least under the aegis of Peter, to introduce into the church at Corinth the Jewish–Christian orthopraxy of the Decree. This means nothing less than the existence of a counter-mission, following the geographical lines of Paul's activity and undermining his authority. Paul's 'views were set aside tacitly by the Decree, but, we may suppose, definitely and clearly in the course of the negotiations among the churches. This meant, however, that Paul's apostolic authority was being contested.'[43]

On this subject I shall here make only one small observation. The promulgation of the Decree, and its introduction at Corinth under the name and with the authority of Peter, afford a complete explanation of 1 Cor. 9 in its present position. In Chapter 8 Paul insists that strong Corinthian Christians shall hold their liberty and their rights in check in deference to the sensitive consciences of their weaker brethren. In Chapter 9 he illustrates this process of self-limitation with reference to his own rights as an apostle. This in itself is intelligible enough, but the example chosen is more than intelligible; it was demanded by the discussion of εἰδωλόθυτα in the light of the Decree. Paul was obliged both to maintain his apostolic authority, and to explain why he had made no use of it; why, moreover, his entire application of himself to the gospel (9.23) led him to behave now in one way, now in another. This is precisely what he does in Chapter 9, and with special reference to Peter.[44] Chapter 9 thus appears to be in place, and there is no reason here to think that in 1 Corinthians we are dealing with fragments of two letters.[45] The transition to Chapter 10 we shall consider later.

(3) Paul's attitude with regard to εἰδωλόθυτα brought him into uncomfortable controversy with the Cephas group; it also brought him into at least equally uncomfortable alliance with the Corinthian 'gnostics'.[46]

Paul uses the word γνῶσις far more frequently than any other New Testament writer: twenty-one times (including once in Colossians), against eight times in the rest of the New Testament (including once in Ephesians, once in the Pastorals, and three times in 2 Peter). Of Paul's uses of γνῶσις sixteen fall in 1 and 2 Corinthians and, of these five are in 1 Cor. 8. If figures can prove anything, these figures show that it was primarily in the Corinthian situation that the idea of γνῶσις developed, and that the γνῶσις was much, though not exclusively, concerned with the problem of εἰδωλόθυτα. The word γνῶσις does not recur in 1 Cor. 10, but the idea makes a veiled appearance in 10.15, where Paul appeals to the φρόνιμοι. This word occurs again at 1 Cor. 4.10; 2 Cor. 11.19, and I have little doubt that it refers to the Corinthian gnostics. The connection of thought in 10.14 ff is clear: Have nothing to do with idolatry. I am aware that it is to φρόνιμοι, who know that an idol has no real existence, that I speak; yet, precisely as φρόνιμοι, consider this point. Can you extend your fellowship with Christ to include evil powers also?

It is impossible to deal here with Corinthian gnosticism in extenso; I propose to glance at it briefly from the viewpoint defined by the subject of this paper, which suggests the following observations.

(a) The γνῶσις was essentially practical; in this respect it is more like the Hebrew חכמה than is the Corinthian σοφία, which has at least a speculative element.[47] We may reasonably trace this practical γνῶσις not only in the treatment of εἰδωλόθυτα but also in the argument of 1 Cor. 6.13, and possibly in the readiness to permit and even encourage the speaking of unveiled women,[48] and to draw the conclusion that since our bodies are not raised—let us eat and drink (cf. 1 Cor. 15.32).

(b) It taught a strict monotheism, on a rationalistic basis. It is probable that in 1 Cor. 8.4 Paul quotes[49] a Corinthian gnostic view: Idols have no real existence, and there remains therefore no God but one. Paul agrees (8.5 f). 10.19 probably reflects the same opinion: Don't think that I am contradicting your correct analysis of idolatry, and the resultant monotheism. It is on this rational ground (as well as on the dualism to be mentioned below) that the gnostics base their opinion: βρῶμα ἡμᾶς οὐ παραστήσει τῷ θεῷ (8.8), and the practical conclusion that a Christian may if he wishes take his meals in an εἰδωλεῖον (8.10).

(c) The γνῶσις was strictly dualistic, and carried its dualism through in a rational and logical way. This appears in its refusal to separate liberty to eat and liberty to commit fornication. It is not on our food laws that we stand before God. The only purpose of food is to satisfy the belly: τὰ βρώματα τῇ κοιλίᾳ, καὶ ἡ κοιλία τοῖς βρώμασιν (1 Cor. 6.13). This is a process with no lasting significance: ὁ δὲ θεὸς καὶ ταύτην καὶ ταῦτα καταργήσει. Analogy suggests the next step: τὸ σῶμα τῇ πορνείᾳ. Why not? Both bodies involved in the transaction καταργηθήσονται. In view of this argument it is after all not surprising that Revelation (for example) should prohibit the eating of εἰδωλόθυτα and fornication in the same breath.

(d) This rationalist dualism led to moral indifferentism. The conclusions drawn are valid in all circumstances, and if others fail to draw them, that is their affair: ἱνατί γὰρ ἡ ἐλευθερία μου κρίνεται ὑπὸ ἄλλης συνειδήσεως; εἰ ἐγὼ χάριτι μετέχω, τί βλασφημοῦμαι ὑπὲρ οὗ ἐγὼ εὐχαριστῶ;[50]

It we ask how Paul reacted to this Corinthian gnosis the answer cannot be a simple one; certainly his response was not a simple negative. The essence of (a) he could accept: action must be governed by doctrine, and doctrine must lead to action; only the doctrine must be sound doctrine. Point (b) also he accepts, though with some qualification. An idol is not God in the sense in which we understand the word; for us there is only one God. Yet the world knows many θεοί and κύριοι (1 Cor. 8.5), and εἰδωλόθυτα are offered to demons. The position is not as simple as Corinthian rationalism suggests, and monotheism needs a firmer foundation than rationalism and the simple denial of spiritual existences can supply. But, on the whole, Paul agrees. When we come to point (c) we find that Paul insists upon a sharp distinction between the free use of all foods, and fornication. A Christian is free to eat what he wills (provided he respects the consciences of others), but he is never free to fornicate. The analogy of 6.13 breaks down because it fails to do justice (in Paul's view) to the relation between physical and spiritual. His understanding of this relation is neither that of Judaism nor that of oriental (or oriental-influenced Greek) gnosticism, but is rooted in his doctrine of redemption, which involves the overthrow of evil powers and the initiation of a new creation.[51] Finally in (d) we find

Paul's fundamental criticism of a position which in many respects he was prepared to uphold: ἀγάπη must always take precedence of γνῶσις (1 Cor. 8.1–3; 13.2, 8, 9, 12 f), and my neighbour's conscience is always more important than my own.

In Corinth, and not here only, Paul had to walk the tightrope between the legalism of Jewish Christianity and the false liberalism of gnostic rationalism. That he was able to do this is one of the clearest marks of his greatness. The church of the next few generations was not so successful, and the tragic gap between gnostic liberalism and legalistically conceived Christianity steadily widened. Paul's attitude to the question of εἰδωλόθυτα was too closely bound up with the gnostic wing for the main body of Christians to accept it. In its quest for safety at any cost the church could see no way of excluding idolatry that did not include rigid abstention from heathen food and from heathen dinner parties, and for full measure many Christians threw in the Jewish laws of butchering as well. Those who did not accept this limitation were dismissed, as we have seen,[52] by Justin and others as the predicted false teachers, and the church as a whole retreated into a narrow religious shell.[53] Jewish Christianity (in this matter) triumphed, though Jewish Christians became less important in the church.

For this unfortunate step there was one piece of justification, in that refusal to eat εἰδωλόθυτα became on at least some occasions of persecution the touch-stone of loyalty to the Christian faith and of the rejection of idolatry.[54] It must be acknowledged, and would have been acknowledged by Paul, that in these circumstances the only proper Christian attitude was to abstain.

NOTES

1 See 1 Cor. 7.1, and cf. 8.1.
2 The material under discussion raises the question of the unity of 1 Corinthians; see below.
3 I believe this to be substantially the original form of the text, but the question is too large for discussion here.
4 But note Kirsopp Lake's hesitation in *Beginnings of Christianity*, v (London 1933), p. 212.
5 Cf. also Sanh. 106a, quoted in S.-B. iii, 793. On 1 Cor. 10. 7, Billerbeck says with reference to παίζειν, 'In der späteren Zeit war es ein feststehender exegetischer Kanon, dass unter צחק in der Schrift nichts andres als Götzendienst zu verstehen sei.' But παίζειν may suggest further overtones of meaning; cf. Arrian's account of Sardanapalus's

inscription (*Alexander* II, 5, 4): ... ἔσθιε καὶ πῖνε καὶ παῖζε ... καὶ τὸ παῖζε ῥᾳδιουργότερον ἐγγεγράφθαι ἔφασαν τῷ Ἀσσυρίῳ ὀνόματι.

6 See for μίασμα Jer. 39.34; Ezk. 33.31; 1 Macc. 13.50; and for μιασμός Wisd. 14.26; 1 Macc. 4.43.

7 In 2 Pet. 2.13 ἀπάταις should be read, and taken as a pun on ἀγάπαις in Jude. So Ewald, quoted by J. B. Mayor ad loc.

8 The κῶμοι objected to in several places in the New Testament (Rom. 13.13; Gal. 5.21; 1 Pet. 4.3) may have been disapproved on religious as well as other grounds.

9 'Social Problems in the Early Church: 1. The Sunday Joint of the Christian Housewife', in *The Framework of the New Testament Stories* (Manchester 1964), pp. 276–90, previously published in the *Festschrift* for Erik Wolf.

10 Cf. H. J. Schoeps, *Theologie und Geschichte des Judenchristentums* (Tübingen 1949), p. 260, n. 1.

11 Cf. 2 Clem. 1.6; 3.1; Preaching of Peter (M. R. James, *The Apocryphal New Testament* (Oxford 1924), pp. 16 f); also the Jewish material referred to on p. 51 below.

12 Ehrhardt (p. 279, n. 2) refers to the Gospel of Thomas 14, but this seems to be of only marginal relevance.

13 See also below on the material contained in the Clementine literature.

14 'La circoncision, le baptême et l'autorité du décret apostolique (Actes 15.28 f) dans les milieux judéo-chrétiens des Pseudo-Clémentines' (*Studia Theologica* ix, 1955, pp. 1–39).

15 Op. cit., p. 34. Where Molland indicates omissions I have completed the quotation, using square brackets.

16 'The Corinthian Correspondence (1) and (2)', in *Studies in the Gospels and Epistles* (Manchester 1962), ed. M. Black, pp. 190–224.

17 The point here does not depend on the acceptance of 2 Cor. 6.14—7.1 as part of this letter.

18 Cf. H. Greeven in *TWNT* vii, pp. 852 f.

19 The *macellum* was in an even wider sense a centre of the catering trade; one could hire cooks there (Pliny, *Nat. Hist.* xviii, 108).

20 Plutarch suggests origin in the Greek μάγειρος, or from a Roman called Macellus, whose ill-gotten wealth was used to build a meat market. We may do better with μάχομαι, μάχαιρα, μάχη, *mactare*; or with *maceria*, an enclosure; or best perhaps with מכלה, a fold, pen, or enclosure.

21 Op. cit. p. 280.

22 H. Lietzmann, *An die Korinther, I, II,* (Tübingen 1949), ed. W. G. Kümmel, pp. 49–52.

23 H. D. F. Kitto, *The Greeks* (London 1951), p. 33.

24 If, as I suspect, the reference is to *The Greek Commonwealth* (Oxford 1931), it is a playful exaggeration of Zimmern's words; but many passages in Greek literature could be quoted more or less to this effect, e.g. Xenophon, *Mem.* iii, 14, 2: ἐσθίουσι μὲν γὰρ δὴ πάντες ἐπὶ τῷ σίτῳ ὄψον, ὅταν παρῇ. The σῖτος is farinaceous food in general, the ὄψον any sort of relish, often fish—and it may or may not be available. The context in Xenophon is worth noting.

25 *Cicero and the Roman Republic* (Harmondsworth 1956), p. 326.

26 Cf. E. Lohse, 'Zu 1 Cor. 10.26, 31', in *ZNTW* xlvii (1956), pp. 277–80, especially p. 279.

27 S.-B. iii, 420.

28 Hence one reason for the existence of religious societies, within which members could be certain of ritual purity without constant inquiry.

29 A. Deissmann, *Light from the Ancient East* (London 1927), p. 351, n. 2.

30 Molland, op. cit.

31 Ehrhardt, op. cit.

32 J. Weiss, on 10.25: 'Damit gibt Paulus eine grossartige Freiheit: gerade jenes vorsichtige Nachfragen ist vom Übel, weil es eine Ängstlichkeit und einen Mangel an Freiheit zeigt, der überwunden werden soll.' E. B. Allo, on 10.27 f.: 'Paul voulait éviter, autant que possible, de troubler les relations de société et d'amitié de ses néophytes, qui pouvaient d'ailleurs servir à la diffusion de l'Évangile. C'était là, dit J. Weiss, un libéralisme extraordinaire pour un Israëlite et un ancien. Le "omnia mihi licent" n'était pas un vain mot, pourvu qu'on le comprît en honnête homme.'

33 W. D. Davies, *Paul and Rabbinic Judaism* (London 1948), p. 321.

34 H. Chadwick, ' "All Things to All Men" (1 Cor. 9.22)', in *NTS*, 1 (1955), pp. 261–75.

35 S.-B. iii, 48–60. Of necessity I omit the texts, which should be carefully studied.

36 A shorter and simpler summary is given by W. A. L. Elmslie, *The Mishna on Idolatry: 'Aboda Zara'* (*Texts and Studies*, viii, 2) Cambridge 1911), pp. 42 f. Elmslie says of the view of 1 Cor. 10.20, that idols are made use of by demons, 'If this idea existed among the Jews, it was confined to the uneducated classes, and, even there, must be ascribed mainly to Greek influence.' He quotes the saying of R. Aqiba, closely akin to 1 Cor. 8.4; 10.19, לבי ולבך ידע דעבודה זרה לית בה משש (Aboda Zara 55a).

37 Cf. the previous note; there seems to be no attempt in Judaism to co-ordinate the various views held.

38 I have discussed this subject in *From First Adam to Last* (London 1962), pp. 83–94 (and see index s.v. Powers).

39 J. Héring, *La Première Épître de Saint Paul aux Corinthiens* (Neuchâtel and Paris 1949), p. 11, gives as one reason for seeing two letters combined in the epistle, 'contradiction entre 10.1–22 qui prend une attitude rigoriste dans la question des sacrifices païens, et 10.23 à 11.1 qui en fait unique-ment une question de charité vis-à-vis des faibles, comme le chapitre 8'. But our discussion suggests that we need not look for two letters to explain the two lines of thought.

40 See the heading of the Psalm in the LXX (τῆς μιᾶς σαββάτων), and Tamid 7. 4.

41 Notwithstanding Acts it is difficult to believe that Paul was present when the Decree was drawn up.

42 I may refer here to my 'Paul and the "Pillar" Apostles' in *Studia*

Paulina (Haarlem 1953), pp. 1–19; and 'Christianity at Corinth' above, pp. 1–27, especially pp. 14–22.

43 H. Lietzmann, *The Beginnings of the Christian Church* (London 1937), p. 199.

44 See above, pp. 28–39.

45 See above, p. 40 and note 39.

46 By 'gnostics' I mean people who made much of the term γνῶσις. I hope this is not an improper use of the word.

47 See above, pp. 6–14. Other literature on Corinthian gnosticism is referred to here.

48 Cf. 9.13 with 10.15; and note how Paul refers to the significance of creation, as in the quotation in 10.26. φύσις (11.14) is scarcely more than a Greek way of referring to 'the order of creation as God made it'.

49 See J. Jeremias in *Studia Paulina* (as in note 42), pp. 151 f.

50 10.29 f. The exact connection of the questions is disputed, but they must in some sense represent the complaint of a strong Christian. A further note might be added here on the sacramentarian interest of the Corinthian gnostics and Paul's response to it (1 Cor. 10.1–11, 16 f; 11.20–34).

51 See above, p. 52.

52 See above, pp. 43 f.

53 Nothing is more striking than that Luke can make Paul himself part-author of the Decree. On this, see E. Haenchen, *Die Apostelgeschichte* (Göttingen 1961), pp. 410–14. Does the fact that the majority, even of Gentile Christians, continued to observe the food laws suggest that the Western text of the Decree sprang from a gnostic source?

54 Evidence in Ehrhardt, op. cit., especially p. 286. cf. J. B. Lightfoot, *Essays on the Work entitled Supernatural Religion* (London 1889), p. 14, n. 2: 'When the season of persecution arrived, and the constancy of Christians was tested in this very way, St Paul's own principles would require a correspondingly rigid abstinence from even apparent complicity in idolatrous rites.'

4

PAUL'S OPPONENTS IN
2 CORINTHIANS

The continuing stream of hypotheses with regard to the Corinthian opposition to Paul will serve as a reminder that this opposition constitutes one of the crucial questions for the understanding of the New Testament and the origins of Christianity. It is not too much to say that a full understanding both of New Testament history and of New Testament theology waits on the right answering of this question. We can see pretty clearly that the development of Christianity in the first three decades after the crucifixion and resurrection of Jesus moved about two poles: on the one hand, the church of Jerusalem, some at least of whose leaders could probably look back to their association with Jesus during his ministry in Palestine, and, on the other, Paul, apostle as he himself but by no means all his contemporaries believed him to be, and the churches he founded in the non-Jewish world. How were these two groups related to each other? Did they act in concert or in opposition? These alternatives are far too simply put, and fail to do justice to the complexity of the facts; but the facts to which justice must be done include the data of 2 Corinthians, where Paul appears to be confronted by a rival apostolate.

This in turn means far more than that Paul was confronted by a rival institution—if indeed it means that at all. Apostleship is bound up with an apostolic message, and Paul's rivals proclaimed 'another Jesus' in a 'different gospel' (2 Cor. 11.4). Doubtless they would have brought the same charge against him. This means that theological conflict runs back into the origins of Christianity, for Paul's adversaries claimed ultimate authority for their beliefs. Historically, topographically and perhaps traditionally they may well have stood nearer than Paul to the historical Jesus.[1] No exposition of New Testament theology that by-passes this problem can be satisfactory, and it is one that runs deep, not only into formal Christology, but into the meaning of history and the nature of authority. As Dr Käsemann[2] rightly saw, 2 Corinthians poses the question how the legitimacy of an apostle, and therewith the legitimacy of the gospel, may be recognized.

These facts may justify me in taking a second bite at this cherry— a cherry that is in truth as big as a football. Since the first bite[3] two major contributions[4] to the subject have been published, and my next step must be to consider these.

In 1964 D. Georgi published his Heidelberg dissertation, *Die Gegner des Paulus im 2. Korintherbrief.*[5] This is a large book, and its subtitle (Studien zur religiösen Propaganda in der Spätantike) shows the broad field in which Dr Georgi—rightly—sets the particular problems of 2 Corinthians. The fact that it is impossible for me here to follow Dr Georgi in his account of Jewish and non-Jewish missions and missionaries, and in his general description of the primitive Christian mission, must not be understood as a depreciation of the contribution he has made in this area. It is inevitable that we should concentrate on the central point, though it should be remembered that, in his argument, Dr Georgi frequently appeals to the background of Paul's opponents as he has described it. Thus his first step is to represent them as θεῖοι ἄνδρες (pp. 220–34), a category of religious persons he has already described. Why does Paul (in 2 Cor. 2.16) so suddenly introduce his question, καὶ πρὸς ταῦτα τίς ἱκανός; (p. 221)? Because his opponents had already affirmed, ἱκανοί ἐσμεν. But ἱκανότης is from and in God alone, and the opponents' bold assertion means that they were claiming to possess divine status, or something like it. The same claim comes out in their confident belief that their gifts, and the signs they perform, verify and establish their position, and is reflected in their readiness (not shared by Paul) to receive financial support from the churches (pp. 234–41), and in their use of commendatory letters (pp. 241–6). Both Moses and Jesus, as themselves θεῖοι ἄνδρες, provide precedent and example for them (pp. 258–65, 282–92).

Diese judenchristlichen Missionare entstammten dem geistigen Raum der hellenistisch-jüdischen Apologetik und suchten—mit Erfolg—das Erbe der jüdischen Mission anzutreten, wobei sie anscheinend überhaupt eine wachsende Tendenz innerhalb der urchristlichen Missionsentwicklung repräsentierten ... Die Gegner versuchten durch den Rückblick auf die Vergangenheit, die Demonstrationen der Macht des Geistes in der Gegenwart und durch den ekstatischen Ausbruch ins Jenseits und in die Zukunft die gegenwärtige Existenz zu überhöhen (p. 301).

The theology and the behaviour of these missionaries belong together and are in radical contrast with those of Paul, who did not need 'aus dem Gang der Geschichte den Geist Gottes zu demonstrieren' (p. 302). In a word, the adversaries were Jewish Christians, but their methods and beliefs were not specifically Jewish, though they had to some extent already entered hellenistic Judaism from the hellenistic world.

The second contribution to the subject is that of G. Friedrich.[6] This was published earlier than Dr Georgi's, but should be taken subsequently, because Dr Friedrich was aware of Dr Georgi's work through the use made of it, while still unpublished, by Dr Bornkamm.[7] Dr Friedrich agrees that the opponents were hellenistic Jews, but is rightly critical of the view that they claimed to be θεῖοι ἄνδρες. This is disproved by their use of epistles of commendation. 'Als göttliche Sendboten brauchen sie keine Empfehlungsbriefe' (p. 196). Instead he points to Stephen and his circle as described in Acts 6 and 7; it is here that we may see the origin of the Corinthian intruders. It is true that the men of 2 Cor. 11.22 are described as 'Εβραῖοι, whereas Stephen and his associates represent the hellenist interest over against the 'Εβραῖοι: no matter—in Paul's usage 'Εβραῖος means only 'Jew'. 'Wie die Männer in Korinth, so sind auch Stephanus und Philippus charismatisch begabte Prediger' (p. 199). 'Die Gegner des Paulus in Korinth legen Wert auf Wundertaten. Sowohl von Stephanus wie von Philippus wird berichtet, dass sie durch die von ihnen vollbrachten Wunder Aufsehen erregten' (pp. 199 f). 'Paulus hat es in Korinth mit Visionären und Ekstatikern zu tun' (p. 200); Stephen and Philip were both ecstatics, and Stephen saw a vision. It is of the lively missionary Hellenists that spiritual gifts are predicated, not of the ordered community of Pharisaic Christians in Jerusalem (pp. 201 f). There are contacts between Stephen's speech and the Christian midrash of 2 Cor. 3 (pp. 202–5). The Corinthian intruders claim to be διάκονοι Χριστοῦ (2 Cor. 11.23) (p. 205). The Hellenists are to be connected with the sharing of goods in Acts; no doubt they took the practice with them in the form of a requirement that churches should provide for their preachers (pp. 205 ff). For Stephen, Jesus was the Second Moses, the Righteous One; he did not think of him as the Servant of God, whose death had atoning power. 'Auch das würde mit der Anschauung der hellenistischen Juden in Korinth übereinstimmen' (p. 208).

Whether Dr Friedrich is right in describing the opponents as hellenistic Jews will be discussed later. In general, his criticism of Dr Georgi is well grounded, for the opponents can be described as θεῖοι ἄνδρες only if the term is even more loosely used than usual.[8] His own views are less convincing. That by 'Εβραῖος Paul means no more than 'Jew' is not supported by the only other occurrence of the word (Phil. 3.5).[9] The contacts between 2 Cor. 3 and Acts 7 might demonstrate a connection between Stephen and Paul rather than one between Stephen and Paul's adversaries. The Seven are not described in Acts as διάκονοι, and Dr Friedrich's attempt to dispose of this difficulty (p. 205) is not more convincing than the many attempts that have been made to find in this chapter an account of the origin of the diaconate. The Seven are connected with the administration of alms in Jerusalem, but (so far as we may depend on Acts) this was in operation before their appointment, and was directed to the benefit of needy classes such as widows, not to the support of the ministry. Paul himself does not seem to have thought of Jesus as the Servant of the Lord; at least, he makes very little use of this identification. According to Acts, the gift of the Spirit was conferred first of all upon the original group of Pharisaic Jewish Christians, and in early Christian circles ecstasy, vision and miracle were too widespread to prove anything. Beyond all this, as Dr Friedrich allows (p. 196), Acts is not a very satisfactory source of information about Stephen and his associates; and it is far from clear how disciples of Stephen found their way to Corinth, and why, if they did so, they should have formed an opposition to Paul. We must, in fairness, not lay too much stress on the Acts account of Paul's participation in Stephen's martyrdom (Acts 7.58), and the contribution this may possibly have made to his conversion (cf. Acts 22.20); but is he likely to have dismissed Stephen as preaching another Jesus, a different gospel? If the answer to this question is, We do not know, then we do not know enough about Stephen to bring him into the discussion at all.

There is, I think, a good deal to learn from both Dr Georgi and Dr Friedrich; I do not think that either of them is completely right. There is room for further inquiry. Before we embark upon such an inquiry three preliminary questions must be considered.

(1) What area of the Corinthian correspondence ought the inquiry to cover? W. Schmithals[10] took in the whole, and there is fairly wide agreement that he was wrong.[11] The situation Paul deals

with in 2 Corinthians is no longer the tendency to division, the free use of the terms wisdom and gnosis, the libertinism, and the misunderstanding of the resurrection that mark 1 Corinthians. The second epistle must not be interpreted in terms of the situation presupposed by the first. If we confine our attention to 2 Corinthians we encounter a literary problem far too complex to be disposed of in half a paragraph of this paper. Dr Georgi seems to me to be right in his view that 2 Cor. 2.14—7.4 and 10—13 are not parts of the same letter, and, though they contemplate the same situation, refer to different stages within it. 'Als Paulus 2.14—7.4 schreibt, droht die Gemeinde bereits den Argumenten der Gegner zu erliegen. Doch sieht Paulus noch eine gewisse Hoffnung, sie vor dem endgültigen Abfall bewahren zu können. Als Paulus 10—13 schreibt, scheint die Gemeinde bereits den Gegnern verfallen und die Lage fast aussichtslos zu sein' (p. 24). With this distinction between 2.14—7.4, and 10—13 I should agree; whether 2.14—7.4 should be lifted out of 1—9 (or 1—7, or 1—8) I am not so sure.[12] For this reason, and because of the severe limits of space imposed by this paper, I propose to confine myself to 10—13. If further investigation were to show that the earlier chapters dealt with the same persons this would further clarify our understanding of the whole Corinthian affair.

(2) This leads to a second preliminary question. Even if we confine our attention to 10—13 is any precision possible? That is, is it possible to find any real coherence in these chapters? This question becomes inevitable if we put side by side 11.22 f, where Paul does not dispute that the persons of whom he is speaking are διάκονοι Χριστοῦ any more than he disputes that they are Jews, but merely adds that, whatever they may be, he is too, and to an even higher degree, and 11.13 ff, where he alleges that certain persons are διάκονοι of Satan, who deceitfully disguise themselves as apostles of Christ and servants of righteousness.[13] We must conclude either that the situation was a complex one, involving at least two groups over against Paul, or that Paul was lashing out blindly, and using language irresponsibly. Of these alternatives I prefer, tentatively at least, to accept the former, though it has been rejected by most recent writers.[14] Dr Bultmann's[15] arguments will be considered later,[16] and it does not seem to me that Dr Georgi has added seriously to their weight. There are difficulties in any view of the situation in Corinth, but they are increased by the attempt to fit all the adversaries referred to into one group.

(3) A third preliminary question is: How is the problem to be tackled? It might be possible to choose one of the current hypotheses, or to construct a new one, and to attempt to establish it from the text; it is however better, and is the course that will be followed here, to take a number of vital and difficult passages, and establish for them as firmly as possible, exegetical results. On the basis of these, one may hope, a picture will emerge with reasonably clear outlines, however vague some of the details may remain. This is a process with which I have made a beginning elsewhere, and my next step will be to recall, and here and there expand, some results already achieved.

(1) One of the most difficult of all passages in these chapters is 10.12–18. All I shall say of it here[17] is that the use of κανών and of μέτρον (with its cognates) raises the question whether it was Paul or his adversaries who had apostolic rights in the Corinthian church, and thus recalls the division of apostolic labour described in Gal. 2.7–10—a division which, as the same chapter shows (2.11 ff), broke down almost as soon as it was made, yet bore witness to Paul's understanding of the apostolic vocation as that of pioneer missionary (cf. Rom. 15.20). He had blazed the trail to Corinth. He made no complaint if others, such as Apollos, came to help him, but the Corinthians could have no more than one father (1 Cor. 4.15), and no attempt to supplant him could be justified. The opponents in mind in this passage are blamed not only for their personal conduct but for not observing a concordat made between Paul and the Jerusalem authorities, notably Cephas.

(2) At 11.13 Paul's opponents are described as ψευδαπόστολοι. The word contains an accusation of falsehood which belongs within the setting of Judaism.[18] What is at issue between Paul and his opponents is the right understanding of Judaism, and especially of its fulfilment in Christianity. This is important, because it means that the dispute is between Paul, who sees in Jesus the fulfilment of the law no less than of the eschatological promises, and Judaizers, who refuse to accept any religion except that of legalism. The word ψευδαπόστολος puts the Corinthian controversy, or at least that part of it to which the word relates (for I have already indicated the complexity of the data), within the Judaizing debate, which elsewhere, but not, explicitly, here, tended to focus on such matters as circumcision and forbidden and permitted foods.

(3) 12.18 refers to the latest stage in the unfortunate bickering

that arose out of Paul's decision to accept no financial support from the Corinthian church.[19] The order of events apparently was: (a) Paul preached without asking his hearers and converts for support; (b) other preachers did make this claim; (c) the argument was used: Paul must know, because he thus tacitly admits, that he is an inferior missionary; (d) Paul replies: No, there is good reason for what I do; (e) the accusation is laid: Paul appears to take no pay, but has in fact swindled us through the collection for the poor in Jerusalem. I shall return to this theme,[20] but it is worth noting here (a) that those who stood on their apostolic rights, as Paul did not, were the other apostles, the Lord's brothers, and Cephas—a Palestinian group (1 Cor. 9.3–6, 15–18, especially 5), and (b) that the accusation presupposed by 2 Cor. 12.18 could most easily have arisen if Palestinian envoys had said (in good faith or bad), We have received nothing so far.

I shall now proceed to a further group of exegetical problems, in the hope that the total exegetical product may, without forcing, lead to a solution of the historical problem.

(1) 10.6: In this verse there is a question which, as Héring[21] observes, not all commentators appear to have perceived. We hear of a παρακοή and a ὑπακοή; whose obedience, and whose disobedience and how are the two related? The obedience is undoubtedly that of the Corinthians, and the ὑμῶν that indicates this is so emphatic that it can hardly be questioned that the disobedience is that of others. Paul is thus seeking complete obedience[22] on the part of the Corinthians in order to take the next step of punishing (ἐκδικῆσαι)[23] the disobedience of others, who, since they are not native Corinthians, must be outsiders who have intruded into the Corinthian church. But if this is so, what can Paul mean by their disobedience? Presumably they were under no obligation to be obedient to Paul, and it is unlikely that he would think of punishing their disobedience to the authority that had commissioned them—unlikely, though not impossible if they had flagrantly exceeded their commission to the detriment of the Christian cause. It is more likely (and a suggestion that could be combined with a modified form of the last) that Paul is again thinking of the agreement of Gal. 2.7–10, and regards the intruders as being in breach of contract (cf. 10.12–18). This verse then underlines the distinction between 1 and 2 Corinthians—for in the former the troublemakers belong to Corinth whereas in the latter they come from outside—and at the same time suggests that

the outsiders represent an alien authority with which Paul is in some relation, though he considers that it exceeds its legitimate powers and rights if it invades his mission field. This is a clear pointer to Jerusalem.

(2) 11.3, 14: The imagery of verse 3 is mixed: on the one hand, Paul thinks of Christ as the last Adam, and the church as in some sense the last Eve, related to Christ in the same way that Eve was related to Adam—derived from him, existing for his sake, and for him only. On the other hand, Paul also has in mind the Old Testament theme of Israel as the bride of God, owing to him pure and exclusive love and loyalty. The mixing suggests that Paul did not begin from, and expound, one of these Old Testament themes; he began from the peril of the Corinthian church, in danger of seduction by false apostles, and thought of the story of Gen. 3 as a means of illustrating it. In this story, the snake deceived Eve; it may be that Paul thought, as some rabbinic teachers did,[24] that the snake seduced Eve; this however is not essential to his argument, and is accordingly not made explicit. It is not Eve's unfaithfulness to Adam so much as her disobedience to God that is in Paul's mind, and it is a similar result that he fears in the Corinthians; their thinking may become corrupt, and they may accept, not the Jesus to whom they have been betrothed, but another Jesus; that is, they may come to believe in a different gospel. The deception comes from the devil, who in Gen. 3 is represented by the snake,[25] and now by plausible envoys. This provides a link with 11.14, where the same charge is made, for in this verse Satan is said to be capable of disguising himself as an angel of light. This is probably another allusion to the story of the deception of Eve. In *Apoc. Mos.* 17 Eve herself recalls the event: 'When the angels ascended to worship God, then Satan appeared in the form of an angel and sang hymns like the angels. And I bent over the wall and saw him, like an angel.' The story then proceeds, with some elaboration, as in Gen. 3. In the related *Vita Adae et Evae* 9.1, Satan was wroth and transformed himself into the brightness of angels, and went away to the River Tigris to Eve. The Slavonic text, 38.1, has: 'The devil came to me, wearing the form and brightness of an angel.'

The beginning of the new age is like the beginning of the old:[26] Satan is at work testing, and where possible destroying, the loyalty of the people of God, and their readiness to find their life where, and only where, God has given it to them.[27] His agent is no longer a snake, equipped with its supralapsarian outfit of legs and human voice, but his servants, who disguise themselves as apostles, as servants of righteousness. These are not specifically mentioned in verse 3, where Paul uses a passive verb and expresses no agent; but the unity of imagery as well as of substance makes it clear that (though this will constitute a difficulty that will have to be considered later —see pp. 70 ff) the persons concerned are the ψευδαπόστολοι.

(3) 11.4: What is the meaning of ἄλλος Ἰησοῦς, πνεῦμα ἕτερον, εὐαγγέλιον ἕτερον? That the answer to this question is bound up with the identity of Paul's opponents has been clearly seen by, for example, Dr Georgi.[28] This passage is fuller and more precise than Gal. 1.6 (which also speaks of a different gospel). In 2 Cor. 11.4 we learn from the additional words (Jesus, Spirit) what distinguishes the new gospel from Paul's. 'Die Differenz liegt vor allem in der Christologie' (p. 285). The use of the simple name Jesus, which points to the earthly Jesus, shows that it is not a question of a gnostic Christology. The true explanation is found, according to Dr Georgi, by turning to 2 Cor. 4. In 4.5, Paul writes: 'We preach not ourselves, but Christ Jesus as Lord,[29] and ourselves as your slaves for Jesus' sake (διὰ Ἰησοῦν).' It is the humble behaviour of Paul that marks him out, over against his adversaries, as a true witness to the lordship of Christ. Thus the interpretation of the earthly Jesus that Paul rejects at 11.4 is one that is bound up with the tradition used by his adversaries and with their own consciousness of spiritual authority. 'Gerade das Letztere führt zu der Vermutung, dass die Gegner eine Christologie vertraten, in der Jesus als ausgezeichneter Pneumatiker, als θεῖος ἀνήρ erschien' (p. 286). Dr Georgi continues the discussion of 2 Cor. 4, and looks also at Chapter 5, without substantially supporting his argument, which all in all is not a very strong one.

It is true that most of the Pauline passages that use the simple name 'Jesus' refer to his earthly life, often with reference to his crucifixion or resurrection or both.[30] Such are Rom. 8.11; 2 Cor. 4.10 (bis—the 'Life of Jesus' is his risen life), 11 (bis); 1 Thess. 1.10; 4.14a. Other passages probably go with these: Gal. 6.17; 1 Thess. 4.14b. In addition to 2 Cor. 11.4, five passages are left (Rom. 3.26; 10.9; 1 Cor. 12.3; 2 Cor. 4.5; Phil. 2.10). The last certainly does not refer to the earthly but to the exalted Jesus; it may however be right to discount it as not Paul's own writing. Rom. 3.26 speaks of God as justifying τὸν ἐκ πίστεως Ἰησοῦ. Some have seen here a reference to the faith, or faithfulness, of Jesus himself; this is un-likely.[31] The parallel in 3.22, which uses Χριστός, shows that in any case the use of the name Jesus alone is not specially significant. 2 Cor. 4.5, notwithstanding Dr Georgi, does not seem to carry a reference to the earthly ministry, since in the latter part of the verse 'Jesus' simply takes up briefly 'we preach Christ Jesus as Lord'; that is, it is because we are δοῦλοι to the Lord Jesus that we offer ourselves in service to men. 1 Cor. 12.3 (cf. Rom. 10.9), which contains the name Jesus twice, in the opposing clauses κύριος Ἰησοῦς and ἀνάθεμα Ἰησοῦς, remains, and gives an important lead to the interpretation of 2 Cor. 11.4. True, the situations contemplated are not identical. In 1 Cor. 12 Paul gives guidance for the distinguishing of spirits.[32] The confession κύριος Ἰησοῦς is an indication that the Spirit of God is at work; the assertion ἀνάθεμα Ἰησοῦς proves that the in-spiration in question, whatever its source, does not come from the Spirit of God. By this test the Corinthians may judge the provenance and credibility of inspiration manifested in their church. In this and other ways (e.g. 1 Cor. 6.5; 10.15; 11.13) Paul encouraged the Corinthians to reach decisions for themselves, and this they now proposed to do in regard to various claimants to apostleship, among whom Paul was but one. He denied not their right to do this, but the validity of the criteria they employed. It did not trouble the Corinthians if the claimant (ὁ ἐρχόμενος) preached another Jesus and they correspondingly received a different spirit from that which bears witness that Jesus is Lord; they could and did put up with such an apostle—for reading ἀνέχεσθε, not ἀνείχεσθε,[33] the verse is a plain statement of fact: If he comes and preaches, you put up with him. That is to say, the Corinthians do not examine the content of what is preached to them, but consider only the manner, and perhaps the credentials, of the preacher. In recent years it has often been argued[34] that one characteristic of the Corinthian intruders was *Pneumatikertum*, which some have traced to hellenistic, others to Palestinian Christian sources. This may be true: what appears in this passage, however, and we shall see it elsewhere in 2 Cor. 10—13, is not so much that the intruders were *Pneumatiker* as that the Corinthians looked for *Pneumatikertum* in any claimant to apostle-ship, whereas Paul believed that it was the content of the apostolic message that vindicated the apostleship of its bearer.

In this verse Paul is attacking the Corinthians rather than the intruders. J. Munck said rightly,[35] '11.4 spricht daher von den

Korinthern und nicht von den Gegnern und besagt, dass die Gemeinde so schwach ist, dass jede beliebige neue und fremde Lehre sie zum Abfall verleiten würde'. We may add that Paul is making this judgement of the Corinthians in the light not of a hypothetical but of a real situation. Paul's reaction to this situation is to be interpreted from 1 Cor. 12.3 and 2 Cor. 4.5 (though not in the sense given to this verse by Dr Georgi). According to the former verse, the decisively Christian predicate to use with the name Jesus is κύριος. In the latter verse this is taken up in a new situation: We preach Christ Jesus as κύριος. This is not a matter of formal credal orthodoxy. The man who recognizes the one κύριος, Jesus, cannot himself play the κύριος, cannot κυριεύειν over the faith of others (2 Cor. 1.24); he can only be their δοῦλος. The intruders proclaim another Jesus not so much (as far as we know) by heretical doctrine as by the kind of behaviour described in 2 Cor. 11.20 (where the recurrence of ἀνέχεσθαι should be noted): ἀνέχεσθε εἴ τις ὑμᾶς καταδουλοῖ, εἴ τις κατεσθίει, κτλ. In all this there is no hint that Jesus was a θεῖος ἀνήρ (though it is likely enough that there were some who did so regard him), or that the intruders were *Pneumatiker*. In the foreground stands the ethical test of behaviour that is or is not consistent with the gospel—a test which the Corinthians had omitted to apply.

Before we leave 11.4 we must consider its relation with the next verse. This is a major topic of debate between Dr Käsemann[36] and Dr Bultmann[37]. The former (p. 44;24) described the transition from verse 4 to verse 5 as *sprunghaft*. In 11.4, Paul speaks of those who preach another Jesus, of these 'Träger satanischen Truges' (p. 42;21); but in 11.5 he appears to make the incredibly modest claim that he is not less than they. 'Selbst als Spott lässt sich das nicht mehr erklären. Mit Satansdienern gibt es keinerlei Vergleich' (p. 42;21). From this, and from other observations, Dr Käsemann draws the conclusion that the ὑπερλίαν ἀπόστολοι of 11.5, to whom Paul considers himself in no way inferior, are to be distinguished from the ψευδαπόστολοι of 11.13, whom Dr Käsemann takes to be the preachers of a 'different gospel'. In his view the ὑπερλίαν ἀπόστολοι are the primitive apostles, Peter and his colleagues, and the ψευδαπόστολοι are envoys of the Jerusalem church. In verse 4 Paul is speaking of the latter, in verse 5 of the former. He does nothing to indicate that he is moving from the one group to the other; hence the *sprunghaft* transition.

Dr Bultmann, who thinks this transition too *sprunghaft* to be credible, and that the comparison with the ψευδαπόστολοι is understandable if done in a sharp attempt to open the eyes of the Corinthians to the truth (pp. 26 f), explains the passage as follows. Paul is asking the Corinthians to bear with him. The request carries with it an implicit charge against his rivals, made explicit in verses 3 and 4. To this the Corinthians could reply: The new apostles have proved their legitimacy, nay, their superiority to Paul, by λόγος and γνῶσις (verse 6); the church may therefore rightly accept them. To this Paul answers, But I am their equal, if not in λόγος at least in the decisive matter of γνῶσις. Verse 5 thus provides a basis for the appeal of verse 1—Bear with me! This appeal is given three grounds: (1) Paul's concern for the church in face of the danger that threatens it (verses 2 f); (2) the fact that the church is willing to put up with Paul's competitors (verse 4); (3) the claim that Paul is not excelled by these competitors. To this last point there is a parallel in verses 18 ff. Verse 6, with its specific reference to γνῶσις, Dr Bultmann argues, must refer to the competitors actually present in Corinth, and this carries verse 5 with it. Thus the ὑπερλίαν ἀπόστολοι and the ψευδαπόστολοι are identical; and this is confirmed by comparison of 12.11 with 11.5, for the aorist ὑστέρησα in 12.11, like the κατειργάσθη of 12.12, points to events that the readers must themselves have observed in Corinth. Throughout Paul is dealing with apostles who have been at work in Corinth.

These arguments would be more convincing if the four chapters did not point to the existence of more than one group of opponents, or rivals. This I have already referred to (p. 64), and I shall return to the point (p. 81). Dr Bultmann's analysis of 11.1–6 is correct in that he sees that Paul is giving three reasons (they are all linked with verse 1 by the word γάρ) why the Corinthians should bear with him. The third reason, however, should be read as: I am not inferior to the greatest apostles of all. This statement was intended to link directly with verse 1, not with verse 4 (hence the *sprunghaft* connection), and verse 6 refers primarily not to the actual characteristics of the ψευδαπόστολοι but to the standards and criteria employed by the Corinthians in estimating the importance of the missionaries who visited them.

This last observation answers the argument cited above from Dr Bultmann. Why should Paul not, Dr Bultmann asks, institute a comparison between himself and the false apostles, 'wenn

es geschieht, um den Korinthern die Augen zu öffnen?' (p. 26).
What he wishes is that, if a comparison is to be made, he should
himself be fairly represented (p. 27). But, on this view, the admission made in the opening words of verse 6 would completely ruin
Paul's case. In fact, in verse 7 he goes on to another theme which
involves comparison between himself and the apostles, the brothers
of the Lord and Cephas (1 Cor. 9.5). On this, see below, pp. 73 f.

(4) 12.5 ff: Grammatically these are among the most complicated
verses in the epistle, and it has long been suspected that the text is
corrupt. The textual witnesses are divided,[38] and the repetition (in
most of them) of the words ἵνα μὴ ὑπεραίρωμαι is often regarded as
suspicious. The only question however with which we are concerned
is, What was Paul's intention in relating the vision of 12.2 ff, and
what light do his comments upon it throw on the Corinthian
situation?

ὑπὲρ τοῦ τοιούτου καυχήσομαι, Paul says in verse 5. τοῦ τοιούτου
points back to the use of the same word in verses 2 and 3; it means
the recipient of the vision, and this is Paul himself. It is an odd way
of referring to oneself, but it is accounted for by the contrast Paul
makes in verse 5, a contrast which he has had in mind throughout.
This is the contrast between the visionary—ὁ τοιοῦτος—and ἐμαυτοῦ.
He could safely boast about the visionary; he would not be caught
out, for he would simply speak the truth (verse 6a). ὑπὲρ δὲ ἐμαυτοῦ,
about himself, however, he will boast only in regard to his weak-
nesses. Why? And why does he in the end forbear to boast about the
one who sees visions? According to Lietzmann,[39] he distinguishes
'Paulus der Apokalyptiker' and 'Paulus der Mensch und Apostel';
this is true as far as it goes, though I do not see how the fact that
Paul's readers were familiar with the distinction between the ἔσω
and ἔξω ἄνθρωπος would help them to understand it. Dr Käsemann
(pp. 63–71; 54–66), followed in this by Dr Kümmel,[40] makes the
point that Paul evaluates his experience of exaltation into heaven,
as he does his speaking with tongues (1 Cor. 14.14) and his ecstasy
(2 Cor. 5.13), in relation to his service to the church. Details of his
rapture to the third heaven have no value for the church; he
therefore sees no value in boasting about them, and suppresses
them. This too is certainly true as far as it goes. It hardly does full
justice however to the explicit μή τις εἰς ἐμὲ λογίσηται ὑπὲρ ὃ βλέπει
με ἢ ἀκούει ἐξ ἐμοῦ. Paul forbears (φείδομαι) to boast about his
visionary experiences lest anyone should form too high an opinion

of him. 'Anyone' (τις) must be a member of the Corinthian church to which he is writing; and the point is that in his treatment of visions Paul is expressing a criterion of apostleship not over against false criteria employed by other so-called, or self-styled, apostles, but over against the Corinthians. Here too[41] it is not necessary to suppose that the false apostles were *Pneumatiker*, only that *Pneumatikertum* was what the Corinthians looked for in an apostle. Their interest in this kind of religion, and in this kind of requirement, stands out clearly in 1 Corinthians, before the intruders appear. No doubt this led to the development of corresponding gifts and interests in visitors less strongminded than Paul; but this aspect of their apostleship may well have been picked up in Corinth rather than brought to Corinth. There may be an allusion to this in verse 6. If Paul boasts about visions he will not be made to look a fool, for he will speak no more than the truth; others may perhaps be caught out claiming visionary experiences they have not had. Paul does not wish the Corinthians to put to his account[42] more than they have seen or heard; others (it may be hinted) were not so scrupulous. Paul himself has been given a sharp reminder of the relative importance of visions and of weakness; the doubled ἵνα μὴ ὑπεραίρωμαι of verse 7, however the grammatical and textual problems are to be resolved, bears clear and eloquent testimony to Paul's own understanding of apostolic ministry; and at the same time indirect testimony to those of whom it might be said, ὑπεραίρονται—flattery has gone to their heads, and they are getting a bit above themselves.

(5) 12.12 f: Dr Käsemann and others[43] have shown that, though σημείοις τε καὶ τέρασιν καὶ δυνάμεσιν must refer to the working of miracles, Paul is careful to place such signs in a context determined by ἐν πάσῃ ὑπομονῇ; that is, the stress lies not on miracles as such but on the fact that they are integrated into the apostolic ministry of service and suffering, in which they play only a subordinate part. It has also been pointed out that σημεῖα τοῦ ἀποστόλου is a phrase Paul does not use elsewhere,[44] and the conclusion has been drawn (for example, by Dr Kümmel)[45] that he here takes hold of a catch-phrase used by his opponents, who applied it to themselves and found in their miracles the warrant of their apostleship. This may be true; it seems to me equally possible and in the light of all the evidence more probable that Paul owed the phrase not to his opponents but to the Corinthian Christians, who certainly regarded themselves as judges of apostles, requiring for example some proof

of the fact that Christ spoke in Paul (2 Cor. 13.3). Of any supposed apostle they demanded σημεῖα, which may have taken the form of visions, miracles or commendatory epistles from recognized authorities.

Paul goes on immediately (2 Cor. 12.13) to say, ironically, that the only respect in which he had given the Corinthians less than the full apostolic treatment was his refusal to take any pay from them. This theme had already received full consideration in 11.7–11, and it is surprising to encounter it again so soon. It is to be noted that in each passage it follows almost immediately upon Paul's emphatic assertion that he does not fall short of οἱ ὑπερλίαν ἀπόστολοι. This is a remarkable pattern; and it becoms all the more remarkable when it is observed that it occurs also in the first epistle (1 Cor. 9). Here too Paul defends his apostleship. 'Am I not an apostle? ... If I am not an apostle to others, to you at least I am.' He must offer an ἀπολογία to those who would put him to the test (τοῖς ἐμὲ ἀνακρίνουσιν) —the Corinthians were already applying their own standards of judgement to apostolic claimants. Almost immediately Paul cites as a clear example of apostolic authority the apostle's right to be supported by the church in which he ministers. Having established the right (verses 7–14) he points out that he makes, and intends to make, no use of it, using language in part very similar to that of 2 Cor. 11.10 (τὸ καύχημά μου οὐδεὶς κενώσει—ἡ καύχησις αὕτη οὐ φραγήσεται εἰς ἐμέ). Now the situation reflected in 1 Cor. 9 belongs to the period before that of the intruders of 2 Corinthians; it is therefore not these intruders who are being compared with Paul to his disadvantage. The persons in question are described in 1 Cor. 9.5 as οἱ λοιποὶ ἀπόστολοι καὶ οἱ ἀδελφοὶ τοῦ κυρίου καὶ Κηφᾶς. It is not easy to define with confidence 'the other apostles'; but we know who Cephas was, and the 'Lord's brothers' included James, one of Cephas's fellow 'pillars' (Gal. 2.9).[46]

Thus we have here not a conclusive proof but at least a strong indication that the ὑπερλίαν ἀπόστολοι of 2 Cor. 11.5; 12.11 were not wandering preachers but high officials in Jerusalem.

(6) 12.19—13.2: These verses contain a number of familiar problems, most of which it will not be necessary to mention here, and also one or two which seem sometimes at least to have escaped notice. It is on the latter that I shall concentrate.

In reading through the epistle one might have supposed that Paul was defending himself, his integrity and also his position and authority. This is not so; what he is doing he does as a responsible Christian and apostle, in the sight of God and in Christ. His is not a human defence of a human being; his language is in the strictest sense theological language, and his objectives are theological. So far as his actions have a human reference it is not to himself but to his readers; the objective is the building up of the Corinthian church. There is reason to take thought for this objective, for Paul fears that the outcome of the present situation may be the reverse of οἰκοδομή, the destruction of such Christian building as has already (cf. 1 Cor. 3.10–17) taken place in Corinth. He fears that when he comes to Corinth he may find the Corinthians to be other than he wishes, and that they may find him to be what they do not wish. The former possibility Paul proceeds to define in precise terms: there may be in the Corinthian church ἔρις, ζῆλος, θυμοί, ἐριθεῖαι, καταλαλιαί, ψιθυρισμοί, φυσιώσεις, ἀκαταστασίαι. It is not necessary to go over this catalogue of sins in detail to see that they all (with the possible exception of ἐριθεῖαι)[47] relate to the sort of situation that would be brought about by the incursion of rival apostles. Strife, anger, and evil-speaking are natural constituents of circumstances in which some sided with Paul, others with his rivals. The same is true of envy, whisperings, and disorders; and most circumstances, even the least promising, seem to have provided the Corinthians with a pretext for putting themselves up with self-importance. Read in their context in 2 Cor. 12 these sins suggest the effect of a rival mission, and though there can be no doubt that they were all to be found in the period of division referred to in 1 Cor. 1.11 the fact that Paul fears that he may find them present when he next visits Corinth shows that he thinks of them as belonging to the time of writing. He continues to consider what may happen on his next visit to Corinth: he fears that God may humiliate him. It is not clear[48] whether πάλιν is to be taken with ἐλθόντος or with ταπεινώσῃ. The point is not one of fundamental importance for the understanding of the verse. However it is resolved it is clear that Paul had previously visited Corinth and had there experienced events that could only be described as humiliating.[49] He fears that this will happen again, and that as an apostle he will appear powerless and ineffective. This, though painful for Paul could fall out for the clarification and furtherance of the gospel;[50] hence he can take God as the subject of ταπεινοῦν. Another aspect of Paul's humiliation would be his mourning over the unsatisfactory members of the church, described as those who sinned previously and did not repent. If the sentence ended at μὴ μετανοησάντων we should still be faced with the problem of settling the time-reference of προ- in προαμαρτάνειν, but this would not be severe. We should think of those who had been guilty of the sins described in verse 20 either before Paul's arrival on the visit in question (ἐλθόντος μου), or perhaps of those who had already been guilty of them on some previous occasion—possibly on the occasion of Paul's second visit, when some may have taken the part of the intruder who attacked Paul (ὁ ἀδικήσας, 2 Cor. 7.12), or indeed back in the period of 1 Cor. 1.11. But after μετανοησάντων Paul goes on to mention three more sins of a quite different kind: ἐπὶ τῇ ἀκαθαρσίᾳ καὶ πορνείᾳ καὶ ἀσελγείᾳ ᾗ ἔπραξαν. Broadly speaking, these are all (unless they are to be violently allegorized) sexual sins of a physical kind, and bear little relation to the offences of verse 20. How is this unexpected continuation to be explained? We must reject the suggestion that προαμαρτάνειν refers to sins committed before conversion; the very fact of conversion means that these sins had been repented of. We must reject also the view that there is no connection between the two verses—that verse 20 refers to sins connected with the intruding false apostles, and that in verse 21 Paul's mind reverts to completely different situations, such as that mentioned in 1 Cor. 5. This view, I say, is to be rejected; it may nevertheless point in the right direction. When Paul wrote 1 Corinthians one of the errors current in Corinth led in the direction of libertinism. The proposition was maintained that, as the belly was intended for food and food for the belly, so the body was made for fornication and fornication for the body (1 Cor. 6.13).[51] In this direction, and towards flirtation with idolatry, the Corinthian gnosis led. The theme of gnosis, and that of sexual immorality, have dropped out of 2 Corinthians;[52] new troubles, doctrinal and moral, have taken their place. Yet not entirely; Paul fears that when he revisits Corinth he may find both new sinners, who in accepting the intruding false apostles have fallen into strife, envy and so forth, and old sinners (προημαρτηκότες) of the gnostic, libertine kind, who have not repented of their fornication.

With this we must continue. Paul is now about to visit Corinth for the third time; the significance of this he brings out with an Old Testament quotation, and then reiterates his warning.[53] It is not the first: προείρηκα καὶ προλέγω. It is not satisfactory to suppose that the προ- in προλέγω is an unintended and meaningless repetition, as if Paul meant to say, 'I have told you previously, and am now telling you.' We must try to make sense of προλέγω as it stands before we think of mending it. This is not difficult. Paul is giving warning that on his third visit he will not spare the offending and recalcitrant Corinthians. He gave this warning in the past (προείρηκα) when actually in Corinth on his second visit (ὡς παρὼν τὸ δεύτερον), and he reiterates it now when absent (ἀπὼν νῦν); it is the same warning on each occasion, and it is delivered τοῖς προημαρτηκόσιν καὶ τοῖς λοιποῖς πᾶσιν; that is, to those whose old errors led them into fornication and kindred sins, and to the rest who, in their reaction to the ψευδαπόστολοι, are now guilty of faction, envy, hatred and the like.

This association and this distinction are both important in the reconstruction of the Corinthian situation.

(7) 13.3–9: We are concerned with only one point in these difficult and important verses. They are full of words that have to do with testing. ἀδόκιμος (3), δόκιμος (1), δοκιμάζειν (1), δοκιμή (1), occur between them six times, πειράζειν and ἐπιγινώσκειν once each. The main content of the paragraph is given in the imperatives of verse 5: ἑαυτοὺς πειράζετε, ἑαυτοὺς δοκιμάζετε. The reflexive pronouns are emphatic: it is yourselves that you should test. The implication is clear: test yourselves, not me. The Corinthians were applying to Paul tests of their own, and this is explicitly stated in verse 3: they seek proof (δοκιμή) that Christ speaks in him. This was the kind of question the Corinthians had asked before (cf. e.g. 1 Cor. 4.3), and they expected an answer in terms which Paul, playing the fool, had briefly allowed himself to use (2 Cor. 11.1; 12.1, 11): vision and ecstasy could justify the apostolic claim to speak in the name of Christ. What the Corinthians were seeking was a demonstration of apostolic authority; that is, they were trying to decide between Paul and his rivals. Paul's first reaction is to take up the challenge. This time he will not spare them (13.2), as he had done in the past, both by meek behaviour when he visited them (10.1, 10), and by abstaining from visiting them (1.23). It was true that Christ was Christ crucified and that it was therefore the business of an apostle to manifest the νέκρωσις of Jesus (4.10); but it was also true that Christ crucified in weakness was Christ risen, who lives ἐκ δυνάμεως θεοῦ, and just as 'we are weak in him' so also 'we shall live with him ἐκ δυνάμεως θεοῦ', and that 'in relation to you'— εἰς ὑμᾶς, awkward words, omitted by B D³ r arm and changed by vg pe go into ἐν ὑμῖν, but undoubtedly genuine, and in an emphatic

position at the end of the sentence. But Paul turns next to a different kind of argument, which he has used elsewhere (cf. 1 Cor. 9.2). Set aside the question whether Christ speaks in me; do you recognize that he is in you? Certainly you do—unless you are ἀδόκιμοι, a conclusion the Corinthians were unlikely to reach. If however Christ is in you, this is the result of my apostolic ministry, and I must hope therefore that you will recognize that I am not ἀδόκιμος. Not that recognition on the part of the Corinthians matters ultimately; it is not their δοκιμάζειν[54] that makes Paul δόκιμος or ἀδόκιμος; indeed, he would be willing to be ἀδόκιμος on their account,[55] and can therefore rejoice in his weakness and their strength, for their strength would constitute his δοκιμή as an apostle speaking in the person of Christ better than his own strength would do; thus he seeks their κατάρτισις (verse 9). Nothing else could so effectively establish his own apostolic status.

The point of this is that the Corinthians have been confronted by two rival apostolates. Not improperly, they wish to determine which is true and which is false, but they have used the wrong criteria. They have looked for written commendations from high authority, and for ecstatic phenomena. Paul in these concluding words says nothing directly about his rivals—he has already dealt adequately, he supposes, with them—but once more points his own people to the only valid criterion of apostolic ministry.

This concludes the exegetical spadework. All that remains is to survey the results, and consider whether, or how far, they enable us to identify Paul's opponents and describe the situation in Corinth.

To go back over the ground we have now traversed, collecting one by one the data relevant to this task, would cost time we cannot spare. We must proceed at once to draw such conclusions as the data permit with reference to the historical and theological questions they raise.

The chief historical question can be set out as follows. Paul's opponents have been identified sometimes as Palestinian and Judaizing, sometimes as hellenistic, Jews.[56] F. C. Baur[57] distinguished between the ψευδαπόστολοι and the ὑπερλίαν ἀπόστολοι; the latter were the Jerusalem apostles, headed by James and Cephas, and the former were their emissaries; all were legalistic Judaizers. In our own time, Dr Käsemann[58] has maintained a similar view, though he takes the ψευδαπόστολοι to be envoys of the Jerusalem church whose task was to bring Gentile churches such as Corinth under the authority of the mother church. The views considered earlier in this paper may remind us however that others have seen in the same opponents some kind of hellenistic Jews, even though working, it may be, from a Palestinian base; and here one may mention names as diverse as those of Schlatter,[59] Lütgert,[60] Bultmann,[61] Schmithals,[62] Georgi,[63] and Friedrich,[64] according to whom the opponents were gnostics, *Pneumatiker*, ecstatics, θεῖοι ἄνδρες, adherents of Stephen and the Hellenists of Acts 6, but in any case Jews whose Judaism had been radically affected by some kind of hellenism. Each set of interpreters could claim to be giving due weight to evidence contained in the epistle. The former group could point to the indisputable evidence that the opponents were Jews, and that it was their Jewishness that Paul singled out for mention. 'Are they Hebrews? So am I. Are they Israelites? So am I. Are they the seed of Abraham? So am I' (11.22). He does not add, 'Have they studied hellenistic thought and religion? So have I.' He disputes their invasion of 'his' Corinthian territory in terms that recall the concordat of Gal. 2.7–10. He rebuts their ἕτερον εὐαγγέλιον as he does in Gal. 1.6. He refers to ὑπερλίαν ἀπόστολοι with the same irony that he uses of the δοκοῦντες εἶναί τι in Gal. 2.6. If we may look so far afield as 2 Cor. 3 we have stronger evidence still, for there Paul uses the story of Moses to show that the glory of the law, though real, was transient, and pointed forward to the even greater glory of the gospel.

There is undoubtedly a good case for the view that the opponents were Judaizers, but it is also easy to understand why it has been attacked.[65] There is no reference in 2 Cor. 10—13 to circumcision; is it conceivable that Judaizers should have omitted this plank from their platform or, if they demanded circumcision, that Paul should have passed over the matter in silence? Paul's reply follows a different line from that of Galatians. It is true, and I think acknowledged by all, or nearly all, students of the epistle, that Paul ultimately grounds his apostolic gospel, and with it his apostleship, in Christ crucified and risen, and refuses any other validation for it. But when, for a moment and for the sake of an *ad hominem* argument, he suffers himself to become a fool and to answer his correspondents in their own terms, he refers to his competence in gnosis (11.6), and boasts of himself in his capacity as a visionary (12.1–6). He knows how to fight not κατὰ σάρκα but (presumably—the words are not used) κατὰ πνεῦμα (10.3 f). He too can work miracles—signs, portents and acts of power (12.12). These pieces of evidence are not unnaturally taken to point to adversaries who lay claim to gnosis, who speak and act in the Spirit, who work miracles and see visions.

Here is the problem to which earlier work on this question has led. It seems to me that our review of material in 2 Cor. 10—13 has shown us the solution. In a sentence: the intruders were Jews, Jerusalem Jews, Judaizing Jews, and as such constituted a rival apostolate to Paul's, backed by all the prestige of the mother church; the Corinthians, confronted by these rival apostolates, proceeded to compare and to judge between them on essentially hellenistic grounds. This explains the fact that the situation with which Paul had to deal, and consequently also his treatment of that situation, contained both Judaizing and hellenizing elements, which give rise to the mixed and even contradictory data which have in turn led to contradictory explanations. It is probable that the situation was further complicated by the readiness of the intruding apostles to accept the criteria proposed by the Corinthians, and thus to adopt a measure of hellenization—one might almost say, of Corinthiani-zation.[66] This is the more probable in that Paul himself did so, though he was careful to bracket his acceptance by the admission, To do this is really to play the fool; that is to say, his acceptance was not a genuine, serious acceptance. He did not acknowledge Corinthian presuppositions as a criterion of apostolicity.

The present discussion has, I think, added some weight to the view that the opponents were Judaizers, and had their roots in Jerusalem. The description of them as ψευδαπόστολοι points to a dispute about the interpretation of the fundamental meaning of Judaism.[67] There was, it seems, a breach of the agreement that Paul had made with the 'pillars' of Jerusalem,[68] and thought relevant to the Galatian dispute.[69] The recurring theme of the apostle's right to payment, and of his right to renounce that right, recalls the non-Pauline practice of Cephas (1 Cor. 9.5).[70] I must repeat[71] that insistence upon circumcision is not an indispensable mark of Judaizing. There were Jewish missionaries who did not insist on circumcision,[72] and we have in Gal. 2 the clearest evidence of a Judaizing movement strong enough to excommunicate the gentile churches which had nevertheless renounced the claim that circumcision was necessary to salvation.[73] At the same time, we have observed repeated indications that the Corinthians were engaged in the task of testing the rival apostles, the old one and the new. You would do better, says Paul, to test yourselves, to see whether you are in the faith (13.5); but the way in which he expresses himself suggests strongly that the Corinthians had thought it more proper to test him, and the context makes this certain. They were impressed by flamboyant and self-assertive behaviour (which, Paul argued, could not possibly be combined with the true gospel of the meekness and gentleness of Christ crucified). They sought proof that Christ spoke in Paul, and this they understood, recalling the old valuation of *glossolalia* to which 1 Corinthians bears witness, to mean the phenomena of inspired speech. A natural accompaniment of this was an interest in visions as a validation of apostolic status.

The evidence is complicated by the fact that at least two groups of adversaries to Paul are to be recognized. I am treading here on familiar[74] though disputed ground, and shall not go over it again. The *sprunghaft* transition from 11.4 to 11.5 when rightly understood is not fatal to a distinction between ψευδαπόστολοι and ὑπερλίαν ἀπόστολοι but rather is entirely coherent with and almost demands such a distinction. The precise relation between the two groups is far more difficult to establish than the fact that they existed. Those who actually visited Corinth brought with them commendatory epistles; from whom, we do not know, but it would be hard to think of more desirable referees than the 'pillars' in Jerusalem, and hard too to think of Jerusalem authorities in a position to act independently of the 'pillars'.[75] At the same time, it must be remembered that Paul himself appears to make a clear distinction between the ὑπερλίαν ἀπόστολοι, with whom he can associate himself, and the ψευδαπόστολοι, who are the servants of Satan. Yet it was presumably not Satan who wrote their testimonials, and we must at this point bear in mind the fact that the intruding pseudo-apostles appear to have accommodated themselves to the requirements made by the Corinthians. Under ancient conditions of communication it must have been virtually impossible to keep a firm hand on one's representatives in distant parts. This is a fact familiar to all students of the political history of antiquity,[76] and it soon entered Christian history too.[77] There is no more convincing hypothesis (though it is not and cannot be more than a hypothesis) than that the ψευδαπόστολοι were agents,[78] unsatisfactory agents who misrepresented their principals, of the ὑπερλίαν ἀπόστολοι, though the latter may also have been such as to give the former some excuse.[79]

This suggestion, or rather the facts that elicited it, may lead to a final observation on the theological significance of the material reviewed in this paper. The chief actors who appeared on the Corinthian stage; under the eye of a Corinthian audience, were Jews; so were those who stood in the wings and were responsible for 'noises off'.[80] They were also Christians, and the kinds of Christianity they represented may be characterized by the ways in which their new faith led them to treat their original Jewish religion.[81] All short descriptions of such complex matters are bound to be misleading, but it will not, I hope, lead us far astray if we speak of conservative Judaism, liberal Judaism[82] and revolutionary Judaism. The first was the Judaism of the 'pillars' in Jerusalem. It was undoubtedly Christian Judaism, for it not only reverenced Jesus and handed on a body of teaching in his name, but believed in his messiahship, and in his resurrection, thus placing him in no common human, or even messianic, category. But it held this faith within a firm framework of Judaism; for example, though it was willing to believe that God would accept Gentiles, it was not prepared to eat with them unless they accepted at least certain basic legal requirements.[83] The second was the kind of Judaism developed in some (but probably not all) areas by the envoys of the Jerusalem church, who retained and sometimes exaggerated the fundamental Judaism of those who sent them out, but accepted—perhaps in good faith and with the excellent intention of commending their Jewish Christian faith to others—a veneer of non-Jewish practice. If they could make a stronger impression by adopting a gnostic framework of thought and the ecstatic accompaniments of pagan religion they were willing to do so, and in Corinth, for example, they reinforced their commendatory epistles by visions, inspired speech and turbulent behaviour. They were making (so it seemed to Paul) the worst of both worlds, and were neither honest Jews nor honest Christians, but ultimately pagan—the servants of Satan, pretending to be apostles and servants of righteousness.[84] His own was revolutionary Judaism. The external features of religion were indifferent to him: 'To the Jews I became as a Jew ... to those outside the law as one outside the law' (1 Cor. 9.20 f). In many respects he remained a Jew; he had been too well trained in rabbinic theology ever to think in radically different forms. But the centre of his faith and of his life was no longer Torah but Christ; and of this proposition there is no clearer example than this theological and ethical response to the Corinthian situation.

The further history of what I have called conservative and liberal Christian Judaism is a fascinating study, but the future was Paul's, though it was and will always continue to be a future threatened by the tendencies that appear in classical form in his rivals on the Corinthian stage. I can think of no stronger justification of my opening remarks about the historical and theological importance of the study of this theme.

NOTES

1 They can hardly have manifested less concern than Paul for the tradition of the words and deeds of Jesus; we probably owe to them part at least of the synoptic tradition.

2 'Die Legitimität des Apostels', *ZNTW* xli, 1942 (reprinted separately Darmstadt 1956), pp. 33–71. In references to this work the pages in *ZNTW* will be given first, then those of the reprint.

3 'Christianity at Corinth', especially pp. 14–22.

4 For further material see the compressed yet lucid survey in W. G. Kümmel, *Introduction to the New Testament* (London 1966), pp. 208–11, and the same author's bibliography in H. Lietzmann and W. G. Kümmel, *An die Korinther (HNT* ix[5]). Tübingen 1969.

5 *WMANT* xi. Neukirchen-Vluyn 1964.

6 'Die Gegner des Paulus im 2. Korintherbrief', in *Abraham unser Vater, Festschrift für Otto Michel (AGSU* v), ed. O. Betz, M. Hengel, and P. Schmidt (Leiden/Köln 1963) pp. 181–215. This article appeared shortly before the lecture 'Christianity at Corinth' was given, and was not dealt with as fully as it deserves.

7 Friedrich, p. 195, referring to G. Bornkamm, 'Die Vorgeschichte des sogenannten Zweiten Korintherbriefes' *(SHAW* Phil.-hist. Klasse 1961), 2.

8 Yet in the end Friedrich comes near to accepting the theory. On p. 196 he writes, 'Dass [die Gegner] aber mit dem Anspruch auftraten, göttliche Sendboten nach Art der griechischen Umwelt zu sein, ist kaum anzunehmen', but on p. 212, 'Weil die Stephanusleute es zugeben, als θεῖος ἀνήρ betrachtet zu werden, darum ist Paulus so scharf gegen sie'.

9 See W. Gutbrod, in *TWNT* iii, 393; also Lietzmann-Kümmel, pp. 150, 211.

10 *Die Gnosis in Korinth (FRLANT*, NF xlviii) Göttingen 1956.

11 See material referred to in note 4 above.

12 The transitions from 2.13 to 2.14 and from 7.4 to 7.5 are perhaps capable of explanation; and see note 25, p. 130 below.

13 Cf. above, pp. 20 f.

14 E.g. Georgi, Friedrich, Kümmel; see the summary material referred to in note 4.

15 R. Bultmann, *Exegetische Probleme des Zweiten Korintherbriefes (SBU* ix) Uppsala 1947.

16   See pp. 70 ff.
17   See above, pp. 17–20.
18   See below, pp. 87–107.
19   See below, p. 127.
20   See p. 74; and the frequent indications (pp. 68–81) that the Corinthians were applying tests to their apostles.
21   J. Héring, *La seconde Épître de Saint Paul aux Corinthiens*, (*Commentaire du Nouveau Testament* viii, Neuchâtel and Paris 1958), p. 79.
22   See G. Delling in *TWNT* vi, 296.
23   See G. Schrenk in *TWNT* ii, 441.
24   For the evidence see, for example, Lietzmann-Kümmel ad loc.
25   For the relation between the devil and the snake cf. Rev. 12.9; 20.2, and see Commentaries on these verses; also S.-B. i, 138 f.
26   Cf. N. A. Dahl, in *The Background of the New Testament and its Eschatology, in Honour of C. H. Dodd*, ed. W. D. Davies and D. Daube (Cambridge 1956), p. 441: 'There exists a real danger, that the deception of Eve shall also find an analogy within the Church, a satanic travesty of the correspondence between the first and the last things.'
27   Cf. P. Bachmann, *Der zweite Brief des Paulus an die Korinther*, (*Kommentar zum Neuen Testament*, ed. Th. Zahn, viii, Leipzig 1918), p. 365.
28   E.g. pp. 284 ff.
29   Georgi, p. 285, rightly points out the emphatic position of κύριος.
30   Cf. W. G. Kümmel, *Die Theologie des Neuen Testaments* (*NTDErgänzungsreihe*, iii, Göttingen 1969), p. 219: 'Paulus' gebraucht 'den Namen des Menschen Jesus in genau derselben Weise für den irdischen Jesus wie für den Auferstandenen.'
31   Cf. the view set forth by K. Barth in his earlier commentary on Romans: 'the faithfulness [of God] which abides in Jesus'. This is abandoned in the later commentary.
32   See my *The First Epistle to the Corinthians* (London 1968), pp. 277–81.
33   On the text see Kümmel in Lietzmann-Kümmel, ad loc.
34   See note 4, and the summaries of the history of interpretation given by Georgi and Friedrich.
35   *Paulus und die Heilsgeschichte* (*Acta Jutlandica*, xxvi, 1, Aarhus 1954), p. 171. cf. Friedrich, p. 188.
36   See note 2.
37   See note 15.
38   See Lietzmann-Kümmel ad loc.
39   Op. cit. p. 155.
40   In Lietzmann-Kümmel, p. 212.
41   Cf. p. 69.
42   For λογίζεσθαι εἰς see Lietzmann ad loc.
43   Käsemann, pp. 62 f; 53; Kümmel in Lietzmann-Kümmel. p. 213; A. Schlatter, *Paulus der Bote Jesu* (Stuttgart 1962), p. 670; cf. L. Goppelt, *Apostolic and Post-Apostolic Times* (London 1970), p. 38.
44   Cf. however Rom. 15.19.
45   Lietzmann-Kümmel, p. 213.
46   See p. 66.

47 For the meaning of this word see my *The Epistle to the Romans* (London 1957), pp. 47 f.

48 See the discussions by H. Windisch, *Der zweite Korintherbrief (Krit.-exegetischer Kommentar über das NT)* (Göttingen 1924), and E. B. Allo, *Seconde Épître aux Corinthiens (Études Bibliques)* (Paris 1956), ad loc.

49 See note 12, and pp. 108–17 below.

50 Cf. Phil. 1. 12. Christ crucified is manifested in the humiliation of his servants.

51 Paul appears to allude to a Corinthian belief; see my Commentary (note 32), ad loc.

52 γνῶσις and γινώσκειν occur 25 times in 1 Corinthians, 14 times in 2 Corinthians; more striking are σοφία and σοφός (28:1), and the πορνεία, πορνεύειν, πόρνη, πόρνος group (13:1). Cf. εἰδωλεῖον, εἰδωλόθυτος, εἰδωλολατρεία, εἰδωλολάτρης, εἴδωλον (15:1).

53 For προλέγειν, 'to warn', see Liddell-Scott, s.v.

54 Or his own; cf. 1 Cor. 4.3 f.

55 Cf. Rom. 9.3.

56 See the accounts of the history of interpretation in Georgi, pp. 7–16, and Friedrich, pp. 191–6; also note 4 above.

57 See e.g. *Paulus, der Apostel Jesu Christi* (Stuttgart 1845), p. 294: 'Da aber diese ψευδαπόστολοι in Corinth sich namentlich auf die Auctorität des Apostels Petrus beriefen, aus Palästina nach Corinth gekommen waren, und ohne Zweifel mit den palästinensischen Judenaposteln in irgend einem Zusammenhang stunden, so sind wohl die ὑπερλίαν ἀπόστολοι, die Apostel selbst, deren Schüler und Abgeordnete zu seyn, die ψευδαπόστολοι vorgaben.' The whole discussion is still of great importance.

58 Op. cit. especially p. 48;30.

59 *Paulus* (see note 43 above); also *Die korinthische Theologie* (Gütersloh 1914).

60 *Freiheitspredigt und Schwarmgeister in Korinth* (Gütersloh 1908).

61 See note 15 above.

62 See note 10 above.

63 See note 5 above.

64 See note 6 above.

65 Friedrich, p. 192: 'Judaisten, wie sie z. B. in Galatien aufgetreten sind, sind die Gegner des Paulus in 2. Kor. auf keinen Fall. Es fehlen alle charakteristischen Merkmale dieser judenchristlichen Nomisten, die Beschneidung, Halten des Sabbats und kultische Reinheit fordern. Sie machen Paulus weder den Vorwurf der Gesetzlosigkeit, noch polemisiert Paulus gegen ihre Werkgerechtigkeit als Hauptmerkmal ihrer falschen Theologie.'

66 It was otherwise in Galatia, where the Judaizers were, it seems, able to state their own terms in their own way, and we have an example of 'pure' Judaizing. It is not easy to say how characteristic of hellenistic Christianity Corinth was; probably more so than the churches of Galatia.

67 See pp. 102 f below.

68   Cf. pp. 65 f.

69   Cf. Gal. 2.7–10. The fact that the Galatians (see note 66) took a less independent line than the Corinthians gives a different shape to Paul's argument in his letter to them.

70   Cf. pp. 66, 74 above.

71   See above, pp. 21 f.

72   See Josephus, *Antiquities*, xx, 40–8.

73   Cf. pp. 95 f below.

74   See above, pp. 64, 70–2.

75   See Käsemann, p. 46;28: 'Nach Gal. 2 sind . . . die Urapostel mehr das repräsentierende Organ der durch die δοκοῦντες verkörperten Leitung der Urgemeinde. Eine Delegation ist schwerlich ohne ihr Mitwirken denkbar, braucht jedoch durch sie nicht mit konkreten Sonderaufträgen bedacht zu sein und hat zum mindesten keine allein auf ihren Namen lautende Vollmacht besessen.' The distinctions drawn here seem to me somewhat too fine.

76   An example taken almost at random: 'The Potidaeans were forced to make overtures for surrender to the Athenian generals . . . The generals were willing to listen to the proposals . . . The Athenians, however, blamed the generals for making the agreement without consulting the government at home (ἄνευ αὐτῶν. . .')') (Thucydides ii, 70; trans. R. Warner. Penguin Classics, London 1954). Note that the generals were acting in good faith; so, it may be, were the ψευδαπόστολοι.

77   Examples of misrepresentation in the New Testament: Acts 15.24 (which should be taken with Gal. 2.12, as well as 2.4); 2 Cor. 4.2; Phil. 1.17 f; 2 Thess. 2.2 (a forged letter); 2 Peter 2.1; Rev. 2.2.

78   It should be remembered that the normal meaning of שָׁלִיח is not 'missionary' (the meaning Paul attached to it), but 'agent'. This linguistic fact may account for some of the bitterness Paul felt about those who claimed apostolic status but did not do the work of pioneers.

79   In Baur's view, Peter and James were downright Judaizers. This they were not; but it is difficult to read Gal. 2 and come to the conclusion that they saw eye to eye with Paul in all respects.

80   Peter himself may have been in Corinth; see pp. 28–39.

81   Cf. p. 64.

82   It is, I hope, clear that I am not using these terms in their modern sense, and would not presume to make any comment on movements within present-day Judaism.

83   See Gal. 2.12, and the Decree of Acts 15.20, 29. This seems to have been a compromise provision for making possible contacts between Jewish and Gentile Christians.

84   That Judaizing Christian Jews thus accommodated themselves to the hellenistic criteria imposed by those who examined their claim to apostleship must have contributed to the development of gnosticism. It is unlikely that it happened only in Corinth. There is here an important field for further study.

5

ΨΕΥΔΑΠΟΣΤΟΛΟΙ
(2 Cor. 11.13)

The problem of the identity of the opponents whom Paul castigates in 2 Cor. 10—13 is no new one, and in the absence of new evidence it may well seem impossible to add to what has already been said on the subject.[1] The present paper makes no attempt to deal with the problem, one of the most important for the history and theology of primitive Christianity, as a whole, but examines one point, in the hope that any light cast by such an examination may prove in the end to illuminate a somewhat wider area.

In 2 Cor. 11.13 Pauls speaks of his adversaries as ψευδαπόστολοι, ἐργάται δόλιοι, μετασχηματιζόμενοι εἰς ἀποστόλους Χριστοῦ. The next verses speak of them as servants (διάκονοι) of Satan (who himself μετασχηματίζεται εἰς ἄγγελον φωτός), and point darkly to their unhappy but deserved end. This is as bitter an attack as Paul makes on any of his adversaries,[2] so bitter that it seems, *prima facie* at least, unlikely that those who are so described should be equated with those who are ironically but more gently described as ὑπερλίαν ἀπόστολοι (11.5; 12.11), and with the 'Hebrews' of 11.22 f, of whom Paul says nothing worse than that whatever claims they make he could make for himself, and with greater right. These comparisons however have been pursued in the past without agreed result,[3] and will not be directly studied here, where attention will be focused on the word ψευδαπόστολος.

This word is not used elsewhere by Paul, nor is it used by any other New Testament writer;[4] Paul does however use a few other ψευδο- compounds. In the same chapter (2 Cor. 11.26) he speaks of ψευδάδελφοι among whom he experienced dangers, and the same word recurs in Gal. 2.4: false brothers crept in to spy out our liberty. At 1 Cor. 15.15 he uses ψευδομάρτυς,[5] but this word contributes little to the present discussion, since it does not refer to Paul's adversaries, but is used hypothetically. If the proposition that God does not raise the dead were true, Paul himself and his colleagues would turn out to be false witnesses, since in preaching Christ crucified and risen they had affirmed that God had done precisely this. It is possible that Paul's word hints at (but it certainly does not itself amount to) a counterstroke, implying that those in Corinth who alleged that God did not raise the dead (15.12) were ψευδομάρτυρες τοῦ θεοῦ. The implication does not become explicit; we may be content to note the genitive (τοῦ θεοῦ), which must be objective (people who bear false witness about God) rather than possessive (since God can hardly be said to possess false witnesses).[6]

These are the only ψευδο- compounds used by Paul. For completeness it may be noted that in the certainly genuine epistles Paul uses the verb ψεύδεσθαι only in vigorous assertions that he himself is not lying (Rom. 9.1; 2 Cor. 11.31; Gal. 1.20). These may suggest a certain sensitiveness to the charge of falsehood, which appears to have been brought against him, and which he on occasion seems to retort; beyond this they do not bear on our problem. In Col. 3.9 Paul (if he be the author) urges his readers not to lie to one another; this is not relevant. At Rom. 1.25 ψεῦδος stands over against the truth of God; at 3.7 ψεῦσμα is used similarly, and in the same context ψεύστης occurs in the quotation from Ps. 116.11. We need not linger over these passages, or over 2 Thess. 2.9, where Paul is speaking of the work of the Man of sin; in verse 11 this eschatological falsehood is brought into the present, where men are induced to believe a lie rather than the truth.

So much for Paul's use of ψεύδεσθαι and its cognates and compounds. The only question we need ask at the moment is: Who were the ψευδάδελφοι? In 2 Cor. 11.26 they must be Christians. The only conceivable alternative is that they were Jews, and this is virtually excluded by the context. The γένος are the Jews, the ἔθνη are the rest; only Christians are left, and it is not surprising therefore that the danger from false brethren forms the climax of the list;[7] it is worse than the peril of the sea. But what was this danger? It does not suffice to say that the legalism of the Judaizers could have destroyed the results of Paul's work as an evangelist of the grace of God. This is true, and there was nothing worse that could have happened; but Paul is here speaking of beatings, shipwrecks, stonings, journeys, rivers, bandits—of personal and indeed physical perils that he encountered in his work, and the perils among false brothers must fit into this framework. With what physical danger could they threaten Paul? It has been suggested[8] that they might have betrayed Paul to hostile authorities: physical danger and the bitterness of treachery would then be combined. Direct physical violence on the part of the false brothers themselves cannot be ruled out. At least it may be said that they were, or claimed to be, or passed as, Christians; that their opposition to Paul was so extreme as to know virtually no limits; and that Paul did not accept that they were genuine Christians.

In Gal. 2.4 also the ψευδάδελφοι were at least persons who passed as Christians. They were not themselves products of Paul's Gentile mission or they would not have needed to spy out the liberty enjoyed by Paul and his converts. The words used in this verse— not only κατασκοπεῖν, but παρείσακτος, παρεισέρχεσθαι and κατα- δουλοῦν—are all significant, and all pejorative. According to Schlier[9] παρείσακτος means that they deceitfully made their way into the church at large, falsely claiming to be Christian brothers, παρεισέρχεσθαι that they proceeded to infiltrate into local com- munities.[10] They can hardly be other than Jewish Christians (or possibly Jews, making themselves out to be Christians) who wished to put a stop to Paul's work. It is to be noted that they are distin- guished from those 'who were reputed to be pillars'—James, Cephas and John, the leading authorities in the Jerusalem church.[11]

Turning to the rest of the New Testament we find that Paul's ψευδομάρτυς is used at Matt. 26.60, of those who at his trial bore false witness against Jesus. This is a merely verbal variation on Mark's use (14.56, 57) of the cognate verb ψευδομαρτυρεῖν.[12] There is nothing to remark on here; the words were current[13] in legal usage. As was pointed out above[14] in the reference to 1 Cor. 15.15, the meaning of ψευδομάρτυς is not 'one who pretends to be a witness but is not', but 'one who as a witness bears testimony that is false'. Thus in Plato, *Lg.*, 937 B, C it appears clearly that ψευδομαρτυρεῖν is equivalent to τὰ ψευδῆ μαρτυρεῖν.[15] According to 2 Pet. 2.1 the rise of false teachers, ψευδοδιδάσκαλοι, is to be expected.[16] These are the Christian counterpart of the ψευδοπροφῆται[17] of the Old Testa- ment. Study of the rest of 2 Pet. 2 reveals little more than that the author disapproves as much of their morals as of their teaching, and believes that severe punishment is in store for them. The Old Testament analogy suggests that the word ψευδοδιδάσκαλος may mean both that the persons in question were unauthorized, arro- gating to themselves an office to which they had no right, and that the content of their message was false. The context gives us little ground for choosing one rather than the other of these possible interpretations of the word, and it may well be that both are in mind;[18] this however reveals little more than the author's abhorrence of his adversaries, which is hardly in doubt anyway. That no clear distinction between ψευδοπροφῆται and ψευδοδιδάσκαλοι is intended appears from the Apocalypse of Peter, which is dependent on 2 Peter.[19] It is however probably a true reflection that the ψευδοδιδάσκαλος represents a further[20] stage of thought than ψευδοπροφήτης. 2 Peter's ψευδοδιδάσκαλοι (and though the word is not used the same thought, and perhaps the same persons, are present in, for example, the Pastorals) represent deviation from the Christian norm in the world of dogmatic theology that began to open up through the impinging of gnosticism upon Christianity; ψευδοπροφῆται, however, belong rather within the field of primitive Christian apocalyptic, and their error is the wrong identification of the apocalyptic history. The word indeed continues to be used for false teachers of any kind, but its roots lie in the Old Testament and apocalyptic. To the evidence for this we must now turn.

In Luke 6.26 and 2 Pet. 2.1 the ψευδοπροφῆται are those of the Old Testament; the word is used in the LXX,[21] and occasions no difficulty. The primary apocalyptic connotation is found in Mark 13.22, with the parallels in Matt. 24.11, 24. The false prophets announce the coming of the false Christs, as if these were the true Christ returning to his elect, whom they thus (as far as this is possible) mislead. Their error consists in anticipating the time of the end, which in any case (according to the context) is not remote. At the other end of the scale, 1 John 4.1 shows[22] the word ψευδοπροφήτης lingering in a decidedly gnostic context, though it should be noted that John chooses to interpret the gnostic pheno-menon in apocalyptic terms: the false teachers are a manifestation of Antichrist; this may be not unrelated to John's choice of ψευδοπροφήτης as a term by which to describe his opponents. In Acts 13.6 ψευδοπροφήτης is used to describe a person who is also said to be a μάγος. This seems to relate him to Simon the Magus (Acts 8.9, μαγεύων), traditionally regarded as the father of gnosticism, though Acts does not so describe him. The right interpretation is given by Haenchen:[23] 'Da für Lukas das entscheidende Kenn-zeichen des Propheten die Erkenntnis des Zukünftigen ist, wird sich Lukas den Bar-Jesus als den Hofastrologen des Sergius Paulus vorgestellt haben, der zugleich die Zauberformeln zu kennen behauptet, welche den Schicksalszwang brechen'. This is on the way to gnosticism, but it has not yet arrived.

The most difficult passage for the use of ψευδοπροφήτης is Matt. 7.15.[24] It is almost certainly right that the false prophets in question here are Christian false prophets, not, for example, Pharisees. It seems to me however very questionable whether they are gnostics. For the interpretation it is better to go back to Matt. 5.19: Whoever breaks one of these least commandments[25] and teaches men so, shall be called least in the kingdom of heaven. This is consistent with the theme of 7.15 ff: By their fruits you shall know them. It is of course possible that the antinomianism to which Matthew is opposed had a gnostic motivation, but if this was so Matthew does not refer to it and was probably unaware of it. The matter is of some importance to us, because Matthew's material may reflect (though hardly in Matthew's own use of it) a Jewish–Christian charge against Paul. Perhaps those of his opponents whom he regarded as ψευδαπόστολοι thought of him as a ψευδοπροφήτης.[26]

Finally, ψευδόχριστος is to be noted. This occurs at Mark 13.22, taken over in Matt. 24.24. The meaning is in no doubt. The false Christs are persons who wrongly claim to be the one true Christ. In addition, they presumably give a false representation of what it means to be Christ, but this is secondary, and simply derives from their false personal identification. They claim an office to which they are not entitled.

This sketch of ψευδο- compounds in the New Testament at large, in addition to providing illustrative material, raises the question of the precise force of ψευδο- in composition. This is a question that has evoked a surprising amount of controversy, which arose out of a discussion between R. Reitzenstein and K. Holl on the origin of the idea of martyrdom, and the early Christian use of the word μάρτυς.[27] In this, the meaning of ψευδομάρτυς will evidently play a significant though subordinate part. If the ψευδομάρτυς is simply a witness who tells lies, the word will contribute nothing to the history of the development of μάρτυς; but if the ψευδομάρτυς is one who pretends to be a μάρτυς though he is not really one, then the μάρτυς must be a person with definable properties and status. Fifty years ago some hot words were engendered; in a cooler atmosphere it can be seen that though Reitzenstein had the better of the linguistic argument no invariable rules can be laid down. ψευδο- may serve as object to the verbal idea with which it is compounded, as in ψευδολόγος, *speaking what is false*, and ψευδομαρτυρεῖν, *to testify what is false, to bear false witness*. But 'ψευδό-χριστος, ψευδ-απόστολος, -ἀδελφος sind sicher als Determinativkomposita mit adjektivischem Anfangsglied empfunden worden'.[28] That is to say, Holl[29] is wrong in saying, 'Die Erklärung, die Paulus hier [2 Cor. 11.13] von ψευδαπόστολοι gibt, lässt sich unmittelbar auf unsern Fall übertragen: die ψευδομάρτυρες τοῦ θεοῦ sind μετασχηματιζόμενοι εἰς μάρτυρας τοῦ θεοῦ,' and Reitzenstein[30] is right in distinguishing between ἀπόστολος as a *Titel* and μάρτυς as a *Bezeichnung*.[31]

We should start then with a presumption that Paul's ψευδαπό-στολοι were (as the context and especially the use of μετασχηματίζεσθαι suggest) claiming an office they did not hold; this however is complicated by the close relation Paul sees between the apostle's vocation and his message. To say that the apostle is constituted by his message would exaggerate, for it was possible to hold and preach the true Christian message without being an apostle, and it seems that in Paul's view as well as in Luke's it was necessary for an apostle to have seen the risen Christ (1 Cor. 12.29; 9.1; 15.8; Acts 1.22); but an apostle would certainly lose his status if he were to preach a false gospel (Gal. 1.8). Note also the parallel-ism of Gal. 2.7, 8 where the passive 'I have been entrusted (πεπίστευμαι) with the gospel' is expressed in the active as '[God] acted (ἐνεργήσας) for me with a view to apostleship (εἰς ἀποστολήν)'. Genuine apostleship and right doctrine were inseparable.

What is clear is that Paul's use of ψευδαπόστολοι implies not simply error in preaching (which, though harmful, might be com-mitted in good faith) but intended deception; that is, not simply theological error but moral fault. There is a world of difference between the two.[32] Where divergent opinion exists Paul is content to think and let think. 'Let each one be fully convinced in his own mind' (Rom. 14.5—even though the question is one that can rend the church in two!). 'Let all of us who are perfect be so disposed; if you look on things at all differently, this too will God reveal to you. Only, at the point which we have already reached, we must stand in line by that' (Phil. 3.15 f, F. W. Beare's translation). It is the more striking therefore that there are other passages where Paul is not content to disagree, but accuses his opponents of deceitfulness, not only of error but of moral perversity. There are also passages where Paul himself appears to be on the defensive against a similar charge brought by others against himself. It will be profitable to investigate this material. 2 Cor. 11.13 is the natural starting-point. Here the 'sham apostles' are further described as ἐργάται δόλιοι,[33] μετασχηματιζόμενοι εἰς ἀποστόλους Χριστοῦ. They made themselves look like[34] (and this must include, They claimed to be) apostles of Christ when they were no such thing. We shall of course return to this passage. Among others that fall into the same category are the following.

2 Cor. 2.17: οὐ γάρ ἐσμεν ὡς οἱ πολλοί,[35] καπηλεύοντες τὸν λόγον τοῦ θεοῦ. Whether this passage should be included here is not quite certain; the issue turns on the meaning of καπηλεύειν.[36] The κάπηλος is a small trader, and καπηλεύειν is accordingly to act as such a person; to sell for personal profit. Paul might thus be referring to people who, in a mercenary spirit but without falsification or intent to deceive, take pay for preaching the word of God. This interpretation can be supported by (a) a long tradition of philosophical usage,[37] in which the sophist is rebuked for selling his intellectual wares for cash, and (b) Paul's criticism elsewhere of those who take pay for preaching, and his own purpose not to be paid, at any rate in Corinth, for his work.[38] That Paul meant this is certain, and significant, for, as 1 Cor. 9 shows, it points at the Jewish–Christian apostles as the κάπηλοι in question. Did he intend also to accuse them of falsifying the word of God, which they took pay for preaching? The habits of the Greek petty trader undoubtedly gave the word this meaning, and associated it with the other; this is particularly clear in Lucian, Hermotimus 59: φιλόσοφοι ἀποδίδονται τὰ μαθήματα, ὥσπερ οἱ κάπηλοι, κερασάμενοί γε οἱ πολλοί, καὶ δολώσαντες,[39] καὶ κακομετροῦντες. That Paul did intend the charge of perversion is suggested by 2 Cor. 4.2 (δολοῦντες τὸν λόγον τοῦ θεοῦ), and also by the claim that he himself acts ἐξ εἰλικρινείας, with the implication that 'the many', whom he attacks, did not so act.

Paul thus claims that the majority[40] of his fellow-preachers and missionaries pervert the message they should proclaim—a staggering thought, which most[41] students of early Christianity do not take seriously. The context does not permit us to identify the false teachers with certainty. That they were Judaizers of some sort[42] is strongly suggested by the next chapter, in which Paul contrasts his own ministry with that of Moses.

The next passage, 2 Cor. 4.2, goes closely with that already discussed. In it Paul says of himself and his colleagues,[43] ἀπειπάμεθα τὰ κρυπτὰ τῆς αἰσχύνης, μὴ περιπατοῦντες ἐν πανουργίᾳ μηδὲ δολοῦντες τὸν λόγον τοῦ θεοῦ. It is a reasonable inference, though not more, that Paul has in mind others who do walk in craftiness, and do falsify the word of God; it is also possible[44] that Paul is rebutting a charge of craftiness and falsification that had been made against him;[45] the probability is that the charge had been made on both sides—if such a charge is made at all it can hardly be other than reciprocal. It includes, and distinguishes, perversion of the true message, and craftiness in propagating the perversion. That the midrash (2 Cor. 3) on the Moses narrative is still in mind is shown by τῇ φανερώσει τῆς ἀληθείας (verse 2) and εἰ δὲ καὶ ἔστιν κεκαλυμμένον (verse 3). Paul is thus still dealing with Judaizing opponents.[46]

2 Cor. 5.12; 10.12–16 may be mentioned here, though they are not as direct charges of deceit as the passages already considered. A man may glory in that in which he ought not to glory—in appearance rather than in fact, in the achievements of others and not his own—out of folly rather than out of deliberately chosen deceitfulness. But the context, especially in Chapter 10, suggests much more than ignorance and folly. 2 Cor. 11.18 falls into the same group.

2 Cor. 11.3 f suggests a plain accusation of deception, though it will be noted that the accusation is not actually made. The parallelism of the statement requires something like: I fear lest

As the serpent deceived Eve
So he who comes[47] should deceive you.

In fact, the second clause is inverted:

So your thoughts may be corrupted.

Perhaps Paul prefers to avoid the active verb and the subject it would require because here he has in mind not the ψευδαπόστολοι but the ὑπερλίαν ἀπόστολοι (verse 5); it seems however more probable that verse 5 is rather loosely attached; ὁ ἐρχόμενος must refer not to an apostle resident in Jerusalem, but to an envoy who actually arrives in Corinth.[48]

2 Cor. 11.26 has been discussed above. Its most probable meaning is that Judaizers, though they claim to be Christians, are only dissemblers; they are not genuine Christian brothers, but a dangerous sham.

There is a considerable quantity of material in Galatians. 1.7 should probably be included, since it is claimed here that Paul's adversaries wish (θέλοντες) to pervert the gospel; they do this not out of ignorance or incompetence as preachers but with full intent. μεταστρέψαι of course is Paul's word; perhaps they claimed to put a perverted version of the gospel right. The context suggests that they claimed authority to make the changes they introduced, since Paul replies, Even if they had the authority of angels they would have no right to change the gospel; probably they had (with or without justification) claimed the authority of the Jerusalem church, and the original apostles. At least, Paul goes on to deal with these supposed authorities.

In what follows, the inner groups of Jerusalem apostles are described as οἱ δοκοῦντες (2.2, 6), οἱ δοκοῦντες εἶναί τι (2.6), οἱ δοκοῦντες στῦλοι εἶναι (2.9). I have discussed these expressions elsewhere;[49] in view of the common usage of the Greek verb, and especially of 6.3 (εἰ δοκεῖ τις εἶναί τι μηδὲν ὤν, φρεναπατᾷ ἑαυτόν) it is very probable that some kind of deception is involved; it may however be not morally worse than unconscious self-deception. The men in question are not ψευδόστυλοι—men who give themselves out to be pillars when they are, and know themselves to be, no such thing. It is simply that they enjoy (possibly in both senses of the word) a higher reputation than the facts warrant, without acting in bad faith.

Gal. 2.4 has been discussed above;[50] here as in 2 Cor. 11.26 the ψευδάδελφοι, who appear to be but are not Christian brothers, are Judaizing Christians.

Gal. 2.12, 13 form a particularly important example, which raises more questions than can easily be answered. The situation is as follows. Cephas, in the mixed Jewish and Gentile church of Antioch, adopted the custom (which Paul also followed—if he did not initiate it) of eating with uncircumcised Gentile Christians. This common eating would no doubt include the specifically Christian gathering at the Lord's Supper, though it need not have been confined to this. In this situation certain people[51] came from James, in Jerusalem. These (or those whom they represented) were the Jewish Christian party (οἱ ἐκ περιτομῆς), and so frightened Cephas (presumably by threats of breaking off fellowship[52]) that he changed his earlier practice, and withdrew into exclusively Jewish–Christian communion, leaving the Gentiles to themselves. This action was caused not by conviction but by fear; it was not conscientious but prudential, and is for this reason described by

Paul as hypocrisy (συνυπεκρίθησαν, τῇ ὑποκρίσει). It carried away all the other Jewish Christians in Antioch, including even Barnabas, and their action is described by Paul in the words οὐκ ὀρθοποδοῦσιν πρὸς τὴν ἀλήθειαν τοῦ εὐαγγελίου. The precise meaning of this is disputed, but, taken with the words cited above from verse 13, it can hardly mean less than that, in some sense, the persons in question were accommodating truth to their own ends. This is confirmed by Paul's words to Cephas;[53] the latter's attitude is fundamentally insincere. He is expecting of the Gentiles the Jewish kind of life that in the recent past he himself has not been living. One may feel, perhaps, for Cephas more sympathy than Paul himself shows. He may have been less frightened for his own skin than for the outward unity of the church and its relationship with the parent Judaism for which he had a special responsibility (2.7 f); he may have panicked, and acted in a hurry in a way that did not do justice to his considered opinion. Whatever excuses may be made, however, Cephas had fallen into an attitude inconsistent with the gospel he professed to believe and preach, and knew that he had done so. This important event cannot have been the origin of Paul's charge of falsehood against the Judaizers since[54] 'false brothers' had been at work at an earlier stage (2.4); it must however have given it a powerful boost, and it is easy—and almost certainly right—to conjecture similar incidents which had led to the Jerusalem discussions of this chapter.

Other passages in Galatians refer to events that happened, and to persons who were active, in Galatia itself: 3.1; 4.16 ff; 5.3; 6.12 f. The first of these is too allusive to permit firm inferences, but the metaphor was no doubt suggested by the events Paul had in mind. To lay a spell upon someone is hardly to treat him with openness and honesty; and the result of the action was disobedience to the truth (that is, the truth of the gospel). It is at least a possible interpretation of 5.3 that the Judaizers had deceitfully withheld from those whom they wished to have circumcised that they would henceforth be under obligation to keep the whole law. Ζηλοῦν (in 4.16 ff) is the despair of commentators and especially of translators.[55] But it may at least be said that ζηλοῦν οὐ καλῶς is regarded as opposite to ἀληθεύειν: Paul speaks the truth to his Galatian converts, whether they like it or not; others, those who would have them circumcised, flatter them, pay court to them, and suppress or pervert the truth. A similar charge is made in more general terms in 6.12 f, where the motives of the Judaizers are impugned. They may profess a concern for your salvation, but in fact (a) they wish to make a good show in the flesh; (b) they wish to escape persecution; and (c) they do not themselves keep the law,[56] so that all their insistence on legal observance on your part is hypocritical. There is deceit at the heart of the Judaizing mission; it is in Paul's view neither honest Christianity nor honest Judaism.

There is less material in other epistles. Phil. 1.17 taken alone hardly amounts to an accusation of bad faith, but does so when read in the light of the next verse, where πρόφασις and ἀλήθεια stand over against each other. προφάσει, standing between ἀγνῶς, (verse 17) and ἀληθείᾳ, can hardly mean less than insincerity of motive; but it would be hard to say in precise terms how much more it means.

2 Thess. 2.2 f[57] raises one entirely new point: the possibility of a forged epistle. The passage however is not clear enough (even when 3.17 is brought in) to enable us to deduce that a forged epistle was already in circulation, and the deception referred to in 2.3 is rather a matter of deluded *Schwärmerei* than conscious deceit. At Rom. 3.8 Paul explicitly claims to have been misrepresented; the disclaimers of 6.1, 15; 7.7 may reflect the same situation.

A quick survey of the evidence shows at once that it is Jewish, or rather Judaizing, Christians whom Paul accuses of deliberate falsehood. The evidence is inadequate—inevitably so, since it occurs in personal letters, addressed to those who were far more familiar with the facts than we, readers to whom Paul could therefore write allusively—and it is not easy to weld it into a whole. This may serve as a useful reminder that Jewish Christianity was not a unitary phenomenon. It seems possible to distinguish the following.

(1) The hypocrisy of those who were driven by circumstances they did not foresee or fully understand into action inconsistent with their own principles. 'Hypocrisy' may seem a hard term for error of this kind, which could possibly be described as an honest mistake, or even as a well-intentioned compromise. It is however Paul's term, and it is justified by Peter's change of coat; he had shown that he fully understood the significance of justification by faith apart from works of law, and was now engaged in building up again what he had previously destroyed.

(2) An unjustified claim to a special and authoritative status,

which gave the right to pass judgement on and interfere in the Christian activity of others. The ψευδαπόστολοι presumably made such a claim, perhaps more forcefully than the Jerusalem apostles.

(3) Falsification of the Christian message. It is easy to see how this could arise out of the attitude described in (1) if this were not quickly rectified. It is very easy to find oneself committed to a false position in such a way that it takes a good deal of grace to withdraw. It is easier still to see its connection with (2), and with the ψευδαπόστολοι.

More light is thrown on the situation when we consider the evident parallel fact that Paul himself was accused of duplicity. It is due in part to his vigorous manner that from time to time he asserts that he is not lying, and calls on God to act as witness to his truthfulness; but such passages[58] are too numerous to be a mere trick of style. People had said: He is lying; he does not really wish to visit Rome, or Corinth; he does not really yearn for the Philippians; he has not had so little contact with Jerusalem; and so on.[59]

Of particular interest to us are passages where Paul asserts the genuineness of his own apostleship. Thus 1 Cor. 9, especially the opening verses, may be regarded as an answer to the charge, Paul is not a genuine apostle, which is not far from the proposition, Paul is a ψευδαπόστολος. The same may be said of Gal. 1.1; if it is argued that Paul's apostolic ministry lacks the proper pedigree he can assert that it came directly from God. 1 Cor. 15.8[60] may amount to the same thing: Paul is an ἔκτρωμα, a freak, and no true apostle. There is more in the Corinthian letters (especially in 2 Cor. 10—13), and in Galatians, to the same effect. It is evident that Paul took great precautions against any possible misinterpretation of his activities in regard to the collection (1 Cor. 16.1–4; 2 Cor. 6.3; [7.2]; 8.20, 21, 23), but that even so charges of sharp practice were brought against him (2 Cor. 12.16 ff).

Gal. 1.10; 5.11 raise familiar problems, which cannot be discussed in detail here. It is by no means clear how Paul is (wrongly) thought to be 'pleasing men', but this is evidently regarded as an insincere act on the part of a servant of God; and if 5.11 implies that Paul was in some way 'preaching circumcision', it must imply that he had dishonestly said one thing to the Galatians while elsewhere he had said another. Similar charges of dishonesty appear to underlie 1 Thess. 2, not only in the verses referred to above,[61] but also in verses 3 and 4. Verse 4 is similar to Gal. 1.10, and there seems no good reason why Paul should in verse 3 say that his preaching had not been deceitful if there had not been at least a whisper that it was so.

From this evidence the following points emerge.

(1) Paul was not truly an apostle; if he had made himself out to be one this was contradicted by the facts, and he became not an apostle but a ψευδαπόστολος.

(2) His work lacked integrity; he won men's favour by telling them what they wished to hear.

(3) He perverted the original message of Jesus in an antinomian sense, and was a traitor to his own people, whose salvation he no longer sought, since he directed his mission to the Gentiles.

(4) He made dishonest use of the money he collected, ostensibly for Jerusalem.

Before we sum up the significance of these results for the understanding of Paul and the history of the primitive church we must pause for a moment to consider whether there exist in the Jewish world any parallels to the charges and counter-charges we have examined.

There is a good deal of controversy in the halakic parts of the rabbinic literature. Even where narrative interest is completely absent the form in which rules and interpretations are presented is often: Rabbi X spoke as follows; Rabbi Y spoke differently; the *halakah* is according to Rabbi X. There is much controversy; teachers do not hesitate to disagree; but it seems to be true that broadly speaking accusations of deceitfulness or bad faith do not occur. For example, I have counted in the Mishnah 249 cases[62] of dispute and discussion between Beth Hillel and Beth Shammai; in none of these is there any accusation of bad faith. For all their disputes, the two schools stood, and knew that they stood, not only within the same religion, but within essentially the same interpretation of that religion.[63]

What of the controversy between Pharisees and Sadducees? Again it will be convenient to examine the material in the Mishnah. This controversy is sharper in tone, but moral accusations are scarce. In Erubin 6.2; Hagigah 2.4; Makkoth 1.6; Yadaim 4.6, 7 differences of opinion are recorded, and in the last passage mentioned these opinions are positively, even aggressively, held;[64] but this does not amount to insincerity, or to a charge of insincerity, and in Makkoth 1.6 in particular due weight is given to the Sadducees' point of view.

Berakoth 9.5 is more difficult to handle, partly because of a variant reading; some MSS relate the matter to Sadducees, others to the *minim*.[65] The Mishnah recalls the former practice of concluding benedictions with the words עַד הָעוֹלָם. This was changed to the full form מִן הָעוֹלָם וְעַד הָעוֹלָם, because of opponents (Sadducees or *minim*) who maintained that there was only one עוֹלָם.[66] Of the opponents it is said that they קִלְקְלוּ. This is evidently a word of abuse,[67] but does not seem necessarily to imply an accusation of deceitfulness. It is however not impossible that this is included. The Sadducees (or *minim*) twisted the simple benediction formula to mean that there was but one age (and no age to come); this had to be guarded against.

There remain Parah 3.3 and 7. In 3.3 there is implied a Sadducean objection to excessive scrupulosity; this is not dishonesty. 3.7 as it stands notes only a difference of opinion; but behind it, in Tosephta Parah 3.8,[68] is an incident which expresses the disagreement in an act of Johanan b. Zakkai's which implies a misleading of the Sadducean high priest. In general however there is bad feeling rather than accusations of bad faith between Pharisees and Sadducees.[69]

Evidence from the Mishnah about relations between orthodox Jews and Samaritans is mixed and contradictory. This reflects the fact that the relations themselves varied from time to time and place to place.[70] In some passages the trustworthiness of the Samaritans is asserted. Thus at Berakoth 7.1, a Samaritan may make one of the three who if they eat together must say the Common Grace;[71] at Demai 3.4 a Samaritan is trusted[72] where a Gentile is not; cf. 5.9; 6.1; at Terumoth 3.9 it is said that 'Heave-offering or Tithes or Hallowed Things that are given by a Gentile or Samaritan are valid'.

Other passages suggest the reverse. Berakoth 8.8 is particularly clear: They may answer 'amen' after an Israelite who says a benediction, but not after a Samaritan until they have heard the whole benediction. That is, you cannot be sure that the Samaritan will not include in his benediction some false doctrine to which you ought not to give the affirmation of an amen. His Benediction, however, may be sound (otherwise there would be a simple prohibition of saying amen), and it is not suggested that he intends to deceive his Jewish neighbour into affirming what he does not mean to affirm. Demai 7.4 apparently means that it cannot be safely assumed that a Samaritan wine merchant will have paid Heave-offering, First Tithe, and Second Tithe on his product. In Shebiith 8.10 R. Eliezer is quoted: He that eats the bread of the Samaritans is like to one that eats the flesh of swine—presumably because one cannot assume that it is clean.[73] Here and in Shekalim 1.5 (the Shekel is not accepted from Samaritans) distrust is implied but not the intent to deceive. Neither is this necessarily implied in Rosh ha-Shanah 2.2: Before this they used to kindle flares [to indicate the time of the new moon], but after the evil doings of the Samaritans they enacted that messengers should go forth. The Samaritans also, it seems, had kindled flares, and these proved to be misleading. The Mishnah assumes malicious intent on the part of the Samaritans, but this need not have been so; there may have been honest differences of observation, calculation, and practice. Gittin 1.5 (No writ is valid which has a Samaritan as witness excepting a writ of divorce or a writ of emancipation) comes nearer to implying a moral charge; cf. Oholoth 17.3; Niddah 4.1, 2.[74]

Of greater importance than any of these Mishnah passages is the accusation that the Samaritans have falsified Torah. See Sanhedrin 90b (a baraita, attributed to R. Eliezer b. Jose); also Siphre Numbers 15.31, § 112 end; Jer. Sotah 7.21c.29; and on all these passages Strack-Billerbeck, i.893 f; iv.1109.

The case of the *minim* is clearer. Their sayings are misleading, and it is at least suggested that their motive is to mislead. Berakoth 9.5 may be mentioned again,[75] 5.3 quotes sayings which, though they sound innocent enough,[76] contain heretical implications, and might therefore be taken to be deliberately misleading. Rosh ha-Shanah 2.1 speaks for itself:[77] Beforetime they used to admit evidence about the new moon from any man, but after the evil doings of the heretics[78] they enacted that evidence should be admitted only from them that they knew. Hullin 2.9 opposes the method of slaughtering adopted by the *minim*, but this is stated as a simple difference of opinion. Megillah 4.8 has to do with the shape, placing, and decoration of the phylacteries. The reasons given for the familiar and 'orthodox' square shape of the Tephillah are so absurd[79] that it seems probable that the variant shapes and manner of wearing constituted the badge (at first perhaps a secret sign) of *minuth*.

A more serious accusation against the *minim* (which does not appear in the Mishnah) lies behind the introduction of liturgical variations in the synagogue service.[80] Evidently it was thought that (a) *minim* might give their own heretical interpretation of words used in the synagogue; hence the introduction of a 'test-benediction' invoking an imprecation upon *minuth* which they could not possibly bring themselves to utter; and (b) in parts of the liturgy originally spoken in an undertone *minim* might introduce their own erroneous statement of belief; hence the requirement that those passages should henceforth be spoken aloud.

Even when all this material is taken into account we are still a long way from the accusations and counter-accusations that occur in the Pauline literature. There are closer parallels in the Qumran literature,[81] especially perhaps in the Habakkuk pesher, which sets over against the Teacher of righteousness one who is variously described as the Preacher of falsehood[82] and the Man of falsehood.[83] This person is apparently the Wicked Priest, who when he first arose had a reputation for truth,[84] but subsequently led others into unfaithfulness.[85]

The conclusion that should be drawn from these observations is clear, and in no way surprising. Broadly speaking, Jews were prepared to argue among themselves on the basis of assumed good faith. An opponent's opinions might be grievously mistaken and roundly disagreed with, but he could still be regarded as no worse than an erring brother. Beth Hillel and Beth Shammai disagreed, but at the same time could regard one another as belonging not merely to the same nation but to the same party within the nation. To a smaller extent this was true also of Pharisees and Sadducees. But inevitably there is a point, hard to place precisely because it was never defined but rather felt, at which the debating opponent becomes a traitor, because he has transgressed the limits of permissible disagreement and betrayed his people. This is felt all the more if, as at Qumran, his defection is taken to be part of the eschatological process.[86] He lies; he is a false brother; his teaching deceives; worst of all, he is used by Satan to stir up the troubles of the last times.

When we return to Paul the following conclusions can be drawn. They are quickly stated, but not without importance.

(1) It would be understandable if the accusation of falsehood was first thrown at Paul; by his life and doctrine he was playing false to the ancestral religion. Once the charge was made it would be both natural and easy, and almost inevitable, to return it; it was not Paul but his opponents who were resisting the destiny

appointed by God for his people. But only Jews, and in particular Jewish Christians, would be open to this kind of accusation. Gentiles could not be, and were not, attacked in this way. The real question is the fulfilment of Judaism, though it issues in practical questions, such as circumcision and food laws. The charge falls within the Jewish area just examined.

(2) This means that the ψευδαπόστολοι of 2 Cor. 11.13 are Judaizers; it follows that the trouble in Corinth was a Judaizing trouble. This in turn means that Judaizing is not a matter of circumcision only, and that there is a close relation between 2 Corinthians and Galatians. The dispute between Paul and the Judaizers, the rivalry between his apostolate and theirs, was not comparable with those between Beth Hillel and Beth Shammai, but touched the roots of both religions.

(3) Paul viewed the ψευδαπόστολοι, and Jewish perversion of the gospel as well as Jewish rejection of the gospel, as an eschatological phenomenon. It would be difficult to account otherwise for the passionate feelings that evidently were evoked on each side.

NOTES

1　See especially G. Friedrich, 'Die Gegner des Paulus im 2. Korinther-brief', in *Abraham unser Vater, Festschrift für Otto Michel* (Leiden-Köln 1963), pp. 181–215; D. Georgi, *Die Gegner des Paulus im 2. Korintherbrief* (*WMANT* 11), Neukirchen 1964.

2　Cf. Gal. 5.12; Phil. 3.2.

3　See e.g. E. Käsemann, 'Die Legitimität des Apostels,' in *ZNW* xli (1942), pp. 33–71 (repr. Darmstadt 1956); against this, R. Bultmann, *Exegetische Probleme des zweiten Korintherbriefes* (SBU ix), Uppsala 1947; also pp. 1–27 above.

4　Nor in the rest of the early Christian literature covered in Bauer's *Wörterbuch*.

5　Liddell-Scott write ψευδομάρτυς, Bauer, *Wörterbuch*, ψευδόμαρτυς. See the philological discussion below, pp. 91 f. Liddell-Scott's accentuation seems to be preferable.

6　See pp. 91 f. It could be maintained that God has witnesses who, not being infallible, fall into error with good intention.

7　So Lietzmann-Kümmel, ad loc.: 'Das ist eben die Steigerung: das Schlimmste, gefährlicher als das Meer, sind die ψευδάδελφοι!'

8　For example, by Allo and Héring.

9　The distinction is somewhat fine, but Schlier's conclusion is certainly right: 'Es ist mit der Wiederholung, die in dem παρεισῆλθον gegenüber dem παρεισάκτους liegt, bewusst die starke Geringschätzung ausgedrückt, die Paulus für seine Gegner hat.'

10 Schlier sees in the article τούς with ψευδαδέλφους a sign that the false brothers and their works were known in Galatia.

11 This is not without relevance to the question whether the ψευδαπόστολοι are to be identified with the ὑπερλίαν ἀπόστολοι.

12 Used in parallel at Matt. 19.18; Mark 10.19; Luke 18.20, in the quotation of Exod. 20.16.

13 As was especially ψευδομαρτυρία (Matt. 15.19; 26.59).

14 See also below, pp. 91 f.

15 For the noun cf. Plato, Gorg., 472 B; Philo, Decal., 138: [ψευδομάρτυρες] φθείρουσι τὴν σεμνὴν ἀλήθειαν.

16 The following verses indicate that the false teachers have already appeared; that is, the 'prediction' is a literary form. Cf. e.g. 1 Tim. 4.1.

17 On this word see pp. 89 ff.

18 So Michael Green, ad loc.—'the men were as untrustworthy as the message'.

19 Apoc. P., 1.1 f. : πολλοὶ ἐξ αὐτῶν ἔσονται ψευδοπροφῆται καὶ ὁδοὺς καὶ δόγματα ποικίλα τῆς ἀπωλείας διδάξουσιν. ἐκεῖνοι δὲ υἱοὶ τῆς ἀπωλείας γενήσονται.

20 Not necessarily later in a chronological sense.

21 Once in Zechariah, nine times in Jeremiah—always as an interpretative rendering of נביא. Josephus uses the word frequently in this sense.

22 So for example C. H. Dodd, R. Bultmann.

23 On Acts, p. 340.

24 See the discussion by W. D. Davies, The Setting of the Sermon on the Mount (Cambridge 1964), pp. 199–204.

25 Probably the Ten Commandments (as small in compass); see G. Schrenk, in TWNT, ii, 544.

26 Apoc. 16.13; 19.20; 20.10 contain a use of ψευδοπροφήτης so specialized that it cannot, and need not, be considered here. It is not likely that there is an allusion to Paul.

27 It has blown over so completely as to leave no trace, so far as I have noticed, in W. H. C. Frend, Martyrdom and Persecution in the Early Church, Oxford 1965.

28 Blass-Debrunner, § 119, 5. cf. also A. Debrunner, Griechische Wortbildungslehre (Heidelberg 1917), p. 57.

29 Hermes 52 (1917), p. 307.

30 Ibid., p. 449.

31 Most of the literature is referred to in the article ψευδόμαρτυς in Bauer's Wörterbuch. The summaries in Indogermanisches Jahrbuch (by P. Wahrmann) are particularly useful, and to vol. v (referred to by Bauer) should be added vol. vi (1918, published 1920).

32 A Protestant contributor to this Festschrift designed to honour a Roman Catholic scholar may be allowed to remark that it is precisely this difference that is found in the new ecumenical situation of the present time; serious theological disagreement continues to exist, and it would be foolish to ignore it, but we no longer accuse, or have reason to accuse, one another of wilfully and perversely corrupting truth in the interest of falsehood.

33 It is interesting that in the only other place where Paul uses the word ἐργάτης (Phil. 3.2) it has an equally bad sense; there is nothing in the make-up or biblical or non-biblical usage of the word to suggest this. Paul uses ἐργάζεσθαι and ἔργον (κυρίου) in a good sense (e.g. 1 Cor. 16.10), and the ground of his anger in these two passages may be that his adversaries contrive to look so much like good Christian workers.

34 For μετασχηματίζεσθαι, I may refer to my note on 1 Cor. 4.6.

35 Instead of οἱ πολλοί, P⁴⁶ D G sy Mcion and the Koine text have οἱ λοιποί. This reading, if not simply an accidental error, may be due to Marcion, to whom Paul was the only true apostle; others may have been unwilling to draw the conclusion referred to on p. 93.

36 See above all Windisch, in *TWNT*, iii, 606–9.

37 Details in Windisch; see especially Plato, *Protag.*, 313 CD, and Philostratus, *V.A.*, 1.13.

38 1 Cor. 9.12–18; 2 Cor. 11.7–11.

39 Cf. 2 Cor. 4.2. καπηλεύειν was specially used of the wine trade, where dishonesty would easily take the form of watering the product, as well as using false measures.

40 Lietzmann-Kümmel, ad loc., is no doubt right in saying, 'man darf das οἱ πολλοί nicht pressen', but Paul cannot mean less than a very considerable proportion.

41 It may be that my word, like Paul's, ought not to be pressed; but I doubt whether it is far wrong.

42 Cf. Windisch, ad loc.: '. . . das Einfälschen einer "anderen" Lehre . . . (11.4), vermutlich judaistischer Irrlehre'.

43 The plural is probably a genuine plural and refers to a group, but the group was one in which Paul was a dominant figure.

44 Lietzmann-Kümmel, ad loc., cannot decide between the possibilities.

45 See below, pp. 98 f.

46 2 Cor. 3.13 (πρὸς τὸ μὴ ἀτενίσαι . . .) is probably a virtual accusation of deceit on the part of the Mosaic (Jewish) ministry.

47 Ὁ ἐρχόμενος, the 'incomer' who preaches another Jesus etc.

48 The fact that Paul is writing prose, not verse, means that it is not worth while to look for examples of parallelism in which a change from active to passive (or vice versa) occurs; these seem to be less frequent than might have been expected.

49 'Paul and the "Pillar" Apostles', in *Studia Paulina in honorem J. de Zwaan*, (Haarlem 1953), pp. 1–19.

50 P. 89.

51 The variant τινα (singular) has been perhaps too easily dismissed by some, but need not be discussed here.

52 Or were they capable of more forceful measures? cf. 2 Cor. 11.26, and pp. 88 f above.

53 It is not certain where these come to an end. We do not need to go beyond verse 14, but if more should be included they confirm the view taken here.

54 Assuming that the material in Gal. 2 is given in chronological order, which is usually but not universally accepted.

55   At least, of translators into English. The NEB's 'honest envy' is not very happy.

56   J. Munck, *Paulus und die Heilsgeschichte* (Aarhus-Copenhagen 1954), pp. 79 ff, thinks the persons in question to be Gentile Christians. I am not convinced by this view, but if it is true the situation must have been in Paul's judgement so much the worse. Gentiles had been converted not to the truth but to a lie.

57   An alternative possibility (assuming the genuineness of 2 Thess., which cannot be discussed here) is that Paul was correcting a possible misunderstanding of 1 Thessalonians.

58   God as μάρτυς: Rom. 1.9; 2 Cor. 1.23; Phil. 1.8; 1 Thess. 2.5, 10; οὐ ψεύδομαι (or the like): Rom. 9.1; 2 Cor. 11.31; Gal. 1.20.

59   Cf. the defence against the charge of ἐλάφρεια in 2 Cor. 1.12–19, also accusations in Acts, e.g. 9.26; 16.20 f; 17.7; 21.28; 24.6.

60   See my commentary on 1 Cor. ad loc.

61   See note 58.

62   Counts may well differ, because it is often difficult to decide where a really fresh subject of discussion begins.

63   For the fundamental unity of the two groups, note, in addition to cases of agreement and changes of view on one side or the other, Yebamoth 1.4 = Eduyoth 4.8.

64   'We cry out against you, O ye Pharisees (Sadducees) . . .'.

65   A third variant is *Epicureans*. For details see O. Holtzmann, *Berakot* (Giessen 1912), p. 103. See also p. 101 below.

66   This view might fit Sadducees better than *minim*, if the latter are Jewish Christians.

67   Danby, 'taught corruptly'; O. Holtzmann, 'Schaden anrichteten'; Dalman, *Handwörterbuch*, 'verderben'; Jastrow, 'to upset, disarrange, damage, ruin; to be corrupt'.

68   See D. Daube, 'Three Notes having to do with Johanan ben Zaccai', *JTS* xi, 1960), pp. 53–62 (56–62). See further L. Finkelstein, *The Pharisees* (Philadelphia 1938), pp. 121–8.

69   This is borne out by the discussion of the differences between Pharisees and Sadducees in Finkelstein, op. cit., pp. 101–85, 281–91.

70   See Strack-Billerbeck, i, pp. 538–60. 'Die Stellung, die die alte Synagoge in religionsgesetzlicher Hinsicht den Samaritanern gegenüber eingenommen hat, ist nicht zu allen Zeiten die gleiche gewesen' (p. 538). Among Mishnah passages, not cited in the text, Nedarim 3.10; Ketuboth 3.1; Kiddushin 4.3 may be mentioned here.

71   But so would be one who e.g. ate *demai*-produce.

72   Here the Samaritan appears on equal terms with an '*am ha-'aretz*.

73   For this obscure saying cf. Jer. Shebiith 8.38*b*.60, quoted in Strack-Billerbeck, i, p. 542.

74   Cf. Niddah 7.4, on the Samaritan method of disposing of abortions.

75   See p. 100 above.

76   To a bird's nest do thy mercies extend; May thy name be remembered for the good [which thou hast wrought]; We give thanks, we give thanks.

77 Cf. 2.2, for the Samaritans.
78 Danby, 'Who tried to confuse the Sages by hiring false witnesses'.
79 A nut-shaped box might cause a wound if one knocked his head against some object!
80 See my Delitzsch Lectures of 1967, published in English as *The Gospel of John and Judaism* (London 1975), pp. 47–50.
81 Whatever precise date be assigned to the Qumran writings they can hardly fail to provide material relevant in age for the study of Paul.
82 מטיף הכזב, 10.9.
83 איש הכזב, 2.1 f; 5.11; cf. 11.1.
84 נקרא על שם האמת, 8.9.
85 הבוגדים, 2.1, et al.
86 Cf. 2 Thess. 2.11, where also belief in untruth is seen as an anticipation, or fulfilment, of an apocalyptic myth.

6

Ο ΑΔΙΚΗΣΑΣ
(2 Cor. 7.12)

The course of events in which the writing of the Corinthian epistles is embedded is a notorious New Testament problem.[1] Between the beginning and the end no light is thrown upon it by Acts, and it can be deduced only by following up more or less obscure clues found in the epistles themselves. Even those events that can be most confidently reconstructed leave plenty of scope for divergent opinions about details, but it seems reasonably clear that, after the writing of 1 Corinthians, Paul paid a second visit (not recorded in Acts) to Corinth, a visit that caused him—and the Corinthians—pain (2 Cor. 1.23; 2.1; 12.14; 13.1); that either on this occasion (and responsible for the pain), or in close connection with it, an unfortunate and reprehensible incident took place (2 Cor. 2.5, 6, 7, 8; 7.11, 12); that Paul wrote to Corinth a severe letter, over which he shed many tears (2 Cor. 2.4; 7.8, 12); and that Titus (possibly as the bearer of the letter) visited Corinth, and on his eagerly awaited return brought Paul good news of the Corinthian reaction to his letter (2 Cor. 7.6, 7, 9, 11, 13, 14, 15). An excellent account of the many variant forms of this outline of events is given by E. B. Allo in a series of excursus.[2] An outline of this kind is presupposed by the present essay, which is directed towards a particular question within this general area of discussion. What was the unfortunate incident that for a time poisoned the relations between Paul and the Corinthian church? Who was the man who caused pain (2.5), and was punished (2.6), but should now be forgiven and loved (2.7 f)? Or, since there seems to be no good reason to doubt that Chapter 2 and Chapter 7 refer to the same person, who was the man who did wrong, and who was the man who was wronged (ὁ ἀδικήσας, ὁ ἀδικηθείς); and what was the wrong?

These are not easy questions. K. Lake[3] wrote: 'The first question is, who was the offender, and what was his offence? The one thing which is here certain is that no confident answer can ever be given.' T. W. Manson[4] somewhat similarly says, 'What exactly happened

on this occasion we do not know and have no means of discovering.'
Manson does however go on to consider the Corinthian situation
generally, and his general view of it is one with which I should
agree. In fact the problem is not quite so impenetrable as these
quotations suggest. Allo[5] gives a list of ten 'traits précis' which stand
out in the general obscurity. These may be summed up as follows.

(1) The offence, whatever it was, was not in the realm of doctrine.
This conclusion Allo justifies by citing 2 Cor. 1.24 (τῇ γὰρ πίστει
ἐστήκατε), but this passage will not bear the weight of proof, for
(a) it does not mean, 'You are sound in the faith',[6] and (b) if it did
mean this it would refer to the time of writing, and not to the time
of the offence. We cannot say more than that in the chief passages,
2 Cor. 2 and 7, Paul does not raise specific doctrinal issues, as he
probably would have done if such issues had been the main point.

(2) It was a clear *act* of injustice or aggression committed by one
Christian against another. Allo cites 2 Cor. 7.12 (τοῦ ἀδικήσαντος ...
τοῦ ἀδικηθέντος), and this point appears to be established.

(3) It was committed by a single individual; at least, one such
person was primarily responsible (2 Cor. 2.5, εἴ τις λελύπηκεν; 6.7,
τῷ τοιούτῳ, ὁ τοιοῦτος; 8, εἰς αὐτόν; 10, ᾧ δέ τι χαρίζεσθε; 7.12, τοῦ
ἀδικήσαντος).[7]

(4) The fault was a grave one, for it led Paul to give up a journey
he had planned, and write a severe letter (2 Cor. 1.23; 2.1, 3, 4).
This point also seems to be established.

(5) It had in some measure affected the whole community, not
only the member[8] directly injured. Allo cites 2 Cor. 2.5; but this
verse raises the question in what sense 'all' had been pained (λυπεῖν)
by the event. Does Paul mean that the offender had by his own act
injured all when he injured one? Or does he mean that to have
such a person in its midst was already an injury to the whole group?
This question may be left for the moment.[9]

(6) It was an offence that Paul could consider a personal injury
(2 Cor. 2.5, οὐκ ἐμὲ λελύπηκεν; 10, ὃ κεχάρισμαι, εἴ τι κεχάρισμαι);
presumably it involved disobedience (2.9, εἰ εἰς πάντα ὑπήκοοί ἐστε).
Of these two propositions of Allo's the former is established, though
it remains to be asked in what sense the offence was a personal
attack upon Paul—an attack on the gospel he preached and on the
church he had founded could be regarded as an attack on him
personally. The reference to obedience is ambiguous. It could mean:
I wish to know whether you are now all, including the offender,

obedient; or, I wish to know whether you have reacted to the situation created by this act as obedient Christians should.

(7) Its gravity had not been recognized by a part—large or small—of the Corinthian church. Hence 2 Cor. 2.5, ἀπὸ μέρους, ἵνα μὴ ἐπιβαρῶ. That is, if Paul is to speak of the offence as committed against *all*, he must immediately, in order not to exaggerate, qualify his statement by a 'partially'. Allo notes also ὑπὸ τῶν πλειόνων in 2.6—not all, but a majority of the Corinthian Christians had punished the offender. Here Allo's conclusion may be right, but it should be drawn with caution. If in 2.5 λελύπηκεν ... πάντας ὑμᾶς means 'he has hurt you all' in a sense other than 'his action has offended and grieved you' it might in the interests of accuracy require qualification without the implication that some of the 'all' had failed to estimate the act at its full weight;[10] and in 2.6 οἱ πλείονες could be taken to mean 'the community as a whole', without suggesting a dissident minority.[11] It is, however, worth noting that subsequent events suggest that the community was not united behind Paul.

(8) Because of the existence of the dissident minority, Paul thought it well to test the obedience of the whole group (2 Cor. 2.9). From this proposition Allo looks back to his sixth point: the incident 'avait le caractère d'une désobéissance'. The conclusion, though possible, is not certain. It may be that what Paul was looking for was not a penitent return to obedience, but an obedient reaction to the situation.[12]

(9) The guilty person had repented, though some of the pain caused by his action remained (here Allo seems to lay too much weight on the perfect tense—λελύπηκεν—in 2 Cor. 2.5). Moreover, the danger of internal conflict remained (2.10). It is surprising that Allo does not at this point explicitly say that punishment (ἐπιτιμία, 2.6) had been inflicted (or at least resolved upon) by the majority of the community (οἱ πλείονες), and that Paul now called for forgiveness and love. These reactions do not in themselves define the crime, but are part of the material available to us for understanding it.

(10) 'Ce délit n'avait pu se produire qu'*après la visite intermédiaire*, si l'on admet, comme nous avons cherché à l'établir, que c'est en cette visite que Paul avait annoncé le projet de voyage dont il est question 1.15, 16 ... C'est en effet lorsqu'il l'eut appris que Paul renonça à son projet, et le remplaça par l'envoi d'une lettre.'[13] It

appears at once that this last point of Allo's does not stand on the same level as the others. It is not a simple observation of fact but a deduction from a conclusion previously drawn, with which not all would agree.[14] We must be content at this stage to say that the incident took place either during or soon after Paul's second visit to Corinth.

Students of the question must be grateful to Allo for his clear exposition of the facts. It will be noted however that he makes use almost entirely of material drawn from 2 Cor. 2. If we turn to Chapter 7, in addition to points that will be made below, it appears that Paul wrote his sorrowful letter not with a view to taking sides, even his own,[15] but ἕνεκεν τοῦ φανερωθῆναι τὴν σπουδὴν ὑμῶν τὴν ὑπὲρ ἡμῶν πρὸς ὑμᾶς ἐνώπιον τοῦ θεοῦ (7.12).[16] This is not quite the same as obedience (see above); it is a matter of personal loyalty to and enthusiasm for the apostle, which the unhappy incident must have called in question, but which, Paul thinks, needed only a suitable opportunity to manifest itself afresh.

What then was the incident? The main suggestions are as follows.[17]

(1) The sin was that of πορνεία referred to in 1 Cor. 5.1. In terms of 2 Cor. 7.12, ὁ ἀδικήσας was the man who had taken his father's wife, ὁ ἀδικηθείς the father. This view, though widely supported in the past, is now almost universally, and rightly, abandoned.

(2) The verb ἀδικεῖν has been given full legal force, and the offence seen to consist in disregard of the teaching of 1 Cor. 6: a Christian had taken legal action against a fellow-member of the church. This interpretation has had few supporters. An incident of this kind would hardly suffice to explain Paul's strong language and his change of plan.

(3) The most common view is that Paul had been resisted and attacked by a member[18] of the Corinthian church, either (a) face to face, during the second visit, or (b) in his absence, by an act of flagrant disobedience and revolt, or (c) in the person of one of his assistants, such as Timothy.[19]

The third of these views seems to me to be nearly correct,[20] and it is not my intention to re-examine all the material that has now been briefly sketched, but rather to ask one or two questions that seem to me to have escaped attention. Some difficulties will never be removed: Paul's narrative of the event, or rather his allusion to it, is full of obscurities, most of which arise simply because he knew what had happened, and knew that his readers knew what had happened, and could therefore allude rather than narrate. But there are difficulties of another kind.

We may begin with the last sentence in 2 Cor. 7.11: ἐν παντὶ συνεστήσατε ἑαυτοὺς ἁγνοὺς εἶναι τῷ πράγματι. It is probably the oddness of the simple dative τῷ πράγματι after ἁγνοὺς εἶναι that led to the addition of ἐν in many MSS; this addition, and the conjecture that εἶναι is an error for ἐν, can safely be rejected. The construction is unusual rather than difficult. The dative is a dative of respect: as far as this affair[21] was concerned, the persons in question were ἁγνοί. In this verse (to the earlier part of which we shall return shortly) Paul is describing the response of the Corinthians to Titus's mission[22]—a response which, when he heard of it, had filled Paul with (perhaps premature) joy. The aorist συνεστήσατε therefore refers to the time when Titus was in Corinth. The verb συνιστάναι,[23] which has a wide variety of senses,[24] is used by Paul in two. Very characteristic of 2 Corinthians (and occurring also at Rom. 16.1) is the meaning 'to commend':[25] see 3.1; 4.2; 5.12; 6.4; 10.12, 18; 12.11. In several of these passages the object of the verb is (as in 7.11) the reflexive pronoun. In another group of passages the meaning is 'to prove' (Rom. 3.5; 5.8; Gal. 2.18, παραβάτην ἐμαυτὸν συνιστάνω). This is not a remote meaning, since *to commend convincingly* is *to prove*, especially when the verb is used reflexively. The question of senses however is important, and vital in 7.11; there is a world of difference between 'You submitted that you were . . .' and 'You proved that you were . . .' The word συνιστάναι itself and its usage are, as we have seen, indecisive; what is decisive is the context and from this there is no doubt that the Corinthians convinced Titus of their point. In respect of the trouble that had taken place they were ἁγνοί.

ἁγνός is not a common word with Paul.[26] The use of ἁγνός at Phil. 4.8 is scarcely relevant here. At 2 Cor. 11.2 it is used of a pure virgin, and its meaning is clear. The sense at 7.11 is not identical, but corresponds to this. The Corinthians had proved (at least, to their own and to Titus's satisfaction) that they had had as little to do with the matter in hand as a pure virgin has had to do with a man. They proved their complete innocence. This does not mean that they had been involved but had now repented and drawn out, any more than a woman who has cohabited with a man but left him is a pure virgin. Whatever anyone else may have done, they were not guilty.

This conclusion is supported by words used to describe the Corinthian attitude as Paul saw it through the eyes of Titus. His severe letter had awakened in them ἐπιπόθησις, ὀδυρμός, ζῆλος (2 Cor. 7.7), σπουδή, ἀπολογία, ἀγανάκτησις, φόβος, ἐπιπόθησις (*varia lectio*, ἐπιποθία), ζῆλος, ἐκδίκησις (7.11). Some of these are, as far as the Corinthians' innocence or complicity is concerned, neutral words: ἐπιπόθησις means that, in his absence, they longed for Paul's presence; φόβος means that they showed him respect and reverence; σπουδή and ζῆλος mean that they fervently and energetically took his part. These words might or might not indicate a change of heart. But ἀπολογία, ἀγανάκτησις, and ἐκδίκησις are all what may be called defensive words: they defended themselves against a charge, they were vexed that it should be brought; they vindicated themselves.[27] If ὀδυρμός stood alone it might indicate a confession of guilt—bewailing one's sin; but the other words in the context exclude this, and the word must have the neutral sense of lamentation.

Thus Titus, and Paul after him, accepted that the Corinthians were innocent in the affair that had caused so much pain. This is confirmed by the fact that they had punished the offender—hardly a proper act if they shared his guilt. This means that some accounts of the sorrowful visit will have to be corrected. It will hardly be possible to say (unless the offensive act is separated from Paul's visit and a new cause of trouble discovered), 'Er hat die Gemeinde in völligem Aufruhr gegen ihn vorgefunden. Einer aus ihrer Mitte hat ihm schweres Unrecht zugefügt, und der Apostel hat Korinth wieder verlassen müssen, ohne die Gemeinde zurückgewonnen und zur Ordnung gebracht zu haben.'[28] We are however left with a serious problem, which is best set out in a pair of contradictions, or apparent contradictions:

1 (a) The offender was a Corinthian Christian;[29] yet
   (b) You—Corinthians—were ἀγνοὶ τῷ πράγματι;
2 (a) Paul's severe letter evoked repentance (2 Cor. 7.9); yet
   (b) You—Corinthians—were ἀγνοὶ τῷ πράγματι.

There seems to be only one solution of this problem: the man who committed the wrong, ὁ ἀδικήσας, was closely associated with the Corinthian church but was not himself a Corinthian. As a visitor to Corinth, claiming superior rights for himself, he had challenged the apostle's position, belittled his authority, and had thus both injured and insulted his person. He was not strictly a Corinthian, so that the Corinthians might be ἀγνοί while he was not: they were ἀγνοί, yet they had not taken Paul's part with that ζῆλος, that σπουδή, they should have shown, and of this they repented. This suggestion satisfies the fundamental terms of the problem, and it is fully consistent with what we know of the Corinthian situation. It remains only to review the epistle in the light of it, and so to consider whether it helps us to understand the text and its historical setting.

In the earlier part of the epistle there are two passages to consider. In the former of these (Chapter 2) we may begin from an observation that is not infrequently missed. Paul wrote a sorrowful, often called a severe, letter; and indeed it will appear later (7.8 f) that it caused pain (though this was not Paul's intention, and his first reaction was to regret it). Yet Paul wrote the letter πεποιθὼς ἐπὶ πάντας ὑμᾶς ὅτι ἡ ἐμὴ χαρὰ πάντων ὑμῶν ἐστιν (2.3). He wrote with tears, yet only to manifest his love. The position recalls that of Gal. 4.19 f: 'My children, with whom I am in travail again, until Christ be formed in you; I could wish to be present with you now, and change my tone.' The delicately balanced situation becomes clear, if it is true that the real offender was not a Corinthian, but that Paul was uncertain how far this outsider had carried the Corinthians with him. The letter was tearful, not angry; it caused pain because the Corinthians were sorry both that Paul should have been ill used and that they had not defended him more vigorously. The obscurities of 2.5 also become clearer on this view. Certainly an intruder of this kind has hurt Paul; but Paul can stand such hurts; the dangerous possibility is that he may have damaged the church.[30] 2.7–11 shows that Paul, perhaps surprisingly, accepts the good faith of the intruder. When he sees what he has done, that the Corinthians are loyally standing by their apostle (verse 9), and that they are ready to forgive him, he will be overcome by remorse.

The latter passage is 7.5–16. Paul was comforted by the safe arrival of Titus, about whom he had been anxious,[31] and more than comforted by the news[32] Titus brought of the Corinthians and of their reaction to Paul's letter. Paul had probably been uncertain how far the Corinthians had themselves been implicated in the action of the intruder; had he written too strongly? Would they be further estranged from him in injured innocence? No; they had taken the letter in the right way, and his confidence had been made good (verse 14). The letter had hurt them, but it had hurt them to good effect; they repented that they had ever listened to the anti-Pauline intruder. They now manifested ζῆλος ὑπὲρ ἐμοῦ. (7.7); it is hard to see what this means if not eagerness to take Paul's part when he was attacked. The significance of 7.11 has already been pointed out. 7.12 comes into clear focus when it is grasped that neither ὁ ἀδικήσας (the intruder) nor ὁ ἀδικηθείς (Paul) was in the ordinary sense a member of the Corinthian church. Inevitably they had played a large part in the letter, which might on that account have been misunderstood. Paul's real purpose was not with these wanderers, himself and another, but with the local church, of which he had made his boast to Titus (7.14).

Chapters 10—13 were probably written after 1—9.[34] They are of great importance to us because by showing how the situation developed they help to make clear the earlier stage represented by Chapters 2 and 7. Here there is no doubt about the presence of intruders, or the fact that they preach another Jesus and a different gospel, and behave in a different way from Paul's. References to these persons—ψευδαπόστολοι rather than ὑπερλίαν ἀπόστολοι[33]—are too numerous to collect here; but it may be worth while to note that some passages are expressed in the singular. These may be nothing more than one way of expressing a generalization, but they may point to a leading opponent—such as ὁ ἀδικήσας. There is someone who is confident that he belongs to Christ (10.7). In 10.10 we learn what 'he says', unless φησίν is to be taken in the sense 'the saying goes'.[35] The man who says this kind of thing should think again (10.11). 10.18 (ὁ ἑαυτὸν συνιστάνων) probably, but not necessarily, is a generalization. 11.4 (ὁ ἐρχόμενος) may point to a particular intruder; so may 11.20, with its repeated τις. By this time, however, there are more intruders, their attack on Paul is more violent, the atmosphere is more bitter, Paul's reply is less restrained. But the position is a development of that alluded to in Chapters 2 and 7, and presupposed by the severe letter. Our hypothesis is confirmed by the fact that it helps to make good sense of the whole epistle.

NOTES

1 Probably the best introduction to and summary of the problem is that of W. G. Kümmel: *Introduction to the New Testament* (ET, London 1966), pp. 198–215. I have discussed various aspects of it in 'Christianity at Corinth', pp. 1–27 above; *The First Epistle to the Corinthians* (Black's New

Testament Commentaries, London 1968); 'Titus', pp. 118–31 below; and on pp. 87–107 above.

2 *Seconde Épître aux Corinthiens* (Études Bibliques, Paris 1956); La visite intermédiaire, pp. 48–54; La faute commise à Corinthe, pp. 54–63; La lettre 'écrite dans les larmes', pp. 68–73; La première mission de Tite et la punition de l'offenseur, pp. 74–6.

3 *The Earlier Epistles of St Paul* (London 1911), p. 169. Among older works this one is still worth reading.

4 *Studies in the Gospels and Epistles*, ed. M. Black (Manchester 1962), p. 213.

5 Op. cit., p. 55.

6 Better, with A. Schlatter, *Paulus der Bote Jesu* (Stuttgart 1962), p. 485: 'ihr durch den Glauben steht'. The (in human terms) strange relation of an apostle to the church (οὐχ ὅτι κυριεύομεν ὑμῶν τῆς πίστεως) is due to the fact that Christians stand (before God) not on the dignity of their apostle but by faith.

7 One or two of these singulars might possibly be taken to refer to a class of persons—'the wrongdoer'; but it is impossible to take them all in this way.

8 Usually, and rightly, taken to be Paul himself. See p. 111.

9 See p. 114.

10 It could mean: 'Such unchristian behaviour has shaken the faith of some but not all of you'.

11 οἱ πλείονες could be used in the sense of *rabbîm*, the total company. This however is far from certain; and even if it were established it would not demonstrate, as some have thought, a connection with the Qumran literature (where this use of *rabbîm* occurs). See H. Braun, *ThR*, NF 29 (Tübingen 1963), p. 218.

12 See pp. 111 f, 114.

13 Allo (see note 2), p. 55.

14 e.g. Kümmel (see note 1), p. 208.

15 Assuming that Paul himself was ὁ ἀδικηθείς (7.12).

16 I give the text as in Nestle. In addition, (1) ἡμων τὴν ὑπὲρ ὑμῶν, (2) ἡμῶν τὴν ὑπὲρ ἡμῶν, and (3) ὑμῶν τὴν ὑπὲρ ὑμῶν are found in the MSS. Of these, (2) and (3) scarcely make sense, but are easily explained as accidental errors; (1) makes sense, but very trite sense in comparison with the reading accepted here.

17 See the full account in Allo (see note 2), pp. 54–63.

18 So, e.g., Kümmel (see note 1), p. 208: 'Obviously the evildoer was a member of the church, for the congregation had passed judgment upon him'. The reasoning is not quite conclusive.

19 According to Allo the assistant cannot have been Timothy, since nothing in the epistle suggests that he had had recent dealings with the Corinthian church, and Paul would have defended his beloved colleague more vehemently and explicitly. Nor, according to Allo, was the injured person Titus.

20 I have assumed it in my paper on Titus: 'Paul made this journey, and was surprised and hurt to encounter a personal insult' (see below p. 128).

Further consideration has led to, I hope, a more exact appraisal of the situation.

21 πρᾶγμα, 7.11. cf. 1 Cor. 6.1.

22 See below p. 125.

23 Also the late formation συνιστάνειν.

24 Liddell-Scott have six main meanings for the active of συνιστάναι, with a total of 17 subdivisions.

25 Cf. the use of συστατικός (2 Cor. 3.1).

26 ἀγνότης occurs at 2 Cor. 6.6; 11.3 (*si vera lectio*); ἀγνῶς at Phil. 1.17; ἀγνεία, ἀγνίζειν, and ἀγνισμός not at all.

27 ἐκδίκησις comes near to meaning that they brought a counter-charge.

28 G. Bornkamm, 'Die Vorgeschichte des sogenannten Zweiten Korintherbriefes' (*SHAW* Phil.-hist. Klasse 1961), p. 9.

29 As is usually supposed; see note 18.

30 It is not easy to be sure of the meaning of λυπεῖν. It may refer to pain of body or to pain of mind; thus it may mean that the Corinthians were hurt in their feelings, or that there was actual damage to the church. 7.10 suggests that both meanings were in Paul's mind.

31 See note 33, p. 131.

32 Ibid. I may mention here as relevant in this paper that in the earlier one I pointed out that Titus had been sent to Corinth not to quell a riot but to make a collection.

33 The more common view is that they were part of the 'severe letter' and were therefore written before Chapters 1—9. The argument of 'Titus' shows, I think, that the usual view is not easy to maintain; I deal with the question in my commentary on 2 Corinthians.

34 See 'ψευδαπόστολοι', pp. 87–107 above.

35 φησίν can be used impersonally, but after the singular of 10.7 there is no sufficient reason for thinking that it must be so used in 10.10. The reading φασίν shows that the singular was understood as a singular, and, in view of the plurals that follow, found difficult.

7
TITUS

The literary and historical problems evoked by 2 Corinthians are too well known and too complicated to be enumerated here. It will suffice to mention three outstanding questions:

(1) Can Chapters 10—13 belong to the same letter as Chapters 1—9? If they form part of a different letter, is this to be dated before[1] or after Chapters 1—9?

(2) Do Chapters 8 and 9 belong together, or are they two separate notes dealing at different times with different aspects of the collection?

(3) Is 2.14—7.4 to be regarded as a misplaced insertion which divides up a single reference (2.13; 7.5) to Paul's encounter with Titus?[2]

The present essay will not provide answers to these questions, which are in fact wider open today than a generation ago, when a fair measure of agreement seemed to have been reached, at least on the proposition that 6.14—7.1 was originally part of the 'previous letter', and Chapters 10—13 part of the 'severe letter'.[3] In all probability, the questions never will be finally settled; and we are unlikely to make much advance towards their solution by surveying them as a whole and trying to think out a comprehensive hypothesis capable of explaining everything at once. If advance is to be made at all it will be made by the pursuit, and eventual integration, of a number of details. Among such details we may count the career of Titus. 'Career' is indeed a somewhat grand word for one of whom we know so little, but it is precisely from 2 Corinthians that we learn most about this evidently trusted helper of Paul's, and a careful tracing of his probable movements can only serve to clarify the historical background of the epistle. It may also appear that there are some passages where commonly accepted exegesis needs to be revised.

It is surprising that Titus is not mentioned in Acts. W. M. Ramsay[4] suggested the explanation that Titus was Luke's relative, whom the author named as little as himself, and for similar reasons.

Perhaps a more convincing explanation is that Titus was closely bound up with Paul's collection and with Corinth, and that Luke— no doubt for the good reason that both provided insights into the life of the early church that would not have proved edifying for the church of his own day[5]—gives abridged and edited versions of them.

There are however a few passages in Acts which, for various reasons, are worthy of brief consideration. At 13.1 there is evidence[6] for a Latin text that ran as follows:

Erant etiam in eclesia [sic] prophetae et doctores Barnabas et Saulus, quibus imposuerunt manus prophetae: Symeon qui appellatus est Niger, et Lucius Cirenensis, qui manet usque adhuc et Ticius conlactaneus, qui acceperant responsum ab Spiritum sanctum [sic], unde dixerunt, Segregate, etc.

Zahn[7] argued that this was a pure form of the Western text, that it contained a reference to Titus, and that it could claim to be original. The text is evidently corrupt,[8] it was probably based (if Titus was in mind at all) on his connection with Antioch (deduced from Gal. 2.1), and (so far as I know) no one has followed Zahn's suggestion. A. C. Clark,[9] adopting the Ciceronian proverb, says that 'Zahn has attempted *arcem facere ex cloaca*'.

At Acts 15.2 there is no textual evidence, even the slightest, for including Titus's name, but in view of Gal. 2.1 there is a strong case for supposing that Titus may have been among those described as accompanying Paul and Barnabas from Antioch. This however means interpreting Acts by Galatians, and adds nothing of consequence to what will be said below on Galatians.

It was a tortuous eccentricity of criticism that identified the Silas of Acts 15.22 with Titus,[10] and the 'suspicion that' the account in 16.3 of the circumcision of Timothy 'is a confused and perhaps erroneous memory of the story of Titus'[11] does not afford a convincing explanation of what is certainly a puzzling narrative. At 18.7 the reading Titius Justus should probably be accepted: 'Titus Justus' may represent an attempt to get Titus into Acts, and 'Justus' the easiest way of escaping a confusion. According to a popular view,[12] it was at 20.2 that Paul met Titus in Macedonia; it is worth noting that Luke shows no awareness of any such event.

We leave Acts, therefore, having learnt nothing whatever about Titus, and turn to Gal. 2, which, though it does provide explicit mention of Titus, raises more difficulties than can conveniently be

handled here. Titus was taken by Paul (συμπαραλαβών) to Jerusalem
about sixteen years[13] after Paul's conversion. Unfortunately however we can date Paul's conversion only by identifying the events of
Gal. 2, and then working back sixteen years; and the visit to
Jerusalem in Gal. 2 is notoriously difficult to identify with any of the
visits recorded in Acts. It cannot however be earlier than the so-
called 'famine visit' of Acts 11, 12, which may not unreasonably be
placed in about AD 46.[14] It may well be[15] that the Council described
in Acts 15 is a doublet of this visit. If so, we may conclude that
Titus had already been not less than five years in the Pauline group
of missionaries when Paul first reached Corinth;[16] if not, the time
may possibly but not necessarily be reduced by the duration of the
so-called first missionary journey (Acts 13, 14).

Much more important than these dubious considerations (since
there is in any case no doubt that Titus was a trusted assistant of
Paul's by the time of the Corinthian episode) are the facts and,
guesses at facts, provided or suggested by the narrative in Gal. 2
itself.

Titus was a Greek ("Ελλην), that is, in accordance with Paul's
(and others') usage,[17] a Gentile. Why did Paul take him to Jerusalem? He may have been one of the deputation appointed (according to Acts 15.2) by the church at Antioch—possibly the Gentile
member of it; Paul may have chosen him as a second colleague
along with the Jew Barnabas; Paul may even have been acting
provocatively, as Luther (quoted by Schlier[18]) suggests:

> Tunc (hunc?) enim assumpsit, ut probaret gratiam equaliter
> gentibus et Iudeis tam in circumcisione quam sine circumcisione
> sufficere.

None of these suggestions is impossible; some can be combined; the
first might account for the association between Paul and Titus, but
is not needed as an explanation.

What happened to Titus? The question whether or not he was
circumcised is warmly disputed, and by no means settled. It turns
on (a) the text of Gal. 2.4 f; (b) the stress laid on ἠναγκάσθη; and
(c) the view taken of the general probabilities of the situation.

As far as (a) is concerned the question appears to be[19] whether
Paul is more likely to have offended copyists by affirming in ana-
coluthon (οἷς οὐδέ) that he did not yield to false brethren, or by
admitting in correct Greek that he did. It seems to be probable that

he wrote the offending Greek (it is not the only place where his syntax is at fault), that he refused to yield, and that copyists mended his Greek at the expense of the sense. If other considerations seem equal it is surely decisive that the persons in question, to whom Paul may or may not have yielded, are described as παρείσακτοι ψευδάδελφοι, who sneaked in (παρεισῆλθον) as spies. Compromise with those who were reputed to be pillars is conceivable, though verse 11 does not suggest that it was probable; but 'I gave in to the dirty spies, in the interests of truth' is not very convincing.

The same considerations probably settle questions (b) and (c). In any case, the stressed ἠναγκάσθη ('he was not actually *forced* to be circumcised, though in fact the operation took place') involves an artificiality of style[20] that is not Pauline. One further fact, seldom as far as I know, observed, lends some support to this view. We know little about Titus except that he was Paul's confidential agent in the gathering of the collection for poor Jews—the saints in Jerusalem. Now it is not impossible that Paul should have employed a born Jew or a proselyte for this purpose. But we know that he was sensitive about the arrangements he had made (1 Cor. 16.1–4; 2 Cor. 8.20 f; 12.17 f), and if, being himself a Jew, he was careful to have a Gentile as his colleague, this would at least make very good sense. A far less convincing suggestion, though it could be true, is that Timothy and Titus were selected as the 'recipients' of the Pastoral Letters as representing the circumcised and uncircumcised wings of the church respectively.

There is thus a strong probability that Titus emerged from the Jerusalem meeting the uncircumcised Gentile he had always been, and that he would retain from this gathering a keen awareness of the peril of legalistic Judaism and of the activities of false brothers; also that he would be aware of the quite different (even if not wholly satisfactory) attitude of the main Jerusalem apostles.

Before leaving Galatians we ought to note the suggestion that in this epistle we have words from Titus's own pen. In *ExpT* 62 (1950–1), p. 380, D. Warner made the suggestion that Gal. 2.3–8 should be regarded as an interpolation. The following grounds are adduced. (1) Verses 3–8 break the continuity of verses 1, 2, 9, 10. (2) They reveal a different estimation of the Jerusalem apostles; in verses 1, 2, 9, 10 these are οἱ δοκοῦντες, οἱ δοκοῦντες στῦλοι εἶναι, whereas the writer of verse 6 does not care who they are. (3) Verses 3–8 contain words not elsewhere used by Paul (ἀναγκάζειν, διαμένειν, εἴκειν, κατασκοπεῖν, παρείσακτος). (4) The writer of verses 3–8 uses the name Πέτρος whereas Paul elsewhere has Κηφᾶς.[21] The conclusion is that verses 3–8 are an interpolation; that they were written by a Paulinist whose views on the Jewish apostles were more extreme than Paul's; that they were written by a Greek. It is very tentatively that Mr Warner adds the suggestion that the Greek may have been Titus.

If Gal. 2.3–8 is indeed an interpolation its author could as well have been Titus as any other; but there is no adequate reason for not ascribing the verses to Paul. Verses 1, 2, 9, 10 are not in fact continuous; verse 9 may begin in the middle of a sentence. The *hapax legomena* are required in the description of circumstances which Paul did not have to describe elsewhere. The use of the Greek name Πέτρος is interesting, but not in itself convincing.[22] The Gospels and Acts show that it was widely current. Titus was, we may think, a witness but not the recorder of one of the turning-points of Paul's career, which was at the same time one of the most important moments in the history of the church. Part of this event was the request that Paul and his colleagues should remember the poor—essentially the Jerusalem church (Rom. 15.26): an obligation Paul himself was eager to fulfil. His word, ἐσπούδασα, could be rendered as an English pluperfect: I had (already) shown myself eager to do this. There would then be a reference back to the alms brought by Paul and Barnabas to Jerusalem (Acts 11.30; 12.25). In this case it might be correct to render μνημονεύωμεν (verse 10), 'that we should go on remembering'. But these suggestions do nothing to identify the visit to Jerusalem that Paul is describing, or to define further the role of Titus. We may simply take it that Paul records a request that was addressed to a group (μνημονεύωμεν), and his own reaction to it (ἐσπούδασα), though he may well have reflected at the same time that he had begun the work of charity without being asked. This leads us to 2 Corinthians.

It will be helpful first to recall the dates of Paul's own movements in relation to Corinth, in order that those of Titus, as mentioned in 2 Corinthians, may be fitted into them.[23] On a probable view, Paul reached Corinth in the spring (say, March) of AD 50, and stayed there for eighteen months, that is, till about September 51. At this point, according to Acts 18.18, he left for Syria, but the visit was a flying one, and he was probably back in Ephesus (which he had merely touched—Acts 18.19 ff—in the journey east) in late summer 52. In Ephesus he stayed two years and three months (Acts 19.8, 10; cf. 20.31), and it is within this period that most of the Corinthian story, as it can be reconstructed from the epistles, must be accommodated. The Pentecost Paul was anxious to keep in Jerusalem (Acts 20.16) will have been that of 55, and the three months he spent in Greece ('Ελλάς, Acts 20.2 f) will have been approximately January to March 55. This period can hardly have failed to include a visit to Corinth. The Pentecost of 1 Cor. 16.8 is likely to have been that of 54 (less probably, 53), so that 1 Corinthians was probably written early[24] in 54, or possibly late in 53. What happened next? Certainly a great deal in a short time.

There is no reference to Titus in 1 Corinthians, nor anything to suggest that he had had any contact with Corinth. We have seen reason to think that he was already at this time one of Paul's trusted colleagues, and it is very probable that if he had already visited Corinth Paul would have spoken of him—either to send his greetings to the church or to remark on his absence. Before we leave 1 Corinthians it will be worth while to note the earliest reference to the collection, with which Titus was later to be closely connected, in 1 Cor. 16.1–4. It seems that the Corinthians had heard, not directly from Paul himself but perhaps from Galatia, that a collection was being made, and had inquired what steps they ought to take. It is to be noted that the plan Paul suggests—private savings, contributed to a common fund on Paul's arrival in Corinth—does not require or even leave room for the collaboration of Titus, or of any other of Paul's agents. Paul himself and the Corinthians will see to it between them.

The first appearance of Titus in 2 Corinthians is a non-appearance. In 2.12 Paul states that he went to Troas, and there had an excellent opportunity for evangelism. He could not however bring himself to take advantage of it because he was so perturbed by the fact that he did not find Titus, whom presumably he had expected to meet in Troas. Instead he set out for Macedonia, on the other side of the Thracian Sea. It is often supposed that this journey is to be identified with that described in Acts 20.1, according to which Paul left Ephesus at the end of his long ministry there and set out for Macedonia. This journey (on the scheme given above) must have taken place towards the end of 54, immediately before Paul's final visit to Corinth in the spring of 55. It should be noticed however that Acts mentions neither Troas nor Titus, and the identification is far less certain than is often thought. If we confine our attention to 2 Corinthians it appears (a) that Paul had reason to expect that he would meet Titus in Troas; (b) that Paul went into Macedonia, not to evangelize that region, or to look after his churches there, or to reach some other mission field, but simply to find Titus as soon as possible; and (c) that Titus must therefore have been at work possibly in Macedonia, or in some other region beyond, but most probably in Corinth, with an agreed return route.

Unless the route had been agreed in detail Paul's departure from Troas was rash. The most natural way from Troas to Macedonia was by ship to Neapolis, thence by road, but there was also a land route, involving the crossing only of the Hellespont. Whichever way Paul went, he risked missing Titus. If he went by land, Titus might be on the sea; if he went by sea, Titus might be on land, or in a boat that never came in sight of Paul's. It is interesting, if no more, to conjecture that the two did miss each other, and that this is why Paul (a) breaks off the narrative here and does not return to it till 7.5, and (b) continued to be so upset when he reached Macedonia. Alternatively, it may still have been too early for sailing so that only the land route was open and Paul could safely take it, knowing that Titus, if on the way at all, would be found there.

At 2.13 Paul drops the story of his Macedonian journey in search of Titus. It is resumed at 7.5; for it is difficult to doubt that this verse takes up the same incident. The coincidence of wording as well as thought and narrative establishes this.

ἐλθὼν	ἐλθόντων ἡμῶν[25]
εἰς τὴν Τρῳάδα	εἰς Μακεδονίαν
οὐκ ἔσχηκα ἄνεσιν τῷ	οὐδεμίαν ἔσχηκεν ἄνεσιν ἡ
πνεύματί μου	σάρξ ἡμῶν[26]

When Titus at last appeared he brought good news from Corinth. He had himself been comforted by the Corinthians' passionate attachment to and longing for Paul, and Paul was comforted by Titus's satisfaction—comforted, and perhaps, as 7.7 may suggest, a little surprised. Paul had expected to find comfort in Titus's arrival and presence, but in addition to these there was the good news from Corinth. Paul had written a letter;[27] it had cost him many tears, and it grieved the Corinthians when they received it, but theirs had been the right kind of penitent grief, and it had borne splendid fruit.

Paul comes back in 7.13 to the theme of comfort: παρακεκλήμεθα, ἐπὶ τῇ παρακλήσει. These words surely link the new paragraph with verses 6 f (παρεκάλεσεν ἡμᾶς ὁ θεός, ἐν τῇ παρακλήσει)—a most important observation, in view of what follows in verse 14. Paul, it seems, had boasted to Titus about the Corinthians (ὑπὲρ ὑμῶν κεκαύχημαι), and his boasts had been proved true by the favourable response, the recollection of which still kindled Titus's affection for the Corinthian church (verse 15). This boasting of Paul's is to be noted, because it virtually rules out the commonly accepted view that Titus had been sent to Corinth to put down a rebellion, and as the bearer of 2 Cor. 10—13. How could Paul possibly have boasted to Titus about the Corinthians, and at the same time put in his hand a letter containing, for example, the words 'I am afraid lest, as the serpent by his guile deceived Eve, your thoughts may be seduced from single-minded and pure faithfulness to Christ' (11.3); 'I am afraid lest, when I come, I may find you not such as I wish . . . lest, when I come again, my God should humble me before you, and I should mourn for many who sinned before and did not repent of the uncleanness and fornication and wantonness they committed' (12.20 f) ? In these circumstances he would have warned Titus of the Corinthians' vices, not boasted of their virtues.

We conclude, accordingly, that Titus had not, on this occasion, been sent to put down rebellion, and that he carried not 2 Cor. 10—13 but a letter which though less drastic had none the less been painful both to write and to read. It was presumably directed to the incident obscurely described in 2.5, in which it seems that Paul had been insulted; perhaps his apostleship had been questioned.[28] Had Titus any other task to perform on this occasion? To answer this question we must continue through the epistle.

The next reference to Titus is in 8.6, in relation to the collection. The chapter begins with mention of the Macedonian churches: in the matter of the collection they have set a good example, which Paul presumably observed at about the same time that he eventually met Titus and heard the good news from Corinth. In these circumstances it was natural to suggest that Titus should forthwith complete (ἐπιτελέσῃ) the task that he had already set in hand (προενήρξατο). This answers the question asked at the end of the last paragraph: when Titus conveyed the 'severe letter' he was also charged with the task of initiating the collection—that is, the actual gathering together of the money, which Paul in 1 Cor. 16.1–4 had said he would himself carry out when he arrived in Corinth. This is a further indication that Titus had not been sent to quell rebellion: a collecting bag is not the most tactful of instruments for such a purpose. Some exhortation follows, and in verses 10 ff the verbs used above with reference to Titus are used of the Corinthians (προενήρξασθε, ἐπιτελέσατε). The latter has the same time reference in each case, for it is evident that though Titus and the native Corinthians did not have identical tasks, the task of giving and the task of collecting would finish at the same time. προενάρχεσθαι, however, must have different time references, for 1 Cor. 16.1–4 shows that the Corinthians had made a beginning of sorts before Titus appeared on the scene.[29] This point is important because it means that ἀπὸ πέρυσι (verse 10) does not apply to Titus's visit. It is true that 'last year' is a most imprecise term (especially as we do not know which reckoning Paul employed and when he thought the year ended and began), and could be applied to quite recent events; but if applied to Titus's first visit it would make the view of events suggested here if not impossible at least very improbable.

Verses 16 f refer back to verse 6 (παρακαλέσαι, παράκλησιν), and may suggest Paul's relief that what might have seemed a somewhat unreasonable request (that Titus should immediately retrace his steps and return to Corinth)[30] met with a warm welcome. Titus was equally keen (τὴν αὐτὴν σπουδήν), and needed no prompting (αὐθαίρετος). συνεπέμψαμεν in verses 18 and 22 should be taken as an epistolary aorist—'we send herewith'; Titus and his colleagues must have been the bearers of the letter which thus commended them.[31] The two colleagues are not named. The names may have dropped out, or have seemed unnecessary, since the men in question would have the letter in their hands. The different commendations in verse 23 should be noted. Two things are said of Titus that are not said of the brothers—he is on Paul's staff (κοινωνὸς ἐμός), and he has already had contact with Corinth (εἰς ὑμᾶς συνεργός). But all are thoroughly trustworthy.

Titus is not mentioned by name in 2 Cor. 9, but there are a few passages in this second collection chapter that should be noted. In verse 2 Paul is boasting (cf. his earlier boasting to Titus, 7.14) to the Macedonians that Achaea was ready ἀπὸ πέρυσι:[32] this puts Chapter 9 at the same date (approximately at least) as Chapter 8. The tense of ἔπεμψα in verse 3 corresponds to that of συνεπέμψαμεν in 8.18, 22. It is possible to take it as a simple aorist of past time, and to suppose that Chapter 9 was written a little later than Chapter 8, but there seems to be no good reason for this nor for the view that Chapter 9 was addressed not to Corinth but to Achaea in general. Paul moreover asked (παρακαλέσαι, verse 5; cf. 8.6) the brothers to go on ahead and get things ready in advance of his own arrival (ἵνα προέλθωσιν . . . καὶ προκαταρτίσωσιν); that is, he will follow them southward from Macedonia to Achaea and Corinth. There is nothing to suggest that his visit will be long delayed.

There is only one more reference to Titus. In 2 Cor. 12.16 ff Paul faces what must have been as hurtful an allegation as any made against him. He has pointed out that he (unlike others who could be named) has not made himself burdensome to the Corinthians by taking pay from them. No, his enemies reply, he has not been so honest; he has tricked his converts, and defrauded them under cover of a collection for the poor. But the charge can be repudiated. So far he himself has taken no direct part in the collection, and he can trust the behaviour and reputation of his delegates. I asked (παρεκάλεσα; cf. 8.6) Titus to do the work, and I sent with him (συναπέστειλα; cf. the synonymous συμπέμπειν in 8.18, 22) the brother. Their record speaks for itself. The coincidence of language is such that the identity of this visit to Corinth with that described in Chapter 8 is scarcely open to question. There is only one difference; in Chapter 8 Paul sends Titus and two brothers, in Chapter 12 he sends Titus and 'the brother'. But in Chapter 8 one brother was particularly involved from Paul's side (ὃν ἐδοκιμάσαμεν ἐν πολλοῖς πολλάκις σπουδαῖον ὄντα, 8.22); the other was χειροτονηθεὶς ὑπὸ τῶν ἐκκλησιῶν, and therefore did not need Paul's defence. Thus in Chapter 12 Paul is able to look back on the visit which in Chapters 8 and 9 was still in prospect, and appeal to the honourable behaviour of his representatives. It is impossible not to conclude that Chapter 12 was written later than Chapters 8, 9, and it is probable that Chapter 12 was written later than the whole of Chapters 1—9, since we have seen some reasons, and there are others, for thinking that 1—7 belong to the same date as 8, 9.

After this point in the New Testament Titus disappears from view. The epistle that claims to have been directed to him conveys no serious information about him beyond the fact that towards the end of the first century his name was remembered, with Timothy's, as that of an outstanding younger member of the Pauline circle. It may be that he spent some time in Crete; Tit. 1.5 need not be

pure fiction, though it may reflect the provenance of the epistle
rather than recollections of Titus's career.

It remains only to put together as briefly as may be an outline
of Paul's dealings with the church at Corinth as these appear in
our sketch of Titus's work, and to bring these into relation with the
literary problems of 2 Corinthians.

(1) About the beginning of AD 54 Paul wrote 1 Corinthians,
promising that he would come to Corinth quickly (4.19), but not
too quickly, for he would stay in Ephesus till Pentecost (16.8). This
would bring him into the season when the seas were open, and faci-
litate a voyage across the Aegean that would not take long.

(2) Paul made this journey, and was surprised and hurt to
encounter a personal insult (2 Cor. 2.5). For this reason he forebore
to make a third visit (1.23), even though the business of the collection still needed to be set in hand.

(3) There was no reason why Titus should not be sent to do this
work; he was authorized to begin the collection, and also carried a
letter of rebuke that cost Paul many tears in the writing. This letter
has been lost. Its disappearance confirms the belief that it was
essentially personal, and dealt mainly, or even exclusively, with one
member of the church. Of the Corinthians in general Paul could
boast to Titus (2 Cor. 7.14).

(4) Paul went to Troas to meet Titus. Because he did not find
him there[33] he was troubled and went on into Macedonia, where
the two met. It was a joy to meet Titus again, but especially to hear
how enthusiastically the Corinthians had embraced his cause.

(5) Paul, happy on the personal issue and indeed anxious that
the punishment proposed for the offender should be mitigated, but
not, it seems, satisfied that the Corinthians understood fully the
apostolic gospel and the nature of the apostolate, sent Titus straight
back to Corinth to finish the work on the collection (which he may
have interrupted because he was so pleased with the Corinthian
response—though this may have been a superficial judgement)
and to convey 2 Cor. 1—9. This was partly a commendation of the
collectors (who were only now about to convey money away from
Corinth), but it also contained instruction in matters the Corinthians
still understood none too well.[34]

(6) Titus came back, this time with the bad news that evoked
2 Cor. 10—13. It is easy to understand the difference between 1—9
and 10—13, even if Titus had not to some extent misjudged the

earlier situation. The agony of 10—13 is due to the fact that false apostles have entered the Corinthian church (perhaps not for the first time) and swept the Corinthians off their feet. Who conveyed 2 Cor. 10—13 we do not know; in view of the fact that 12.18 is the only reference to him, presumably not Titus. In the course of this letter Paul threatens a third visit.

(7) This visit took place, and is referred to in Acts 20.1. Apparently it took three months (if we can accept the figure in Acts) to deal with the trouble.[35] Rom. 15.26 shows that Achaea did produce a contribution for the collection, but we may infer from the absence of an Achaean name in Acts 20.4 that the sum was not large. It may have been the false apostles who infiltrated into Corinth who awakened Paul's fears regarding the way in which his gift might be received in Jerusalem (Rom. 15.31); the narrative in Acts suggests that his fears were not groundless, and the discreet silence of Acts 20.2 f about the church in Corinth, and the reference to a plot made by the Jews, may reflect the strife that preceded Paul's success in winning the church there to his side.

NOTES

1 It is often thought to be, or to be part of, the 'severe letter' of 2 Cor. 2.4; 7.8.
2 Within this section a special problem is raised by 6 14—7.1, which some think to be part of the 'previous letter' (1 Cor. 5.9), and others believe not to have been written by Paul.
3 Detailed bibliography would be out of place in this essay; see W. G. Kümmel, *Introduction to the New Testament* (London 1966), p. 205.
4 *St Paul the Traveller and Roman Citizen* (London [10]1908), p. 390. See also *BC* v, p. 490.
5 This does not imply falsification, but a practical, pastoral intent; and Luke's knowledge was probably limited.
6 A ninth-century Latin manuscript, *Prophetiae ex omnibus libris collectae*, in the library at St Gall (Codex 133).
7 Zahn's views are briefly and accessibly stated in *BC* v, pp. 492 f.
8 Zahn supposes that *Ticius* should be *Titus*, and that between *Ticius* and *conlactaneus* the words *Antiocensis, Manaenque Herodis tetrarchae* have fallen out.
9 *The Acts of the Apostles* (Oxford 1933), p. 350.
10 For an account of this view, and of some other curiosities, see the article on Silas by P. W. Schmiedel in *Encyclopaedia Biblica* (London 1914), cols 4514–21.
11 *BC* iv, p. 184.
12 See below, pp. 123 f.

13 By the inclusive reckoning of antiquity, the 'three years' of Gal. 1.18
means probably two and a fraction, the 'fourteen years' of 2.1, thirteen
and a fraction. Adding them together we reach fifteen or sixteen years.
It is possible that the fourteen of 2.1 includes the three of 1.18.

14 See *BC* v, pp. 452–5, 468.

15 See *BC* v, pp. 201–4.

16 Probably in AD 51; see below, pp. 122 f.

17 Rom. 1.16; 2.9, 10; 3.9; 10.12; 1 Cor. 1.22, 24; 10.32; 12.13; Gal.
3.28. Rom. 1.14 and Col. 3.11 are not so clear. See also e.g. Mark 7.26;
Acts 14.1; 16.1; 18.4; 19.17; 20.21.

18 H. Schlier, *Der Brief an die Galater* (Göttingen 1949), p. 34.

19 Notwithstanding B. W. Bacon, 'The reading οἷς οὐδέ in Gal. 2.5',
(*JBL*, xlii 1923), pp. 69–80.

20 Unless A. D. Nock, *St Paul* (London 1938), p. 109, was right in suggesting that Titus, to keep the peace, had himself circumcised without
consulting Paul, and to Paul's embarrassment.

21 Wherever Κηφᾶς occurs in this epistle (1.18; 2.9, 11, 14) the Western
text has Πέτρος.

22 See Lietzmann and Schlier, ad loc., with the reference to Holl's
suggestion that, for Paul, Peter was the name of the missionary, Kephas
that of the Jerusalem apostolic official. Moreover, though in verses 3,
6, 7, 8 the references to Paul in the first person singular could come
from a glossator they can hardly have stood in Titus's own account.

23 I have discussed these dates in *A Commentary on the Epistle to the Romans*
(London 1957), pp. 2–5 and *A Commentary on the First Epistle to the
Corinthians* (London 1968), pp. 3 ff, 22 f, and here state the results
without giving the arguments.

24 1 Cor. 5.7 has led some to think that Paul was writing at Passover time.
This is possible, but the reference to Christ as our Passover could have
been made at any season.

25 The change from first person singular to first person plural does not
mean that a different event is being described, but it furnishes an
argument against the view that 2.13 and 7.5 were originally continuous
2.14—7.4 being an interpolation from another letter.

26 πνεῦμα and σάρξ are here (though not usually) almost equivalent psycho-
logical terms; cf. 7.1, where the similar parallel use is often, but
wrongly, taken as proof that Paul was not the author of 6.14—7.1.

27 References to this letter, like those to Titus, have the effect of binding
Chapters 2 and 7 together.

28 It had already been questioned (e.g. 1 Cor. 1.12; 3.4; 4.9–13, 15; 9.1 f;
15.8), and the theme continues to play a vital part in 2 Corinthians
(1.17, 24; 3; 4; 6.1–10; 10—13 *passim*).

29 We may find here an explanation of the puzzling οὐ μόνον τὸ ποιῆσαι
ἀλλὰ καὶ τὸ θέλειν (8.10). At first sight this seems inverted: 'not only to will
but also to do' would make better sense. But all is clear if, as seems reasonable, we can take the meaning to be, 'You not only began (under the
guidance of Titus) to make the collection; you had already last year,
and without prompting, formed the intention of joining in the collection'.

30 To judge from 1 Cor. 16.1–4 the collector's task ought not to have been a big one, and Titus might have shown resentment at the interruption, and at being made to travel a long way back for a duty that could be very quickly discharged.

31 Commendatory letters play a large part in the Corinthian correspondence (e.g. 2 Cor. 3.1 f). It was the intrusion of credible (and, in some sense, accredited) outsiders that caused most of the trouble in this church.

32 In 8.10 they had *begun* last year. This does not mean that Chapter 9 was written a year or so later than Chapter 8, but only that to the Macedonians Paul had enthusiastically overstated the case; hence his embarrassment (9.4).

33 τῷ μὴ εὑρεῖν με Τίτον τὸν ἀδελφόν μου (2.13)—not because of anxiety about affairs in Corinth. Paul may well have been anxious about Titus. If the collection had (as Paul might have expected) been completed, Titus would have been carrying a considerable sum of money, and would have been a likely prey for robbers (cf. 2 Cor. 11.26).

34 See note 28. Their present vigorous support of Paul probably betrayed their mistaken notion that an apostle should be a figure of imposing and aggressive dignity.

35 It was, however, Paul, not Titus, who dealt with it. This makes better sense than the common reconstruction of the Corinthian story, according to which Paul failed to control his own church, withdrew in disorder, and left it to his junior colleague to redeem his failure.

8

ROMANS 9.30—10.21
Fall and Responsibility of Israel[1]

It is unnecessary here to remark on the immense body of literature that this passage, and this theme, have evoked; equally unnecessary, I hope, to point out that a review of this literature, even if I were competent to make it, is out of the question. At the most I shall be able to refer here and there to other points of view in the hope of making my own understanding of the passage clearer. This will unfortunately have the effect of laying more stress on my disagreements with other students of the epistle than on what I have learnt from them. My debt to many is in fact great.

(1) Our first task must be to establish the place of the present paragraph (9.30—10.21) in the section of the epistle under general consideration (Rom. 9—11); later we shall see that Chapter 10 is not without relation to other parts of the epistle—a fact that may usefully remind us that it is an error to isolate Chapters 9—11 from the epistle as a whole. Undoubtedly it forms a unit, but (even though Paul may have worked the material out and used it on other occasions before he wrote Romans) it is an integral part of the epistle as we have it, and part, though a relatively independent part, of the argument of the whole.

(a) Perhaps the most common view is that, after a predestinarian account of the fall of Israel in 9.1–29, 9.30—10.21 provides a complementary account of the same lapse in which the fault is laid squarely at Israel's door, and in turn leads to a synthesis in Chapter 11 in which Paul states his hope for Israel's future. There is a good deal of evidence to support this view. The theme of Chapter 9 is stated in the words that follow upon the exordium in praise of the privileges of Israel (9.4 f): οὐχ οἷον δὲ ὅτι ἐκπέπτωκεν ὁ λόγος τοῦ Θεοῦ (9.6). God's word is victorious, and is only verified by the course of events. It is his promise, not natural procreation, that constitutes the seed of Abraham that is to inherit blessing (9.8). God is not unjust; he is as free as the potter to make vessels for whatever purpose he chooses (9.21). He pities whom he chooses to pity, and hardens whom he chooses to harden (9.18). It follows that man's will and effort play no effective part; only God's mercy determines man's election and achieves God's purpose (9.16). Only God's predestinating love pronounces who are and who are not his people (9.25 f); and if he chooses to cut Israel down to a bare seed, scarcely distinguishable from Sodom and Gomorrah, there is nothing to prevent his doing so; indeed, he has publicly declared through the prophet that precisely this is his purpose (9.29).

The new paragraph does nothing to relieve the tragedy of the situation; Paul must still, as in Chapter 9, supplicate for the salvation of his people, which, if not excluded, is evidently anything but secure (10.1). It is not insignificant that Israel is zealous for God, even though their zeal is ineffective because it is uninstructed (10.2). Implicitly and explicitly men are invited to have faith (πιστεύειν), and are blamed when they adopt some other course (9.32; 10.4). The issue of justification and salvation is expressed in a conditional clause in which the protasis is in the second person singular: ἐὰν ὁμολογήσῃς ... καὶ πιστεύσῃς ..., σωθήσῃ· καρδίᾳ γὰρ πιστεύεται εἰς δικαιοσύνην, στόματι δὲ ὁμολογεῖται εἰς σωτηρίαν (10.9 f). It is implied, it is for you to believe, and to confess your faith. Why then has Israel not done this? Not because God sent no preachers of the gospel; not because the preachers and their message were not heard; not because Israel did not know, or understand what was being done (10.14–19; there is a minor contradiction between 10.19 and 10.2). The fault lay with Israel, who did not call upon the God who sent his messengers, and did not obey (ὑπήκουσαν, probably equivalent to ἐπίστευσαν) the message. God thus desired their response and took every possible step, through all their history, to secure it, and declared as much in the Old Testament: ὅλην τὴν ἡμέραν ἐξεπέτασα τὰς χεῖράς μου πρὸς λαὸν ἀπειθοῦντα καὶ ἀντιλέγοντα (10.21).

Chapter 11 works out the conflict between divine predestination and human freedom in terms of election and remnant. A remnant of Israel has in fact believed; the rest have not stumbled so as to fall absolutely (11.11); God has not forgotten his gifts and call (11.29), and the broken off branches will be restored to the parent olive (11.23). The full complement of the Gentiles will come in, and all Israel will be saved (11.25 f), when God finds means of dealing with all men, as he intends, in mercy alone (11.32). Predestinating grace will be received by faith (11.22 f).

This, broadly speaking, is the view adopted by many writers on Romans and on Pauline theology; there is much to be said for it, and it is at least arguable that if to some extent the logic fails in Chapter 11 the fault is Paul's rather than the commentator's. This is a question not to be pursued in this paper; the relation of 9.30—10.21 to 9.1–29 is, and the answer that in the two chapters predestination and free choice are set over against each other as two equally necessary elements in a complete discussion of the matter is attractive.

(b) It is however vigorously disputed by J. Munck.[2] His fundamental objection is that this kind of interpretation of Romans 9—11 rests upon false presuppositions. 'It is wrong because it is incorrect to assume that Paul shared the modern view that divine purpose and human responsibility are two separate parts of existence, which work independently of each other but which can be united if they can be made to agree with modern, anthropocentric ideas of divine justice' (p. 60/75). There are, according to Munck, two features of the biblical notion of election; first, election is something that has happened in history, and of which therefore the fruits are to be seen; and secondly, it is not an irrevocable decision. It is this visibility and variability that are important for Paul. The event of Christ has manifested in history the meaning of the Old Testament, and the manifestation continues through the vicissitudes of the mission to the Jews; 'God's election is not an axiom but a fact which can be described' (p. 61/77). Behind it is an unvarying purpose of salvation, but the purpose is adapted to varying situations. 'The description that follows in 9.30—10.21 does not analyse the responsibility and guilt of the Jews. It merely catches up on details of what has happened to the Jews, details not supplied us at the beginning of Chapter 9 (or since then, for that matter)' (ibid.). 10.21 shows that God's purpose has always been one of salvation.

Thus 9.30—10.21 is not to be regarded as a mere recapitulation of 9.6–29 from another point of view, providing no real advance in thought. Analogies are to be found in other groups of three Chapters, 1 Cor. 8, 9, 10 and 12, 13, 14, where in each case the middle chapter contains the heart of the message. This is so, according to Munck, here also. The problem is stated in 9.1–29; the solution is sketched in 9.30—10.21—the one way of salvation is that of justification by faith, and 'God never tires of issuing the call to salvation' (p. 62/79); and Chapter 11 is a detailed practical application of the solution.

There is not a little that is persuasive and salutary in this characteristically fresh view of Munck's. It is up to a point true that for
Paul the doctrine of election arises out of missionary experience
rather than out of speculative theology, that it is flexible rather than
rigid, and that God wills salvation. But it is also true that Paul read
the doctrine of election in his fundamental textbook of theology—
the Old Testament, and though his views on the subject cannot be
called rigid they were held with sufficient firmness to drive him to
difficult exegetical and theological expedients in the attempt to work
out the synthesis of Chapter 11. Munck, moreover, seems himself to
be aware that the use he makes of 10.21 is one-sided. True, God's
outspread hands represent a purpose of love and salvation; but the
people with whom he pleads are disobedient and recalcitrant, and
this goes further than a report of what has happened to the Jews.
By describing them in this way it states their responsibility and guilt.
Further, it is mistaken to describe the distinguishing of the divine
purpose and human responsibility as a 'modern view'. The distinction was clearly made in antiquity. It will suffice to quote the
famous saying of Aboth 3.16, to which, as everyone knows, there
are many parallels: 'All is foreseen, but freedom of choice is given'.
That Aqiba, to whom the saying is ascribed, was no more successful
in combining the two points of view than others who have discussed
them at very much greater length is not the point; the point is that
he distinguished them.

(c) G. Maier[3] takes a view similar to that of Munck, to whom
he refers with approval. Of Chapter 10 he says, Paul 'zeigt jetzt die
geschichtliche Auswirkung und Erfahrung der Prädestination, die
bei den Juden seiner Zeit auf Verhärtung lautet' (p. 384). He goes
further, however, than Munck does, taking as his next step the
observation that there are parallels between Rom. 10 and the
Qumran literature. The Manual of Discipline, he maintains, shows
the same combination of election and freedom of choice that we
find in Paul. The tractate is full of the notion of predestination, yet
the members of the sect are described as נדבים, 'die Willigen'
(1QS I 7), whereas in 1QS II 25 ff it is said of the non-member
'jeder, der sich weigert, einzutreten in den Bund Gottes, um in der
Verstocktheit seines Herzens zu wandeln, soll nicht in die Gemein-
schaft seiner Wahrheit kommen. Denn abgewiesen hat seine Seele
Unterweisung der Erkenntnis der gerechten Satzungen. Er hat den
nicht festgehalten, der sein Leben zur Umkehr brachte, und unter

die Rechtschaffenen darf er nicht gerechnet werden'.[4] Other references are given, and the conclusion drawn: 'Qumran zeigt also, dass im Rahmen des Judentums, das unter dem Einfluss der Weisheitstradition stand, eine grundsätzliche Prädestinationslehre mit freiheitlich strukturierten Aussagen zusammengehen konnte' (pp. 384 f). Returning to Romans, Dr Maier draws the conclusion, 'Rö. 9.30—10.21 steht nicht neben Rö. 9.1–29, sondern unter ihm. Darin offenbart sich wieder der "essenische" Charakter der Gedankenführung in diesen Kapiteln' (p. 385). A further point of resemblance between Paul and Qumran is that each 'das Erkennen der Gerechtigkeit Gottes mit der Prädestination in Beziehung setzt' (p. 390).

This argument is self-defeating. I shall not discuss the alleged parallels, though they are perhaps less close than is supposed by Dr Maier's argument; if we allow them full weight they mean that the train of thought in Rom. 9. 10 is analogous to that which is common to Qumran and Wisdom treatments of predestination. But it is, as Dr Maier himself has convincingly shown, characteristic of these literatures to set side by side the themes of predestination and free choice, and to sharpen the contrast between them. Thus if Paul is writing in this vein a juxtaposition of the themes of election and freedom is precisely what we should expect to find.

In fact, the view of the majority seems, at least on this occasion, to be right. The unbelief of Israel may be looked at from two points of view, that of divine election and that of human choice, and Paul looks at it first from the one and then from the other. To say this is not to deny that something can be learnt from the different views that have been summarized. It is natural that when Paul deals with human choice rather than with the purpose of God he should give more detail of what has happened; it is through the human choices of which history is made up that the progress of the divine plan becomes visible. Munck is right therefore in noting that 9.30—10.21 provides a factual account of what is discussed only in theoretical terms in 9.6–29. 'What if. . .?' Paul asks in 9.21 ff; in Chapter 10 we learn what God did, and how man responded. Dr Maier too is right in saying that Chapter 10 is in a sense subordinate to Chapter 9. God's choice is by definition prior to man's decision, whatever the logical relation between them may be. Whether there can be a logical reconciliation of the two freedoms, God's and man's, is a question to which Paul does not address himself; so far as he has an answer it is expressed in eschatological terms in Chapter 11. In Chapter 10 he is still laying down the terms of the problem, and, in particular, insisting upon the responsibility of Israel for a wrong decision.

(2) This leads to the second major division in this paper. The chapter contains many problems, but, like Chapter 9, it stands firm on one basic fact: Israel has, at least for the present, fallen from the destiny appointed for the people of God. Paul's reaction to this lapse is expressed less emotionally than in 9.1 ff, but is nevertheless clear. The restrictive force of μέν *solitarium* in 10.1 seems to be this: Even though the fall of Israel has happened in accordance with what God himself has declared, even though it was the Lord who laid the stone of stumbling in the path of his people, it remains my desire and my prayer that they may yet attain salvation[5]. This goal, however, is not assured; and at the moment Israel is moving in the wrong direction.

All this is clear and undisputed: throughout Rom. 9—11 Paul is wrestling with the problem of the unbelief of Israel. This simple observation leads directly to the basic exegetical question raised by our chapter. It is an exegetical question, because it can be answered only by eliciting the meaning of the text, but it is also a question with historical and theological aspects and consequences. Granted that Israel has made a wrong choice and rejected the divine offer made to it, how, when and in what historical circumstances did the rejection take place? There are three possible answers to this question.

(a) Israel has rejected the apostolic message of Paul, his colleagues and his predecessors. We know this to have been at least partially true, though the event was perhaps less clear-cut than Paul thought—or perhaps we should say that he showed exceptional foresight in seeing, when many of his contemporaries could not do so, that before long Jewish Christians would be no more than a small and not very highly regarded minority in the church. Paul himself allows that the rejection was not complete—'for I myself am an Israelite, of the seed of Abraham, of the tribe of Benjamin' (11.1). We must remember too (and Paul cannot long have forgotten) that there was a Jewish wing of the church that seems to have claimed superior rights even within his own churches (Gal. 2; 2 Cor. 10—13). Acts is perhaps not far from the truth in suggesting sometimes that the Jews had rejected the gospel (e.g. 13.46; 18.6; 28.25–8) and

elsewhere that considerable numbers of Palestinian Jews were converted (e.g. 6.7; and especially 21.20: πόσαι μυριάδες εἰσὶν ἐν τοῖς
Ἰουδαίοις τῶν πεπιστευκότων). Possibly (but this is a theme we cannot
follow up historically) what Judaism had at this stage decisively
rejected was Paul's understanding of the gospel (note Acts 21.20 c;
πάντες ζηλωταὶ τοῦ νόμου ὑπάρχουσιν). This hardly affects Rom. 10
from the theological angle, though it is not unimportant in any
attempt to understand the development of the primitive church.

(b) A second possibility is that Israel had rejected the ministry,
and the person, of Jesus. As a historical proposition this too is not
without some obscurity, and the extent to which the Jewish population of Palestine was behind the crucifixion is a question on which
more opinions than one, not to mention wild historical romances,
are current. For us it is sufficient that the crucifixion was a fact, and
that Paul knew that it was a fact. The immediate outcome of the
work of Jesus was complete failure, in the sense that he did not receive the active and effective support of his people.

(c) There is a third possibility. The defection of Israel may run
further back into Israelite history. Certainly Paul sees it as predicted
by the prophets; was the prediction simply of what was to happen
after the period of prophecy had ended? Or was the attitude that
culminated in the rejection of Jesus and of Paul's gospel one that
was manifested more or less clearly in the response made by Israel
to all the approaches made to them by God? This is suggested by the
words already quoted from 10.21; not at one point only, but all day
long—and this may well mean through the whole of Old Testament
history—God stretched out inviting hands to a people who returned
only misunderstanding and rebuff. Can the same principle be
detected at various points, or as a continuous thread, in the story
of Israel?

The three possibilities mentioned are not mutually exclusive;
indeed, the third, if we adopt it, almost necessarily implies the first
and second, and the first and second make much better sense if the
third can be accepted too. We have good reason for thinking that
Paul's mind was moving on these lines, for in Chapter 11 they become explicit. If at the present time there is a believing remnant this
is precisely what happened in the time of Elijah (11.2–5). We shall
not however assume the conclusion before studying the paragraph
in detail, though we may at this stage note that if we include the
third possibility as an element in Paul's argument we shall be

confronted with some important theological questions, notably the meaning of the law and its relation to the gospel.

(3) I shall now proceed, not, of course, to study the chapter in detail, but at least to look at some of the major exegetical problems, in the hope of winning some firm ground on which to stand.

At the end of the preceding paragraph Paul uses Old Testament quotations to demonstrate the fact that the number of Israelites included in the true people of God is being cut down to a bare remnant. His quotations also have the effect of showing that a number of Gentiles are being included (9.25–9). His main concern in Chapters 9—11 is with the Jews, but in 9.30 he takes up again the calling of the Gentiles, not so much for their own sake (they immediately fall out of consideration) as to establish certain terminology and terms of reference. The metaphorical language (διώκειν, καταλαμβάνειν) is that of running a race, and may look back to the figure of the runner in 9.16. The Gentiles were never in the race; that is, they did not make righteousness their objective. Yet, not knowing what they did, they caught up with it. Whatever this δικαιοσύνη may have been, it was certainly a δικαιοσύνη ἐκ πίστεως, for the Gentiles were by definition doing no works that could have served as the ground for righteousness. Historically this means that they became Christians, members of God's people, thus granted the status of righteousness in the presence of God. This status they had accepted as a gift; this is the meaning of πίστις. The righteousness in question was therefore not God's faithfulness as creator but a standing which they possessed (not indeed in their own right) in his judgement.

With this Paul leaves the Gentiles and resumes his main theme. The failure of Israel is summed up in verse 31: Ἰσραὴλ δὲ διώκων νόμον δικαιοσύνης εἰς νόμον οὐκ ἔφθασεν. Unlike the Gentiles, they have been running hard, but their quarry has escaped them; it is to be noted however that what Paul says in this verse about the Jews does not balance exactly what he says in verse 30 about the Gentiles. He says that the Jews were pursuing not δικαιοσύνη but νόμος δικαιοσύνης, and that they did not come up with νόμος. What does he mean by νόμος δικαιοσύνης? Calvin (who is here following an old line of interpretation, and also the Koine and Vulgate text, which has νόμος δικαιοσύνης in both parts of the verse) thinks that νόμος δικαιοσύνης is to be understood as if Paul had written δικαιοσύνη νόμου. 'In the first part of the verse he has, I think, put *law of righteousness* by hypallage to mean *righteousness of the law*, and when he repeats the phrase in the second clause, he has understood it in a different sense to mean the form or rule of righteousness.'[6] He concludes from this: 'Paul's use of contrasted expressions is striking, when he informs us that legal righteousness was the reason why Israel fell from the law of righteousness' (ibid.). This is, theologically, an illuminating comment, but as exposition of the text it will not do. It fails textually, for in the latter part of the verse we must read simply νόμον, and not νόμον δικαιοσύνης;[7] and it fails exegetically, first because one ought not to assume without very convincing argument that when Paul says νόμος δικαιοσύνης he really means δικαιοσύνη νόμου, and secondly because it is unwise to assume that νόμος changes its meaning within half-a-dozen words—Rom. 7.22 f, sometimes invoked as a parallel, carries no weight, because there Paul makes quite clear what he is doing by means of the expression ἕτερος νόμος. This passage, incidentally, does throw light on the understanding of law with which Paul is working here. We must, however, unless some strong counter-reason presents itself, suppose that the νόμος which Israel did not reach was the νόμος δικαιοσύνης that it pursued. νόμος is not often, in the Pauline epistles, followed by a genitive (except Θεοῦ and Χριστοῦ, and even these are not common). Rom. 8.2 (νόμος τοῦ πνεύματος τῆς ζωῆς, νόμος τῆς ἁμαρτίας καὶ τοῦ θανάτου) provides a parallel of sorts, but not one that can be usefully employed—it would involve explaining *obscurum per obscurius*. The simplest and best suggestion, though it does not seem to have been often adopted, is that δικαιοσύνης is an adjectival genitive: the law in question is a righteous law. This claims no more, and not much less, than Paul has already said in Rom. 7.12: the law is ἅγιος, the commandment ἁγία, δικαία, ἀγαθή. Compare also Gal. 3.21, where the only fault found with the law is that it lacks the power to give life; had it had this power, righteousness would truly have been derivable from the law. Israel thus pursued its law, and it was a righteous law—it commanded what was right, and did not command what was wrong. Moreover, it required that men should be righteous; this seems to be the meaning of τὸ δικαίωμα τοῦ νόμου (Rom. 8.4). This law Israel pursued, but εἰς νόμον οὐκ ἔφθασεν; this can hardly mean anything other than that Israel essayed to keep the law, and to achieve the righteousness it required, but failed to keep the law. Here Paul invited contradiction, not only from his fellow-Jews but also, in a sense, from himself, for in Phil. 3.6 he claims that with regard to the righteousness that is in the law he was himself ἄμεμπτος. The self-contradiction, however, is apparent only, for in Phil. 3.9 he goes on to describe the righteousness he gets out of the law (ἐκ νόμου) as ἐμὴ δικαιοσύνη; this corresponds to the ἰδία δικαιοσύνη which in Rom. 10.3 is contrasted with the δικαιοσύνη ἐκ θεοῦ. It was, as Calvin would say, legal righteousness, or, as we might even more plainly say, legalistic righteousness that men had achieved by means of the law, and this was not the righteousness that the law itself had required. In the proper sense, it was no righteousness at all. Thus Israel pursued the law, but, though they were circumcised, kept the Sabbath, observed the rules of cleanness, and so on, they were in all this not achieving the law—εἰς νόμον οὐκ ἔφθασεν. The same distinction is made in Rom. 2, where the proposition is laid down: περιτομὴ μὲν γὰρ ὠφελεῖ ἐὰν νόμον πράσσῃς (verse 25)—as if being circumcised and doing the law were two separable possibilities! And in Rom. 3 Paul shows that the law, understood in the wider sense of the Old Testament, declares that οὐκ ἔστιν δίκαιος οὐδὲ εἷς (3.10). We cannot take this further and establish what it was that the law required and Israel failed to achieve, and what Israel, mistakenly, did achieve, unless we proceed to the next verse.

Characteristically Paul omits to provide the next sentence with a verb: διὰ τί; ὅτι οὐκ ἐκ πίστεως ἀλλ' ὡς ἐξ ἔργων. It is not difficult, and not incorrect, to supply some such verb as ἐδίωκον; they pursued their goal by the wrong means. 9.30 has already suggested the point: the only way to achieve righteousness (which is what the righteous law requires) is by faith. This way the Gentiles, who really had no choice in the matter, had adopted, when they were surprised by the gospel; thus κατέλαβεν δικαιοσύνην. Israel had not done this. They had been given the law (3.2; 9.4) and had sought to do what they understood it to mean; but they had misunderstood their own law, thinking[8] that it was to be obeyed on the principle of works, whereas it demanded obedience rendered in, consisting of, faith. This is the fundamental observation on which the understanding of our theme rests. Israel tried to catch up with the law, that is, to obey the law, by the principle of works. This was a not unnatural misunderstanding. It has been repeated in countless books and articles, and is quite true, that תורה is not identical in meaning with νόμος or with lex; yet Torah as we see it in the Pentateuch (not to mention the developments in oral Torah) contains not a few statutes, ordinances and judgements, and ἔργα are actions performed in obedience to such rules. Thus, on the one hand, the law (if we may take this to mean the law of Moses) presents itself as a collection of holy, righteous and good precepts, each requiring obedience for which in return a reward is promised; on the other hand, the law rightly understood calls for a response in terms not of such ἔργα but of πίστις, by which alone man can truly achieve the law. In view of this Paul might well ask the question (Gal. 3.19), τί οὖν ὁ νόμος; What purpose was the law intended to serve? The answer, or part of it, appears in our paragraph, which is illuminated by the discussions in Gal. 3 and Rom. 5.

At this point we may speak, with P. Stuhlmacher,[9] of Paul's *Gesetzesdialektik*, though I should not myself use this term to mean exactly what it does for Dr Stuhlmacher. For him (if I understand him rightly) the νόμος δικαιοσύνης is the Torah as 'eine zum Zwecke des göttlichen Rechtes und seiner Findung gestiftete Gebotsmanifestation' (p. 92). 'Sie ist ursprünglich die den Menschen vor Übertretung schützende, weil den Weg des Gotteswillens weisende Erwählungsurkunde des Gottesvolkes' (ibid.). It is to this Torah that Israel οὐκ ἔφθασεν. Instead Israel 'ist der durch die Sünde entstellten und ins Gegenteil ihres ursprünglichen Sinnes verkehrten Tora, dem Gesetz des Moses, verfallen' (ibid.). The dialectic thus appears to be between an original Torah and its relative perversion in the law of Moses. This does not seem to me to correspond with Paul's usage of the word νόμος and his view of the law of Moses. Paul can use the word νόμος in a generalized sense (e.g. Rom. 2.14), but the law which Israel possesses is the law of Moses. Dr Stuhlmacher rightly refers to Rom. 7.7 ff as a parallel to the 'good' view of the law which appears in 9.31, but this law, which is holy, righteous and good, and also spiritual (that is, inspired by God, 7.12, 14), is unmistakably the law of Moses, since it contains the specific command, οὐκ ἐπιθυμήσεις (7.7; Exod. 20.17; Deut. 5.18). It is with reference to this law that Paul speaks of a ἕτερος νόμος (7.23), an evil counterpart of the good law into which the good law is perverted by sin. Again, the law which, according to Rom. 3.21, bears witness to the righteousness of God that is manifested in the Gospel must be the law of Moses, since it is associated with the prophets—'the law and the prophets' means, substantially, the Old Testament. The fault of the Jews is not that they have pursued the wrong law; they have pursued the right law and there is nothing in the passage before us to suggest that this right, or righteous, law, the νόμος δικαιοσύνης, is anything other than the law of Moses. Their fault is that they have pursued the right law in the wrong way, οὐκ ἐκ πίστεως ἀλλ' ὡς ἐξ ἔργων. This means that the right response to the law of Moses was not works, but faith. Let me here state, with a view to clarity, that it seems to me that this observation will supply the key to (a) the stone of stumbling, (b) the τέλος νόμου of 10.4, and (c) the exegesis of various Old Testament passages used by Paul in this paragraph, and especially of Deut. 30.11–14. I shall return to these propositions in due course as they arise.

Paul immediately (9.32 b, 33) uses the figure of the stone of stumbling, making first, before he uses the citation formula καθὼς γέγραπται, the plain statement, προσέκοψαν τῷ λίθῳ τοῦ προσκόμματος. The verb προσκόπτειν is evidently taken out of the noun given in the allusion, πρόσκομμα; but the statement as such is Paul's own. In fact, even after the καθὼς γέγραπται Paul remains somewhat distant from his Old Testament base—and, incidentally, from 1 Peter 2.4–8, where the addition of a reference to Ps. 118.22 gives a much more clearly christological tone to the passage. The first line of Paul's quotation runs: ἰδοὺ τίθημι ἐν Σιὼν λίθον προσκόμματος καὶ πέτραν σκανδάλου. In the LXX of Isa. 8.14 we encounter the words λίθος, πρόσκομμα, and πέτρα, and these are sufficient to establish the source Paul has in mind; but the setting of the words is entirely different. In particular, there is a negative to reverse the sense: καὶ οὐχ ὡς λίθου προσκόμματι συναντήσεσθε αὐτῷ οὐδὲ ὡς πέτρας πτώματι. This negative is not in the Hebrew, which runs: ולאבן נגף ולצור מכשול; it is natural to suppose that the negative was introduced by the accidental repetition of the letters לא. It may well be that the opening words of Isa. 8.14 (LXX), καὶ ἐὰν ἐπ' αὐτῷ πεποιθὼς ᾖς (which could perhaps have arisen out of a corruption of what we read as the last words of the Hebrew of 8.13, והוא מעריצכם), led Paul to add the next line of what appears as one quotation: καὶ ὁ πιστεύων ἐπ' αὐτῷ οὐ καταισχυνθήσεται. These words recall Isa. 28.16 (quoted later at 10.11), which differ only in having οὐ μὴ καταισχυνθῇ (read in Romans by D G). It is very often supposed that Paul moved from the one passage to the other because each contains the word λίθος (אבן); the fact that he does not quote this word from Isa. 28.16 must throw a little doubt on this common view.

We have little knowledge of how the Jews interpreted Isa. 8.14.

Sanhedrin 38a is quoted by both Strack-Billerbeck[10] and J. Jeremias,[11] but the somewhat intoxicated opinion of Judah and Hezekiah, the sons of R. Ḥiyya, that the passage referred to the Messiah, can hardly be held, even when their father's curious form of the principle *in vino veritas* is taken into account, to justify the belief that a messianic interpretation was generally current.[12] It is hard to make out of the LXX much more than incompetent translation of a defective and misunderstood text; it should however be noted that in the LXX verse 16 (חתום תורה בלמדי) becomes οἱ σφραγιζόμενοι τὸν νόμον τοῦ μὴ μαθεῖν; that is, the recalcitrant persons are those who will not accept Torah. The Targum lends some support to this, (a) by opening verse 14 with the words ואם לא תקבלון, (b) by continuing, His Memra shall be amongst you . . . for a stone of smiting, and for a rock of offence, and (c) by reading in verse 16 (cf. the LXX), Seal and hide the law, they do not wish to learn therein (לא צבן דיילפון בה). I am suggesting that when Paul speaks of the stone of stumbling and rock of offence what he has in mind is primarily the Torah. This cannot be made a clear equation, for when the words ὁ πιστεύων ἐπ' αὐτῷ are repeated in 10.11 αὐτῷ must refer to Christ. There is, however, no insuperable difficulty here. Between 9.33 and 10.11 Paul speaks of Christ as τέλος νόμου—the abolition of the law in the sense that he replaces it, performing more perfectly the purposes it was intended to serve (see below, pp. 146 f; cf. Heb. 8.7, 13); it corresponds with this that in 10.12 he declares that there is no distinction between Jew and Greek (see below, pp. 149, 151). It was a Jewish belief that the law was first offered to all the nations; only Israel accepted it, and to them it became a ἁγίασμα (the LXX word of Isa. 8.14). The other nations, rejecting it, found the law henceforth to be an offence.[13] Paul perceives that Israel, while pursuing its own understanding of the law, was scandalized by its true meaning. Israel did not catch up with the law because it based its observance of Torah not on faith but on works. That is, the law was open to two kinds of response, a faith-response and a works-response. The latter leads to disaster, the former to righteousness and salvation. This recalls to Paul's mind the obscure picture of Isa. 8.14; if you accept the law with faith, or, better perhaps, if you put your trust in God (ἐπ' αὐτῷ), the giver of the law, you will not be ashamed; if you will not hear its true message (see below) you will fall over it, as a stone of stumbling. This, I think, is Paul's real *Gesetzesdialektik*: a faith-response to the law of Moses leads to righteousness, a works-response to the same law, to stumbling and destruction.

This leads to two questions (which are perhaps different aspects of the same question): What is the relation between the law and Christ? What is the relation between the law and the apostolic gospel? It would be wrong to attempt immediate answers to these questions as I have formulated them; we must allow Paul to develop the matter in his own way.

It is at this point that the interjection of 10.1 is made. Is it simply an interjection, or does it play a logical part in the development of the argument? That it springs out of strong personal feeling is not in question, but Michel[14] is probably right in the view that it points forward to the mystery of 11.25 f, and the cross-reference is useful at least in this, that it shows that the question in Paul's mind is how Israel may in the end be brought to make the necessary faith-response. For the moment, Paul is not taking the λίθος προσκόμματος, scriptural though it is, to be the last word: this is the force of the μέν (see above, p. 137). What Paul seeks at present is an explanation of Israel's προσκόπτειν. It is not enough to say *that* they approached and responded to God's word and initiative in terms of works rather than faith; Paul must say *why* they did so.

10.2 does not advance the argument very far. Israel's zeal for God says no more than the διώκειν of 9.31. They were anxious to do what they believed God required of them, but their method was mistaken. It is doubtful whether either ζῆλος or ἐπίγνωσις has a technical sense that would take us further than this. There is in the New Testament no verbal parallel to ζῆλος θεοῦ (unless in Acts 22.3, where however, in view of 21.20, it is probably right to take ζηλωτής with τοῦ πατρῴου νόμου), but Gal. 1.14 (ζηλωτὴς τῶν πατρικῶν παραδόσεων) is a good pointer to what Paul means. The best parallel to κατ' ἐπίγνωσιν is 1 Peter 3.7: no more is meant than sensible and correct appreciation of the situation. The point of 10.2 is thus rightly made by Michel: 'Der Kampf um Israel ist also eine Auseinandersetzung über die Richtung des Eifers' (op. cit., p. 223). It is worth noting that Paul as a Christian does not speak of having ζῆλος θεοῦ.

We come now to 10.3, 4, where both the theological question (How can a lapse determined by God be Israel's fault?) and the historical question (Is Paul thinking of the rejection of the apostolic message, of Jesus himself, or of an earlier relation between God and Israel?) come to a head. ἀγνοοῦντες takes up κατ' ἐπίγνωσιν:[15] what

Israel should have recognized, but failed to recognize, in the law was God's righteousness, the righteousness they might have had as a gift had they been prepared to accept it by faith. Instead they attempted to establish their own righteousness, τὴν ἰδίαν [δικαιοσύνην]. This expression naturally suggests Phil. 3.9, where ἐμὴν δικαιοσύνην is further defined as τὴν ἐκ νόμου. Both definitions are important; taken together they mean a righteousness that I have derived from the law not as a gift received by faith but by means of my own works. In Rom. 10.3 Paul does not describe this righteousness as coming ἐκ νόμου, probably because he is about to describe as the righteousness of God, true righteousness, something which also has or might have had, its origin in the law (10.6 ff). When the Jew looked at the law he failed to see God's righteousness but saw an opportunity of establishing his own. It is probable (though disputed) that ἡ δικαιοσύνη τοῦ θεοῦ here is the same as τὴν ἐκ θεοῦ δικαιοσύνην ἐπὶ τῇ πίστει in Phil. 3.9. This Paul had in fact received διὰ πίστεως Χριστοῦ, since he participated in the all but universal Jewish misunderstanding of the law, which in 10.3c is described not simply in intellectual (οὐ κατ᾽ ἐπίγνωσιν, ἀγνοοῦντες) but in moral terms: τῇ δικαιοσύνῃ τοῦ θεοῦ οὐχ ὑπετάγησαν. The use of ὑποτάσσεσθαι is important. Compare Rom. 8.7: the flesh is not and cannot be subject (ὑποτάσσεσθαι) to the law of God. This subjection is the true relation of man to the righteousness of God in the law; like obedience, it is very close in meaning to faith (see especially 10.16, οὐ πάντες ὑπήκουσαν τῷ εὐαγγελίῳ). Thus Israel's οὐχ ὑπετάγησαν means that they would not let God be God, acknowledge his judgement and that the only righteousness one can have is what he chooses to bestow. 10.3 thus looks back to, repeating and expounding, 9.32a: οὐκ ἐκ πίστεως ἀλλ᾽ ὡς ἐξ ἔργων.

Verse 4 is a notorious crux; the problem centres upon the meaning of τέλος. Is it termination, object, goal or result? It must be recognized that these terms are by no means mutually exclusive. When an instrument has been used to achieve its intended goal it may well, without disparagement, be discarded as no longer useful; and with God object and result are bound to be ultimately identical, since it is unthinkable that he should fail to achieve his goal. One cannot settle the question of 10.4 by simply contemplating the word τέλος and its use in Greek; it is better to begin by recognizing that there are in the Pauline epistles passages that suggest the meaning *termination* (e.g. Rom. 6.14, 15; 7.4; Gal. 2.19; 1 Cor. 9.20), and others that suggest that the law is *established* (notably Rom. 3.31, νόμον ἱστάνομεν; but also the many quotations, including Rom. 13.8 ff where Paul not only cites the commandment of love from the law but assumes that the other commandments, which love fulfils, are valid too). One has to ask, in regard to all these passages, exactly what is being abolished, or established, and how. It is clearly impossible to conduct such an inquiry here, even with reference to the few representative verses that I have mentioned. Rom. 10.4 provides a hint which could be applied to them all. What is established in Christ is the true righteousness of God (εἰς δικαιοσύνην) which was always accessible in the law to faith. Christ is a new initiative on God's part not open to the self-righteous, self-justifying, works-response that the law had by its very form invited. True, he too had been rejected by Israel; the law which should have induced an attitude of humility before God had through sin (7.13) had the effect of educating Israel in self-righteousness. It had proved to be a negative *praeparatio evangelica,* so that the Gentiles who had not had the Jew's advantage (3.1) had stumbled upon the righteousness the Jews had missed (9.30). The point may be defined more sharply by the observation that three reactions to the law were possible: the reaction of faith, the reaction of works and the reaction of unbelief. The coming of Christ reduced the possibilities to two, faith and unbelief. This means that the law was an appropriate instrument of a provisional predestination; the decree *nisi*[16] (if the analogy may be used) became absolute in Christ, who was the end of the law in the sense that the reaction of works was excluded. The righteousness of God was offered not only to Jews but παντὶ τῷ πιστεύοντι (cf. 9.30; 10.11, 13); the works element in law was therefore terminated, though not the requirement that men should be obedient to God.

What Paul has said in 9.30—10.4 amounts to a complete reversal of the way in which Israel in general had understood its Torah. Was it conceivable that he alone should be right?[17] To justify his position he had to supply a new exegesis; and this he proceeds in representative fashion to do, by using Lev. 18.5 and Deut. 30.11–14. It is sometimes thought to be a curious inadvertence or a whimsical paradox on Paul's part that he should quote from Torah to illustrate both ἡ δικαιοσύνη ἡ ἐκ νόμου and ἡ ἐκ πίστεως δικαιοσύνη; but if our argument so far is right it was imperative that he should do precisely this. The law—the law of Moses—could be responded to in terms of works or in terms of faith; it thus became at once a stone of stumbling and a ground of confidence.

Paul's quotation of Lev. 18.5 is close to but not identical with the LXX: ἃ ποιήσας ἄνθρωπος ζήσεται ἐν αὐτοῖς, where the antecedent of ἃ . . . αὐτοῖς is προστάγματα καὶ κρίματα, חקות and משפטי. The change Paul makes covers a difficulty that could only have been straightened out if he had been prepared to write at much greater length. He believes (so we have been led to think) that δικαιοσύνη θεοῦ, true righteousness, could have been had through the law if men had responded to it in faith. But ordinances and judgements are just the things that invite a works-response, and Israel is hardly to be blamed for responding to them in this way. Yet Israel is to be blamed, for the Torah itself bore adequate testimony to the other kind of approach, and, as Paul works out in Gal. 3, since Scripture elsewhere declares that ὁ δίκαιος ἐκ πίστεως ζήσεται (Hab. 2.4; Gal. 3.11), it must be inferred that no one has done adequate works in obedience to the law, which will consequently carry with it not blessing but a curse.

Paul turns to Deut. 30.11–14 in order to demonstrate from Torah the righteousness of faith, producing a new exegesis to support his new understanding of the law. This is at best paradoxical, and may well be thought unjustifiable. The subject of Deut. 30.11 ff is ἐντολή, מצוה; the commandment, it is urged, is not too hard to keep— men should keep it, and earn life by doing so. In other words, Deut. 30 is saying the same as Lev. 18. Is Paul's exegesis honest? Is it sensible? C. H. Dodd (ad loc.) provides part of an answer by recognizing the difference between the Priestly Code in Leviticus, and the Deuteronomic; the two codes did understand law in different ways. But this observation has little validity for Paul, who certainly believed Moses to have been the author of both books. It is probable that the starting-point of his exegesis was the nearness of the word (10.8): 'Paulus argumentiert von der Gewissheit aus, dass ein "nahes Wort" nur ein den Menschen begnadendes Angebot sein kann'.[18] Given this, the rest will follow. The word is the word that we preach, that is, the Christian gospel. The major change that Paul makes (εἰς τὴν ἄβυσσον for εἰς τὸ πέραν τῆς θαλάσσης) shows the firmly Christocentric emphasis of the exegesis. *Heaven* is easily interpreted, but 'beyond the sea' would be meaningless, and, helped perhaps by the thought of תהום, the primal sea, Paul completes the picture of Christ whom men could not bring from heaven because the Father had already sent him, and could not bring up from the underworld because God had raised him from the dead. This means that Paul is arguing backwards from the Christian confession of 10.9, which asserts that the heavenly κύριος has come in the person of Jesus, and that God has raised him from the dead. His exegesis must be Christological, since Christ is God's new initiative, replacing law as the means by which righteousness is conferred.

Paul now uses the confession of faith that he has quoted to emphasize (10.11 ff) that salvation is available for all who believe; if the Gentiles might have it on these terms so also might the Jews; if they have not been automatically included they have not been *a priori* excluded—οὐ γάρ ἐστιν διαστολή (10.12). At this point, under the influence of Joel 3.5, ἐπικαλεῖσθαι comes into use alongside πιστεύειν; there is no change of meaning.

It is not possible to study the rest of the chapter in detail. There are two main points to note. The first is the fastening of responsibility upon the Jews. Whatever the predestinating purpose of God may have been he has done all he could to see that Israel had the opportunity of hearing and understanding his message. He sent messengers, who spoke his word; Israel heard, and understood; the only reason why they did not call upon him was that they were disobedient to his bidding that they should do so. Secondly, we encounter once more the question to what time Paul refers. For the most part he says what he has to say by means of Old Testament quotations; this superficially suggests that he has in mind the history of the Jews before the coming of Christ. He has however prefaced the discussion with an allusion (10.9) to the Christian confession of faith in Jesus (not 'the Messiah' but the historical person) as Lord, and in verse 16, prompted by Isaiah's τῶν εὐαγγελιζομένων (not in fact an accurate quotation of either Isa. 52.7 or Nahum 2.1) he refers to τὸ εὐαγγέλιον, by which he can hardly have meant anything other than the Christian gospel. The question is a proper one, but, as I said above, the quotation of Isa. 65.2 in 10.21 indicates that the answer should be comprehensive: God's hands have always been stretched out to his unresponsive people, a fact that may remind us, before we begin to sum up, that the problem of predestination in relation to guilt and responsibility is a complex one, for if there are predestinarian passages in the Old Testament that suggest the rejection of Israel, or at least its reduction to a small remnant, there are also passages that speak of its election, and, in some cases, of its self-determined refusal to accept its responsibilities. These will be developed in Chapter 11, but we should already have in mind that our theme includes at least the following terms: election to salvation and election to unbelief; a stone of stumbling which invites faith; and a defection of Israel, which in view of Christian Jews such as Paul is at no stage complete.

We must now leave this sketch of a few of the exegetical details to draw the material together, and attempt to state concisely what Paul has been saying in 9.30—10.21.

(4) Chapter 9 deals with the theme of divine election, but, as I have just said, does so in a complex way. The seed of Abraham are elected as God's people, but the composition of the 'seed' cannot be determined by a genealogical table, or even by ethical performance. God will do with his creatures, including the physical descendants of Abraham, exactly what he chooses; and he intends to diminish the number of blood Israelites in his people, and to add to them a number of Gentiles. This sketch of God's purpose Paul develops in order to answer the question that grieves him unceasingly: Why has Israel not accepted the gospel?

The question would not be so heart-breaking if it simply related to godless Esau; in fact it related to the most ardent and most moral theists in the world, and the process by which God's purpose (which, as Paul keeps in mind, is not yet completed) is worked out requires further elucidation. Now the most characteristic feature of Jewish life is the pursuit of the law. It is in this that the interpretation of their history must be found. Approaching the law as a Christian, that is, in the light of Jesus Christ, Paul sees that, as a revelation provided by the Spirit of God, it requires a response in faith—that complete obedience which goes beyond the observance of rules and gives itself in complete dependence on and devotion to God. The law of Moses, however, was cast in the form of precepts and commandments, which, whatever their usefulness in other respects may have been, lent at least some weight to the view that what the law required in response was works—acts of obedience to specific rules, constituting on the part of those who did them a form of righteousness. The law thus provided an instrument by which the purpose of God operated among Israelites. Through the law God was always offering life to his people (see Deut. 30.15 ff), but the offer met with resistance—not least from those who pursued their own mistaken legalistic conception of it with the greatest zeal. The true understanding of the law merges into the 'word of faith, which we—Christians—preach' (10.8). Both under the law and under the gospel, all God seeks is that men should call upon him; all who do so, whether Jews or Greeks, will be saved (10.12 f). There stands out in this section the provisional character of election, and indeed, since God stretches out his hands in vain, the failure of election. Looked at from the other side this means: 'So steht das Erbarmen Gottes ganz allein den Menschen gegenüber: ihre Anklage, aber auch ihre Hoffnung, so gewiss es eben die Gerechtigkeit seines Richters ist'.[19]

How this paradox is worked out must be dealt with when Chapter 11 is studied. It must suffice now to indicate, though it will not be possible seriously to discuss, two of the theological and historical issues that are raised in 9.30—10.21.

(a) The question of Israel's place in the purpose of God will be better discussed when we have before us the material provided by Chapter 11. In the heart of Rom. 10 (cf. 3.22) we have the affirmation that there is no distinction between Jew and Greek; the same Lord will abundantly save everyone who calls upon him (10.12 f)—and it has already become evident that Gentiles even more than Jews are doing this (9.30). The great advantage conferred on the Jews (9.4) has turned out to their disadvantage, for it has led them not to call upon God in faith, but to offer him works. The Jews thus stand out as the great *reductio ad absurdum* in religious history. The best law and the greatest zeal have resulted only in failure. It follows that though a law may serve a temporary (Gal. 3.19) purpose in a useful way, regulating a nation's life and keeping some kinds of inhumanity in check, it cannot be a permanent or final manifestation of the way of God and of his dealings with men; its purpose is negative (Rom. 5.20; Gal. 3.19). It follows equally that though a chosen people, and an elect remnant within that people, may serve a temporary purpose on behalf of mankind as a whole, such a people cannot be a final expression of God's intention for creation. The διαστολή, which, being a product of the law (cf. Exod. 8.23), is affirmed in the Old Testament, and denied by Paul, bears witness to some elements in the truth, but the final truth is the mercy of God for all (11.32). The usefulness[20] both of law and of national election are terminated by the mission of Jesus. This leads to our second question.

(b) What is the place of Jesus in the history of Israel? I mentioned earlier the three forms that Israel's defection might be said to take. In this chapter Paul deals explicitly with Israel's misapprehension of the law, and Israel's rejection of the apostolic message. He says nothing of the historic mission of Jesus, and of his rejection and crucifixion. This, broadly speaking, is true of the Pauline epistles as a whole. Jesus is confessed as the Lord whom God raised from the dead; Christ speaks in his apostolic messenger; he is the end of the law. The story of his life is not narrated. A quick answer to the question might be that for Paul 'Jesus Christ' stands as the supreme symbol or expression of the fact that God deals with men in mercy, and that in consequence they are related to God by faith only. The name, like a mathematical symbol, signifies this grace-faith operation. It is a clearer operator than law, which it replaces, expressing more trenchantly God's requirement that man should love his neighbour, and asserting more persuasively God's love for man even when man fails most signally to obey this radical command. He is the righteousness of God, both in himself and as an offer to man, so that one might as well say that in the gospel the righteousness of God is revealed (Rom. 1.17) as that in the gospel the person, Jesus of Nazareth, is proclaimed. But in fact this will not do. Resurrection implies previous crucifixion; and τέλος, whatever logical nuances it may bear, signifies a historical process. The clue to this process is provided not here but in Gal. 3.16: the historical figure of Jesus is the seed of Abraham, and thus includes in himself the process of election and the law, for he precedes and concludes both.

NOTES

1 This paper was not intended to give a complete account of the contents of the paragraph with which it deals, but to expound the teaching of the paragraph on the theme denoted by the sub-title.

2 *Christus und Israel* (Aarhus and Copenhagen 1956), pp. 60 ff; ET, *Christ and Israel* (Philadelphia 1967), pp. 75–9. References are given to both editions.

3 *Mensch und freier Wille nach den jüdischen Religionsparteien zwischen ben Sira und Paulus* (*WUNT* xii, Tübingen 1971), pp. 382–92.
zwischen ben Sira und Paulus' (*WUNT* xii, Tübingen 1971), pp. 382–92.

4 I use the translation of E. Lohse, *Die Texte aus Qumran*. Munich 1964.

5 See my commentary ad loc., with the reference to Blass-Debrunner, §447, 4.

6 J. Calvin, *The Epistles of Paul the Apostle to the Romans and to the*

Thessalonians, tr. Ross Mackenzie (Edinburgh and London 1961), p. 217.

7 The longer variant occurs in the Koine text, and in the Vulgate and Syriac; not in any of the older Greek MSS.

8 We may deduce this from the word ὡς: 'Das ὡς markiert das subjektiv irrtümliche des israelitischen Strebens'. Lietzmann, *HNT*, ad loc.

9 *Gerechtigkeit Gottes bei Paulus* (*FRLANT* 87, Göttingen 1965), pp. 87, 92.

10 *Kommentar zum Neuen Testament aus Talmud und Midrasch* (Munich 1922–61), ii, pp. 139 f.

11 *TWNT* iv, p. 277.

12 Judah and Hezekiah, the sons of R. Ḥiyya, were sitting at a meal in the presence of Rabbi, without saying a single word. So Rabbi said to the servants, 'Give the young men more wine, that they may say something'. When they were drunk, they rose and said, 'The Son of David will not come until the two dynasties in Israel, the Exilarch in Babylon and the Patriarch in the Land of Israel, come to an end' (Isa. 8.14). Rabbi said to them, 'My children, you are putting thorns in my eyes'. Then R. Ḥiyya said to him, 'May it not seem evil in your sight. Wine (יין) has a numerical value of seventy, and mystery (סוד) has a numerical value of seventy; when the wine goes in, the mystery comes out'.

13 A similar distinction may be found within the family of Abraham. According to the Jonathan b. Uzziel Targum of Gen. 22, Ishmael boasted of his willing acceptance of circumcision at the age of thirteen, whereas Isaac had been circumcised on the eighth day; perhaps, had Isaac had any choice in the matter, he would have refused circumcision. Isaac replies, 'I am now thirty-six years old, and if the Holy One (blessed be he) required all my members I would not refuse'. Thus Ishmael (one might say) boasts of his works in response to God's command, and Isaac offers the total obedience of faith. I owe this reference to an intervention by S. Lyonnet in the discussion of another paper.

14 *Kritisch-Exegetischer Kommentar über das Neue Testament: Der Brief an die Römer* (Göttingen 1955), ad loc.

15 For the correspondence between ἀγνοεῖν and ἐπιγινώσκειν cf. 2 Cor. 6.9.

16 In English law, the first stage of divorce proceedings results in a provisional 'decree *nisi*'; later this is (or may be) made absolute.

17 See e.g. W. Grundmann, 'The Teacher of Righteousness of Qumran and the Question of Justification by Faith in the Theology of the Apostle Paul', in *Paul and Qumran*, ed. J. Murphy-O'Connor (London 1968), pp. 85–114.

18 Michel, op. cit., p. 225.

19 K. Barth, *Kurze Erklärung des Römerbriefes* (Munich 1956), p. 152.

20 In the absolute sense of conveying the truth about God, and access to him.

9

THE ALLEGORY OF
ABRAHAM, SARAH, AND HAGAR IN THE
ARGUMENT OF GALATIANS

That the middle chapters of Galatians constitute a *locus classicus* for the doctrine of the *iustificatio impiorum* is a proposition too familiar to require demonstration. How the allegory of Abraham, Sarah, Hagar, and their children fits into Paul's exposition of the theme is by no means so evident. Many commentators have found difficulty in it—not only in the interpretation of its details but over the question why Paul should have used it at all. Luther, whose love for the Epistle to the Galatians is well known, regards it as mere decoration: 'Allegories do not strongly persuade in divinity . . . as painting is an ornament to set forth and garnish a house already builded, so is an allegory the light of a matter which is already otherwise proved and confirmed'.[1] Calvin writes similarly: 'As an argument it is not very strong, but as confirmation of his earlier vigorous reasoning, it is not to be despised'.[2] This is faint praise.

Modern commentators on the whole treat the passage, or neglect it, in the same way. In his discussion of Justification by Faith Alone Barth[3] has a splendid exposition of Galatians, 'the writing which has a particular importance in this connection as a source and a criterion' (p. 637), but 4.21–31 is passed over completely. Does it contribute nothing to the theme that Christ 'is both the ontic and the noetic principle, the reality and also the truth of both justification and faith'? We come down to earth with Burton[4] who in his summary of the epistle (p. lxxiv) describes the paragraph as 'a supplementary argument, based on an allegorical use of the story of the two sons of Abraham, and intended to convince the Galatians that they are joining the wrong branch of the family.' Compare p. 251, where he writes, 'Before leaving the subject of the seed of Abraham it occurs to the apostle, apparently as an afterthought, that he might make his thought clearer and more persuasive by an allegorical interpretation of the story of Abraham and his two sons . . .'. Schlier,[5] quoting Cornely[6] (*Efficax argumentum addit*) attributes greater weight to the argument of the paragraph: Paul is concerned 'die Frage, die zwischen ihm und den galatischen Christen steht, zuletzt noch durch eine ausführlichere Exegese zu klären' (p. 153). But he quotes Burton, and to the same effect Oepke[7] (the argument gives the impression that it is 'erst nachträglich eingefallen'), and offers no reason why Paul should attempt to clinch his argument in this way.

Other commentators, whose expositions are slighter than Schlier's, are for the most part as silent as he with regard to the motivation and aim of the passage. J. C. O'Neill[8] divides it into parts. As it stands, the paragraph assumes that Judaism and Christianity are two separate entities, which was not true in Paul's time. It is necessary therefore to omit 4.24b–27, 30 as a post-Pauline interpolation. O'Neill is not certain that the remainder can be credited to Paul; if this proves impossible the whole must be regarded as a later comment (pp. 80 f; see also pp. 62 ff). It is in fact very difficult to make any satisfactory sense out of 4.21–24a, 28, 29, 31, when the other verses are removed; the paragraph must stand as a whole. But it is unwise to judge it on the strength of preconceived notions of the relation between Paul's partly Gentile church and Judaism (or Jewish Christianity?) and to follow O'Neill in rejecting Pauline authorship. O'Neill's work does however underline the importance of establishing the place of Gal. 4.21–31 in Paul's argument and thought.

The most thorough attempt to achieve this goal known to me is that of J. Bligh,[9] who argues that the core of Galatians consists of the speech Paul delivered when he confronted Peter at Antioch. This has usually been held to end at 2.14 or at latest at 2.21; Bligh believes that it continues (interrupted here and there by a few interpolations or supplements) as far as 5.13a, and that the allegory of Sarah and Hagar formed the climax of the speech, in which Paul called for the dismissal of the Ishmaels, who were trying to dispossess the Isaacs, the rightful heirs. It is not easy to summarize Bligh's argument because it is scattered over a large number of pages as connections, and the setting of the several sections, are discussed in the course of the commentary. What follows is not a full account, but I hope that, given the necessity of compression, it may seem fair. The argument turns to a considerable extent on the detection of overlapping literary structures. Thus we cannot stop at the end of chapter 2 because there is a chiastic structure which extends from 2.11 to 3.4.

A.	2.11–13	A′.	3.1–4
B.	2.14a	B′.	2.19–21
C.	2.14b	C′.	2.18
D.	2.15	D′.	2.17
E.	2.16a	E′.	2.16g
F.	2.16b	F′.	2.16f
G.	2.16c	G′.	2.16e

H. 2.16d—We too put our faith in Jesus Christ.

The material is further knit together by a smaller chiasmus that runs from the last words of chapter 2 into chapter 3.

A. 2.21 Did Christ suffer death for nothing?   A′. 3.4 Have you suffered so much in vain?

B. 3.1, 2a Foolish Galatians...   B′. 3.3 Are you so foolish?

C. 3.2b   C′. 3.2d

D. 3.2c ... that you received the Spirit.

We cannot however stop at 3.4. Paul has described the vigorous action that he took to deal with the situation in Antioch. He was prepared publicly to confront Peter. We must suppose that he went on to give his reasons for such extreme measures, and these appear as we proceed through chapters 3 and 4. Bligh writes, '3.4 does not make a fully satisfactory ending to the Discourse. One still expects a direct appeal to the Jewish brethren to stop compelling the Gentiles to Judaize and to be faithful to the Pauline gospel. Verses 5–7 take a step in this direction, but do not arrive at the point of drawing the practical conclusion. Thus the question arises whether the Antioch Discourse does not run on much further. The scriptural arguments proposed in 3.5—4.10, which assume familiarity not only with the text of the Old Testament but also with the midrashic traditions based on it, would be much more intelligible to Jewish Christians from Jerusalem than to gentile converts in Galatia; and the first person pronouns "we" and "us" in 3.13; 3.24 and 4.4 are more easily intelligible if their meaning is "we Jews" and "us Jews". Probably, then, the Discourse at Antioch runs on at least as far as 4.10' (p. 235). Bligh recognizes, as of course he must, that 4.11–20 cannot be part of the Antioch discourse. It is addressed directly to the Galatians, and references to them cannot be removed[10] as occasional words added when the speech was transformed into a letter. This paragraph is built on allusions to Paul's ministry in Galatia and can never have belonged to any other setting. 4.8–10 however can be understood as addressed to Judaizers in Antioch—they observed days, months, seasons and years; but verse 10 is too abrupt to have formed the original end of the discourse. The allegory of Sarah and Hagar winds up the scriptural argument and is needed to establish Paul's point. 'Far from being an afterthought the allegory is the climax of St Paul's discussion of the question, Who are the heirs of Abraham?, and contains, in allegorical language, the practical conclusion towards which the whole Discourse has been driving: "Send away the slave-woman and her children!" (i.e., Send away the Judaizers)' (p. 235). 4.31—5.13 is a revised version of the end of the speech, 5.10b–13 being part of the revision added as a suitable conclusion when the speech was incorporated in the letter. Bligh suggests that the original ending, which should be attached to 5.10a, is to be found in 6.16–18. Another chiasmus fastens the allegory in the structure of the whole.

A.	4.11, 12a	A'.	4.30b
B.	4.12b	B'.	4.30a
C.	4.13, 14a	C'.	4.28, 29
D.	4.14b, 15, 16	D'.	4.26, 27
E.	4.17, 18	E'.	4.21–25
	F. 4.19, 20		

But the argument grows unconvincing—so unconvincing as to cast doubt on the whole construction. This last is a clumsy, unbalanced, unconvincing chiasmus; and it involves a paragraph (4.11–20) which, on Bligh's own admission, cannot have been part of the original discourse at Antioch. This of course Bligh has not overlooked. 'The second half was composed first, and the first was skilfully added to form with it the symmetrical pattern of 4.11—4.30' (p. 380). Is it really conceivable either that Paul composed these two apparently spontaneous outbursts (that to the Galatians and that at Antioch) with such refined literary polish, or that by a piece of sheer good fortune they happened to fit together into chiastic form?

Bligh's suggestion, though superficially attractive, fails to carry conviction. It turns Paul into a modern politician reading a prepared statement to a press conference; and it is safe to assume that the incident at Antioch did not happen in this way at all. Paul does not say that he made a speech. He said outright to Peter what he had to say, and there is no reason why this should not end at 2.21; in fact it is probable that the direct address of 3.1, O foolish Galatians, marks the resumption of his letter in the strict sense, and that he now addresses his readers in their own situation. The argument that in what follows some passages (e.g. 3.28; 4.30) are suitable to the Antiochene situation loses force when it is remembered that Paul introduces his account of the Antiochene situation because he saw a parallel between it and the situation in Galatia. The great merit of Bligh's interpretation is that it gives to Gal. 4.21–31 a concrete setting and a very sharp point. Paul introduced the story of Sarah and Hagar not because he thought his Galatian children (4.19) would appreciate a story[11] or because he chose to decorate his serious argument with rhetorical artifice, but in order to lead up to the climax of his Antioch speech and policy: Cast out the slave-woman and her son; Expel the hypocritical Jewish Christians from the church. This would certainly be an impressive conclusion, but we may note, in addition to the points made above, that it leaves 4.27 (the quotation from Isa. 54.1) without any explanation[12]. If Bligh's exegesis is unsatisfactory, can a better be found?

We may begin from the observation that the story of Abraham and his children, and the quotation of Isa. 54.1 which is embedded in it, are by no means the only references to the Old Testament in the central chapters of Galatians. Such references are frequent in Chapter 3; they fall away in Chapter 4, where Paul turns to a non-biblical analogy (4.1–7) and then uses autobiographical material (4.11–20). When the Old Testament material in Chapter 3 is studied an important feature comes to light: in at least three places (and these cover in one way or another nearly all the Old Testament material used) Paul's words can be best explained if we may suppose that he is taking up passages that had been used by his opponents, correcting their exegesis, and showing that their Old Testament prooftexts were on his side rather than on theirs.

Gal. 3.6 begins with a quotation of Gen. 15.6 (cf. Rom. 4.3). It is very awkwardly introduced by the word καθώς, the connection of which is disputed. All that Lietzmann[13] has to offer is: 'Der Übergang von dem Appell an die persönliche Erfahrung zur biblischen Beweisführung ist durch nichts vermittelt als durch das verlegene Flickwort καθώς' (p. 18). From the strictly grammatical standpoint it is hardly possible to do better than this; but may καθώς not be

explained as taking up a passage that Paul's opponents had quoted?
Paul would be saying to the Galatians: I know that the Judaizers
quote Gen. 15.6 to you, but what I have told you is not contradicted
by but is *in accordance with* the true meaning of that verse. That Paul
found it necessary to dispute the common understanding of Gen.
15.6 we know from Rom. 4, where he uses the exegetical device of
the *g͑zērā šāwā* to prove that the verse refers to a non-imputing of
sin which is equivalent to the gratuitous imputation of righteousness,
and not to a careful account-keeping of Abraham's good works.
In Rom. 4 Paul uses Ps. 32 to establish his interpretation; in Gal. 3
he quotes Gen. 12.3; 18.18 to show the interest of the Gentiles in the
promise to Abraham. Since these by definition are not circumcised
and do not keep the law their participation in the promise is due to
faith independently of law, and this both confirms the interpretation
of Gen. 15.6 and leads to the next step in the argument.

The Old Testament quotation in 3.10 was almost certainly used by
Paul's opponents: Cursed is everyone who does not abide in all the
things that are written in the book of the law, to do them (Deut.
27.26). It requires no stretch of the imagination to see how naturally
the passage could be used by Judaizers. 'Paul himself fails to observe
all the things that are written in the law—he becomes all things to
all men, and among Gentiles lives as a Gentile: he is under a curse.
He admits, or claims to admit, Gentiles to the people of God without
requiring them to be circumcised and to keep the law: instead of
enabling them to share in the blessing of Abraham he brings them
under a curse. He would do better to leave them alone.' They may
have added (3.12) the corresponding positive passage from Lev.
18.5 (cf. Rom. 10.5): The man who has done the things prescribed
by the law shall live by them. Verbal contact however ($\zeta\acute{\eta}\sigma\epsilon\tau\alpha\iota$—
$\zeta\acute{\eta}\sigma\epsilon\tau\alpha\iota$) enables Paul to turn the argument by referring to Hab.
2.4,[14] which declares that, like righteousness, life is to be had by
faith; and faith is different from the doing that the law requires.
This not only puts Paul and his Gentile Christians in the right; it
enables him to turn on his adversaries. Since life could be had by
doing yet is in fact, on the witness of Scripture, had only by faith,
it will follow that no one, not even the Judaizers, does the things
prescribed by the law; accordingly they are not merely without life
but (in consequence Deut. 27.26) under a curse.

Cursing leads to the next quotation: Deut. 21.23 in 3.13 (Cursed
is everyone who hangs on a tree); it seems however unlikely that

anyone in any sense a Christian would have used this against Paul. Jews who were not Christians—Paul himself before his conversion—may have used it against Christians, but the suggestion that the crucified Jesus was cursed by God[15] was of no particular use to the Judaizers. We must see here not a quotation wrested by Paul from his adversaries but one that he introduces into the argument because it shows how the curse levelled against those who did not observe the law (whether in the legalistic or ceremonial sense, or in the new sense pointed out by Paul in 5.14) was disposed of—it was borne by the innocent Jesus and thus nullified for those who by faith were now in him. It was the cross that put the promise of Gen. 18.18 into effect.

Paul is back with his opponents in 3.16, which rests on a number of Old Testament passages—Gen. 12.7; 13.15; 17.7; 22.18; 24.7. After the material already surveyed it seems reasonable to suggest that they argued (as is stated in 3.16a): The promises were addressed to Abraham and his seed. This means that the Gentiles have no share in them, unless they are adopted into the Abrahamic seed by circumcision and legal observance. Those who are not Abraham's seed cannot hope to receive what God has explicitly promised elsewhere. To this Paul replies: What do you mean by seed?[16] You will note that the word stands in the singular, σπέρματι, zar'ᵃka; this means that the promises are to be fulfilled in and through a single person. The exposition of this theme occupies the rest of the chapter, for Paul is well aware that σπέρμα and zᵃra' are collective terms, and he cannot bring his exposition to a close until he has re-established a collective seed. It is however a new collectivity, based no longer on physical descent and therefore exposed to racial, social and physical divisions (3.28), but solely upon the one primary seed, Christ, in whom all are one (3.29). Incorporated in the exposition is at least one other, not strictly biblical, point that was probably used by the Judaizers: the law, they said, had the supreme dignity of being delivered on God's behalf by angels. They used this tradition, as (according to Acts 7.53; cf. Heb. 2.2) Stephen did, to magnify the law. Paul replies: Yes, indeed, the law was ordained by means of angels; this, rightly understood, proves its inferiority to the promise which God spoke directly and in person to Abraham.

It is at this point that Paul turns aside from the main line of argument, remembering that though in any context the biblical basis of his position remains of fundamental importance, his readers are in the main Gentiles, and may be expected to be more familiar with other realms than that of the Old Testament, and giving an example from the ordinary legal provisions of the hellenistic world.[17] This illustration occupies 4.1–7; in 4.8–10 he puts together the two realms he has touched upon—the observance of days, months, seasons and years is a return to the στοιχεῖα—and in 4.11–20 he makes a personal appeal based upon his earlier relations with the Galatians. He now takes up again the biblical thread, linking it to the personal appeal by verse 21, which may be paraphrased: If you are so keen on the law you had better pay attention to what it actually says. If you do so, you will find that it is on my side and not on that of the Judaizers who are persuading you not simply to listen to the Old Testament (which Paul himself certainly considered a good thing to do) but to understand it in a legalistic way, which made membership of the people of God dependent upon legal observance rather than upon God's electing grace. When the matter is put in this way the main proposal of this paper is already implied. It is that Paul's opponents in Galatia followed up their quotation of the passages (see 3.16) on the seed of Abraham by an argument based upon the two women, Sarah and Hagar, by whom Abraham had children. The seed of Abraham, understood physically, issued in legitimate and illegitimate children. The Galatians were urged to legitimize themselves.

There are already two hints in 4.22 that Paul is taking up material his opponents had used. The verse begins with the familiar γέγραπται. As a rule this introduces a quotation.[18] Here it does no more than summarize a quantity of Old Testament material spread over a number of chapters in Genesis: Abraham had two sons. γέγραπται allows the genuine Old Testament foundation of the Judaizers' argument; the question is whether they have rightly interpreted the evidence. Paul continues: Of the two sons, one was 'of the slave woman' (ἐκ τῆς παιδίσκης), the other 'of the free woman' (ἐκ τῆς ἐλευθέρας). Of which slave, and of which free woman? The wording implies that the story is already before the Galatians; they will know that the slave is Hagar, the free woman Sarah. The articles are anaphoric in this sense. The Judaizers must have continued their exegesis of the Genesis story on the same lines as Jub. 16.17 f, where it is said to Abraham that 'all the seed of his sons should be Gentiles, and be reckoned with the Gentiles; but from the sons of Isaac one should become a holy seed, and should not be reckoned among the Gentiles. For he should become the portion of the Most

High, and all his seed had fallen into the possession of God, that it should be unto the Lord a people for (his) possession above all nations and that it should become a kingdom and priests and a holy nation'. Both Gentiles and Jews were physically descended from Abraham. Given this distinction the whole story can be readily understood in a way unfavourable to Gentiles. The pregnant Hagar is driven out and allowed to return only on sufferance (Gen. 16.6). When Ishmael is born, both mother and child are banished and left to die in the desert (Gen. 21.10). This is harsh treatment, and Jewish exegesis was concerned to justify it. According to Josephus, Hagar was sent away because she insulted the barren Sarah (*Ant.* i. 188 f); later Hagar and Ishmael were removed lest, when the aged Abraham died, the older boy might injure Isaac (i. 215). The Targum of Pseudo-Jonathan[19] adds some justification for Sarah by representing Hagar as the daughter of Pharaoh the son of Nimrod, and thus of evil ancestry. But no amount of palliation was able, or intended, to alter the fact that Sarah's descendants were the Jews, and elect by God, and Hagar's descendants were Gentiles and stood outside the promise.[20] The Judaizing argument is clear. The true descendants of Abraham are the Jews, who inhabit Jerusalem. Here are the true people of God; and it will follow that Jerusalem is the authoritative centre of the renewed people of God, now called the church. Those who are not prepared to attach themselves to this community by the approved means (circumcision) must be cast out; they cannot hope to inherit promises made to Abraham and his seed.

Two points are clear. (1) This is a part of the Old Testament that Paul would have been unlikely to introduce of his own accord; its value from his point of view is anything but obvious, and the method of interpretation is unusual with him (see pp. 165 f). It stands in the epistle because his opponents had used it and he could not escape it. (2) Its plain, surface meaning supports not Paul but the Judaizers: the Jews, who live by the law of Moses, are the heirs of Abraham and it is to Jews that the promise applies. Paul does not contest the statement that Hagar's child was born κατὰ σάρκα—a purely human arrangement for securing if not legitimate at least legitimizable issue was all that was involved;[21] whereas Sarah's was born διὰ τῆς ἐπαγγελίας—a specific divine word had been spoken in consequence of which the birth, impossible κατὰ σάρκα, took place. So far Paul's Judaizing opponents; they have correctly stated the content of the text, but the question remains how the text is to be interpreted. The Judaizers had given it its straightforward, literal[22] meaning. It is over against this that Paul asserts that the matters in question are ἀλληγορούμενα (4.24). Commentators and others[23] point out, correctly, that ἀλληγορεῖν, as a Greek word, may mean either to speak allegorically, or to interpret allegorically, and if we are to think of Galatians simply as a piece of Greek prose we shall no doubt accept, with Lietzmann, Schlier, and others, the former meaning, though there is little difference in effect between 'These things are written in allegorical form', and 'These things are (here and now) being allegorically interpreted'. Paul however was not simply a writer of Greek prose, and he is nowhere closer to his Jewish background than when he is interpreting the Old Testament.[24] We may accordingly see here a piece of exegesis k^emin ḥōmær[25]. In addition to a number of unnamed doršē ḥ^amūrōt, interpretations of this kind are notably ascribed to Rabban Johanan b. Zakkai and to Rabban Gamaliel II, who stand close enough to Paul to make their examples of special interest. Two points may be brought out from examples of exegesis k^emin ḥōmær. (1) In Sifre Numbers 8, Rabban Gamaliel interprets k^emin ḥōmær a specific word in Num. 5.15: Why must the offering in respect of the suspected adulteress be of barley meal? 'As her acts have been bestial, so her offering consists of the food of beasts.' (2) In Mekilta 83b (Mišpaṭim 2; in Mechilta D'Rabbi Ismael, ed. H. S. Horovitz and I. A. Rabin (Jerusalem 1960), p. 253, 7 f), Rabban Johanan b. Zakkai in interpreting Exod. 21.6 answers the question why the ear rather than any other member should be pierced, as follows: The ear, which has heard: Thou shalt not steal, and went and stole, that is to be pierced rather than all (the man's) members. We see in these examples the reinterpretation of a significant word and the use of an explanatory text. It is precisely these two methods that Paul uses in order to interpret the story of Abraham and his sons in a way consistent with his view of the law and of justification. First, the name Hagar is given a fresh interpretation. The problem of the text of 4.25a is familiar, and too complicated for full discussion in this paper. The only point that we must note is the omission of the name Hagar in P[46] ℵ C G lat sa Orig Ambst. The name is included in B A D﹩ sy. The witnesses are fairly equally divided but a decisive consideration in favour of the long text is that omission of Hagar leaves a bare piece of geographical information of little interest to the readers or relevance to the context: Sinai is a mountain in Arabia (or, Mount Sinai is in Arabia). It is much more to the point that Paul should identify the woman Hagar with the mountain where the law was given. Other interpretations of the name were current;[26] we need not linger over the etymological arguments with which Paul might have supported his.[27] The identification itself is the ground for the statement of 4.24b.[28] Hagar stands for the covenant of Sinai, that is, the covenant of law; she is a slave, and her children are slaves. Those therefore who adhere to the law are slaves and do not inherit the freedom of Abraham and Sarah. This is one main step, though a negative one, in Paul's argument. He agrees that the children of Sarah are to be distinguished from the children of Hagar; but the Jews (and Judaizers), the children of the legal, Sinaitic, covenant, are the children of Hagar—and therefore slaves.

The second step remains. Paul introduces a quotation from Isa. 54.1, which, it seems, had never been associated with the story of Abraham, Sarah, and Hagar. Why does Paul use this passage? The answer probably is that he is making use of a $g^e z\bar{e}ra \ \check{s}\bar{a}w\bar{a}$. The whole story in Genesis proceeds from the fact that Sarah was barren, $^{\epsilon a}q\bar{a}r\bar{a}$. This word provides a link[29] with Isa. 54.1 which enables Paul to make his point.[30] Isa. 54.1 was interpreted with reference to Jerusalem; so for example the Targum (Sing praises, O Jerusalem, who wast as a barren woman that bare not ... more shall be the children of desolate Jerusalem than the children of inhabited Rome—J. F. Stenning's translation). Since however ἡ νῦν 'Ιερουσαλήμ has already been appropriated to the Hagar-Sinai-law-bondage complex it is necessary to introduce the concept of the heavenly (ἄνω) Jerusalem; and Paul's interpretation is not only that 'you, brethren, corresponding to Isaac, are children of promise' (verse 28), but that the future—as promise and inheritance imply—is with the church of justified sinners rather than with law-keeping Judaism. The whole argument is confirmed by one further observation. In the story (τότε, verse 29) Ishmael persecuted Isaac. The foundation for this statement is Gen. 21.9, according to which Sarah saw Ishmael $m^e\d{s}ah\bar{e}q$. The meaning of this word is disputed. The LXX render it παίζοντα, which is reasonable enough but is an inadequate basis for the sequel. Jub. 17.4 offers an explanation: Sarah saw Ishmael playing and dancing, and Abraham rejoicing, and she became jealous. The Pseudo-Jonathan Targum of Gen. 22.1 represents Isaac and Ishmael as disputing, and elsewhere violent attacks are mentioned.[31] Now it could not be maintained that Gentile Christians had persecuted Jews (it might be added, They had not yet had the opportunity), but none knew better than Paul that Jews had persecuted Christians, and that Judaizers were now threatening his life's work (Gal. 2.2; for a different kind of threat cf. 2 Cor. 11.26). It is thus confirmed that the Jewish Christians are, theologically, Ishmaels, the law-free Christians Isaacs, and the next step follows. Cast out the slave and her son; for the son of the slave shall not inherit with the son of the free woman (Gal. 4.30; Gen. 21.10). This is not (*pace* Bligh) a call to the Gentile Christians in the church of Antioch to rise up and expel their Jewish Christian brethren; it is rather the command of God to his (angelic) agents, and expresses what the fate of each party is to be. It is the fact of persecution that leads Paul to conclude (διό) in verse 31 that 'We are children not of the slave but of the free wife'.

So Paul brings his argument to a close. He has run through the quotations that his adversaries have used and shown that they establish not the Judaizing case but his own. He sums up in 5.1: For freedom did Christ set us free; stand fast therefore, and do not become entangled again in a yoke of bondage. He then begins to write freely, and not as a respondent. Look! *I Paul* tell you . . . (5.2). His so-called allegorical treatment of Abraham and the two women was evoked not by a personal love of fantastic exegesis but by a reasoned case which it was necessary that he should answer. In other passages where there is similar exegesis there is probably similar motivation. In Rom. 4 Paul finds it necessary to establish his own exegesis of Gen. 15.6.[32] In Rom. 9.6 ff Paul is countering the view:[33] If what you say is right, God's word has broken down. He answers the objection by asking, What do you mean by Israel? What do you mean by seed? The difference between Isaac and Ishmael, Jacob and Esau, proves that Israel and seed are not to be taken as words of merely physical relationship.

Another example of elaborate typological interpretation of the Old Testament is to be found in 1 Cor. 10. It has been disputed whether in this chapter Paul took up and adapted a Jewish midrash which spoke of a baptism into Moses and of spiritual food and drink, or composed his own midrash.[34] Perhaps the best suggestion might be that Corinthian Christians, who believed the sacraments to have magical prophylactic efficacy, initiated the midrash and that Paul replied by taking the story further: Let us agree that the Israelites had their typological baptism and eucharist; much good did these do them! Finally it may be suggested that behind 2 Cor. 3 lay an exposition designed to glorify Moses; Paul singles out the detail of the veil Moses was obliged to wear, and uses it to show that, great though the glory of Moses was, it was a fading glory, not to be compared with the glory of the new covenant.

There may be some recollection of Paul's polemical use of Isa. 54.1 in a few rabbinic references to it. Thus when the passage was quoted by a *min* to Beruriah (wife of R. Meir) the first part of her answer was perhaps no more pointed than necessary. 'Because she did not bear, should she sing?' 'Fool, look at the end of the verse, where it is written, For more are the children of the desolate than the children of the married wife, saith the Lord'. But she continues with an asperity justified not by the question but the general perverseness of *minim*, 'Sing, O congregation of Israel, which art likened to a barren woman who did not bear sons of your kind (*minim*) for hell' (Berakoth 10a; cf. Midrash Song of Songs 1.37, on 1.5). H. J. Schoeps[35] refers to what he regards as an 'Ironisierung dieser Allegorie'. The passage in Pesikta de Rab Kahana, Piska 22, is translated as follows by A. Wünsche: 'R. Berachja im Namen des R. Levi hat gesagt: Du findest, als unsre Mutter Sara den Jizchak gebar, sprachen die Völker der Welt: Gott behüte! nicht Sara hat den Jizchak geboren, sondern Hagar, die Magd der Sara, hat ihn geboren. Was that Gott? Er ließ die Brüste der Weiber der Völker der Welt vertrocknen, und es kamen die Matronen (reading *wᵉhaju maṭrōnōṯ šællahæm bā'oṯ*) zu Sara und küßten ihr den Staub von ihren Füßen und sprachen zu ihr: Thue uns etwas Gutes ... und säuge unsre Kinder! Unser Vater Abraham sprach zu ihr: Sara, es ist nicht der Augenblick, sich zu verbergen, sondern gehe hinaus auf die Straße und säuge ihre Kinder! heilige den Namen Gottes! So heißt es Gen. 21.7: "Kinder wird Sara säugen". Es heißt hier nicht *ben*, ein Kind, sondern *banim*, Kinder wird sie säugen. Wenn nun schon ein menschliches Wesen, dem eine Freude geworden, sich freute und alle erfreute, wie erst, wenn Gott kommen wird, um Jerusalem zu erfreuen!'[36]

These passages add no weight to the argument, but are at least not inconsistent with the view that Isa. 54.1 played a significant part in Jewish–Christian polemics. This leads to the final question: What light do these observations throw on the opposition to Paul, and on his response to it?

The adversaries did not act out of mere personal spite or jealousy; they held a serious theological position which they supported by detailed biblical arguments. It is no doubt true that they hoped to escape persecution (6.12) and to exercise a visible dominion over the Galatians (6.13); but this is not the whole truth. At the heart of their theology was the concept of the people of God with its origin in Abraham, and the divine promise that constituted it. They probably took the view (expressly controverted by Paul in 3.17) that the Abrahamic covenant had been redefined by the Sinaitic. The promise was made to Abraham and his seed; and the obligations of the seed were revealed in the law, fulfilment of which was made the necessary condition for receipt of the promised blessing. The scriptural argument on which this position rested reached its climax in the story of Abraham, Sarah, and Hagar. Only the Sarah-Isaac line could count as seed; this was the line that included Moses and therefore the law, and it had its seat in Jerusalem. It had found its fulfilment in Jesus and his disciples, notably James, Cephas and John, and was still administered in terms of the law from Jerusalem. If Gentiles were to participate in it they must be adopted into the family by circumcision, and recognize the overlordship of Jerusalem.

This is in some respects a not unattractive legalism, and its arguments are not without some weight; it is the more important to observe how Paul rebuts it. He accepts the authority of the Old Testament, the indefectibility of the divine promise, and the important role played by the people of God. In Gal. 3 (which can receive no detailed discussion in this paper) his main point is that the law, and the Sinai covenant, have only temporary validity. The argument in Chapter 4 is more subtle, and sheds some light on Paul's understanding of the *iustificatio impiorum*. Paul uses Isa. 54.1 to reverse the family relationships of the descendants of Abraham. It cannot be said that this verse provides an unambiguous interpretation of the story in Genesis. It speaks of two women: the *'ᵃqārā* and the *bᵉ'ūlā*. The one is to have more children than the other. In Genesis Sarah is both barren and married. Moreover, each woman has, in the chapters contemplated, one son, and each son has many descendants (Ishmael, Gen. 16.10; 17.20; 21.13; Isaac, 17.16). Paul's use of Isa. 54.1 is thus in a sense arbitrary; he takes from it what he brings to it. But what he brings to it is not arbitrarily chosen, for the theme that he (rightly) sees in Isaiah is the theme of privilege, and of God's concern for the unprivileged. God chooses the foolish, the weak, the base, the despised, even the things that are not (1 Cor. 1.27 f); he chooses the barren and the deserted rather than the privileged and favoured woman. Thus the physical descendants of Sarah become the spiritual descendants of Hagar, and the physical descendants of Hagar (generalized into the Gentiles) become the spiritual descendants of Sarah, who inherit the divine promise. The disputed interpretation of the story in Genesis becomes the root of the argument (also worked out in—somewhat different—Old Testament terms) of Rom. 9—11, and a profound, though obscure, statement of the paradoxical predestinating grace that determines the ungodly to righteousness and life. Paul's insight is at once moral (in that his sympathy is engaged by the unprivileged) and theological (in that he holds fast the freedom of God in grace). If space permitted this dual insight could be traced back to Jesus, and onward to its more elaborate exposition in Romans.

NOTES

1   M. Luther, *Saint Paul's Epistle to the Galatians* (ET 1860), p. 347.
2   J. Calvin, *The Epistles of Paul the Apostle to the Galatians, etc.* (ET 1965), p. 84.
3   K. Barth, *Church Dogmatics* iv 1, 637–42; there is a short reference in ii 2, 215. C. H. Dodd, *According to the Scriptures*, London 1952, does not deal with the passage, and there is hardly more in B. Lindars, *New Testament Apologetic*, London 1961.
4   E. de W. Burton, *The Epistle to the Galatians*, ICC 9, Edinburgh 1921.
5   H. Schlier, *Der Brief an die Galater*, MeyerK vii [10]1949.
6   R. Cornely, *Commentarius in S. Pauli Apostoli Epistolas*, iii (1892). I have not seen this work.
7   A. Oepke, *Der Brief des Paulus an die Galater*, THK ix (1937). I have not seen this work.
8   J. C. O'Neill, *The Recovery of Paul's Letter to the Galatians*, London 1972.
9   J. Bligh, *Galatians*. St Paul Publications, London 1969.
10   As 'O foolish Galatians' can be dropped from 3.1.
11   G. G. Findlay, *The Epistle to the Galatians*, ExpB, n.d., p. 287.
12   J. Bligh (p. 404) asks the question, 'Why does St Paul introduce the quotation from Isaiah?', but his answer shows what Paul makes of Isa. 54 rather than why he turned to it.
13   H. Lietzmann, *An die Galater*, HNT x, [3]1932.
14   Having discovered the importance of this verse Paul will use it on its own in Rom. 1.17.
15   Or was an affront to God—the genitive, $qil^al a\underline{t}$ $^{\prime ae}l\bar{o}him$, was sometimes taken to be objective.
16   Cf. Rom. 9 (p. 165).

17 Evidence is given by H. Lietzmann and H. Schlier, ad loc.
18 Rom. 1.17; 2.24; 3.4, 10; 4.17; 8.36; 9.13, 33; 10.15; 11.8, 26; 15.3, 9, 21; 1. Cor. 1.19, 31; (2.9); 3.19; 9.9.; 10.7; 14.21; 15.45; 2. Cor. 8.15; 9.9; Gal. 3.10, 13; 4.27.
19 Conveniently given in J. Bowker, *The Targums and Rabbinic Literature* (Cambridge 1969), p. 204.
20 It would be possible here to pursue a number of side-issues interesting and important in themselves but not strictly relevant to our theme, notably the question whether the notion of virginal conception was read into the story of Sarah; see J. McHugh, *The Mother of Jesus in the New Testament* (London 1975), pp. 313–21.
21 See J. Bright, *A History of Israel* (Philadelphia 1959), p. 71; G. von Rad, *Genesis* (ET, London ²1963), pp. 186 ff.
22 In the language of a somewhat later time, the *pešaṭ* interpretation.
23 F.g. F. Büchsel, in *ThW* i 260.
24 At this point it may be said that the very extensive allegories of Abraham, Sarah, and Hagar by Philo contribute little, in form or substance, to this discussion, and are therefore in this paper left out of account; they are interesting but not illuminating. Philo's application is 'most like and yet most unlike that of St Paul ... they stand in direct contrast, and their results have nothing in common' (J. B. Lightfoot, *Saint Paul's Epistle to the Galatians* (London 1890), p. 199).
25 On the terminology see W. Bacher, *Die exegetische Terminologie der jüdischen Traditionsliteratur*, 1899, 1905 (= 1965), i 61 ff; J. Bonsirven, *Exégèse rabbinique et Exégèse paulinienne* (Paris 1939) pp. 230, 240, 249 f; Bill. iii 388–99.
26 See J. B. Lightfoot, op. cit., pp. 193–8; Bill. iii 572 f.
27 See the commentaries, especially J. B. Lightfoot, H. Lietzmann, H. Schlier.
28 For this reason we may prefer γάρ to δέ in verse 25a.
29 There is another link in the fact that the Haftarah to Gen. 6.9—11.32 is Isa. 54.1—55.5.
30 Note that as verse 24 rests upon verse 25 (γάρ) so verse 26 rests upon verse 27 (the same conjunction).
31 See R. Le Déaut, *Bibl* xlii, 1961, 37–43. A variety of interpretations of *meṣaḥēq* is given in Gen R 53.11: immorality, idolatry, bloodshed, shooting arrows and other missiles. There is further evidence in Bill. iii 575 f.
32 Cf. Gal. 3.6, and pp. 158 f above. 'Paulus begegnet dem Gesprächs-partner also erneut dort, wo dieser sich am stärksten und unverwundbar fühlt' (E. Käsemann, *An die Römer, HNT* 8a, 1973, p. 98 [³1974, p. 99], on Rom 4).
33 A different view will be found in E. Käsemann, op. cit., p. 249 (³p. 251).
34 See H. Lietzmann, *An die Korinther* i/ii, HNT 9, ⁵1969, ad loc., with the additional notes by W. G. Kümmel.
35 *Paulus* (Tubingen 1959), p. 252.
36 A. Wünsche, *Pesikta des Rab Kahana*, 1885, p. 207; text in B. Mandel-baum, *Pesikta de Rav Kahānā* (New York 1962), i, 326. It is interesting

to note that Piska 20 is based on Isa. 54.1, but beyond noting the seven *ᵃquaroṭ*, Sarah, Rebecca, Rachel, Leah, the wife of Manoah, Hannah and Sion, has nothing relevant to our discussion.

SELECT INDEX

New Testament passages discussed